Lives of Lawyers

Law, Meaning, and Violence

The scope of Law, Meaning, and Violence is defined by the wide-ranging scholarly debates signaled by each of the words in the title. Those debates have taken place among and between lawyers, anthropologists, political theorists, sociologists, and historians, as well as literary and cultural critics. This series is intended to recognize the importance of such ongoing conversations about law, meaning, and violence as well as to encourage and further them.

Series Editors:

Martha Minow, Harvard Law School
Michael Ryan, Northeastern University
Austin Sarat, Amherst College

Narrative, Violence, and the Law: The Essays of Robert Cover, edited by Martha Minow, Michael Ryan, and Austin Sarat

Narrative, Authority, and Law, by Robin West

The Possibility of Popular Justice: A Case Study of Community Mediation in the United States, edited by Sally Merry and Neil Milner

Legal Modernism, by David Luban

Surveillance, Privacy, and the Law: Employee Drug Testing and the Politics of Social Control, by John Gilliom

Lives of Lawyers: Journeys in the Organizations of Practice, by Michael J. Kelly

Lives of Lawyers:
Journeys in the
Organizations
of Practice

Michael J. Kelly

Ann Arbor

THE UNIVERSITY OF MICHIGAN PRESS

Copyright © by the University of Michigan 1994
All rights reserved
Published in the United States of America by
The University of Michigan Press
Manufactured in the United States of America
⊛ Printed on acid-free paper

1997   1996   1995   1994   4   3   2   1

A CIP catalogue record for this book is available from the British Library.

Library of Congress Cataloging-in-Publication Data

Kelly, Michael J., 1937–
     Lives of lawyers : journeys in the organizations of practice /
Michael J. Kelly.
          p.   cm. — (Law, meaning, and violence)
     Includes bibliographical references and index.
     ISBN 0-472-10500-0
     1. Practice of law—United States. 2. Lawyers—United States.
3. Law firms—United States. 4. Legal ethics—United States.
I. Title.   II. Series.
KF300.K45   1994
174'.3'0973—dc20   94-1734
                                                              CIP

To Narindar

There is nothing real in life that is not real because someone described it well.

—Fernando Pessoa, *The Book of Disquiet*

For the first time Lydgate was feeling the hampering threadlike pressure of small social conditions, and their frustrating complexity.... [H]e was inwardly resenting the subjection which had been forced upon him. It would have seemed beforehand like a ridiculous piece of bad logic that he, with his unmixed resolutions of independence and his select purpose, would find himself at the very outset in the grasp of petty alternatives, each of which was repugnant to him. In his student's chambers, he had prearranged his social action quite differently.

—George Eliot, *Middlemarch*

Lives were stories; there was no way out of that. Time and the innate human need to give shape to things, to select so as to find order, meant that any life was just a story, one's own or anyone else's. Like all stories, the story of a life could only be an approximation to the truth, or perhaps a parallel.... The fact that one had acknowledged that life stories were no more than approximations to true stories did not mean that one should stop testing them against such discoverable truths as one could lay one's hands on. For if everyone was to be thought of as more or less an artist by virtue of the construction of these long and sometimes touching tales, redemption for the transient seemed . . . , if there were such a thing, to be not so much in the art as in the continuity of the effort to understand.

—Isabel Colgate, *Deceits of Time*

It is the strangest claim in the world—raised sometimes, but never lived up to even by those who raise it—that one should present experiences without any theoretical link between them, and leave it to the reader, or the pupil, to form his own convictions. But the mere looking at a thing is of no use whatsoever. Looking at a thing gradually merges into contemplation, contemplation into thinking, thinking is establishing connexions, and thus it is possible to say that every attentive glance which we cast on the world is an act of theorizing. This, however, ought to be done with consciousness, self-criticism, freedom, and, to use a daring word, with irony—yes, all these faculties are necessary if abstraction, which we dread, is to be rendered innocuous, and the result which we hope for is to emerge with as much liveliness as possible.

—Goethe, Preface to *Theory of Colours*

Acknowledgments

This book has been so long in gestation that I begin with an apology to the multitudes whom I would want to mention here were it not for the fact they have long since faded from my memory. My primary debt of gratitude is owed to the generosity of scores of people who talked candidly with me and helped me understand, in some small measure, their lives in the law and the character of their organizations. This book is in important respects built on the perceptions and ideas about the practice of law of these indigenous natives to whom I promised anonymity: they helped me construct the rudimentary anthropology of their practices that animates the descriptions and thinking of this work.

A second group of people encouraged me to carry on with this work and in many cases made comments and criticisms and editorial suggestions I found extraordinarily helpful. They include Michael Meltsner, Aviam Soifer, Roland Christensen, Robert Post, John Van Maanen, Michael Tonry, David Luban, Robin West, Roger Cramton, Thomas Palay, Robert Condlin, Gerry Singsen, Daniel Givelber, and Douglas Rosenthal. They are not responsible for the quality of the reasoning in the book, but I am greatly indebted to them for helping it along to completion.

Finally, I am grateful to various assistants over the years who played a vital role in the production of the finished product: Dottie Guthmuller, Keisha Hargo, Jude Howard, Jennifer Kinloch, Flo Smith, Ann Vroom, Grace Won, and many others whose names I cannot recall but whose assistance made it possible to sustain the double life of administrator and writer.

Contents

Chapter 1

Professionalism and the Culture of Practice

The legal profession in the United States at the close of the twentieth century is changing at a precipitous pace. Over twice the number of lawyers practice in the 1990s as did in 1960.[1] The profession is increasingly specialized. It is distinctly more heterogeneous, as women and ethnic and racial minorities enter the profession in relatively large numbers.[2] Lawyers as a group are markedly younger,[3] more competitive, and more combative than perhaps at any time in the history of American law.

Although the demographic transformation, increased specialization, and declining civility of the American legal profession represent change, it is the growing power of the practice organization that chiefly drives the metamorphosis of the contemporary legal profession.[4] During the 1970s substantial organizational growth occurred in government law divisions, law departments operating within corporations,[5] legal-aid bureaus, and other agencies providing legal services

---

1. The 1960 figure is 285,933. The 1985 figure is 723,189 (United States Census Bureau 1992, 192, table 314). The *estimate* of lawyer population for 1990 is 805,000 (Curran et al. 1985, 5). "Between 1970 and 1985 the legal profession grew 141%, compared to 46% growth for the professions in general and 34% for the entire work force" (Sander and Williams 1989, 432). "By 1988, the ratio of lawyers to the general population was far more than twice its historic average (up to 1970)" (Sander and Williams 1989, 433 n. 4).

2. From 1971 to 1987, the population of female lawyers increased from 3 percent to an estimated 16 percent of the bar (Curran and Carson 1991, 2).

3. The median age of lawyers in 1988 was forty. In 1971 it was forty-five (Curran and Carson 1991, 3). Lawyers under thirty-six years of age made up 39 percent of the 1980 lawyer population and only 24 percent of the 1960 lawyer population (Curran et al. 1985, 8).

4. In 1960, 36 percent of private practitioners were in firm settings (Curran et al. 1985, 14). By 1988, the proportion of lawyers in firm settings had increased to 54 percent (Curran and Carson 1991, 6).

5. The total number of lawyers employed in private industry grew from 39,000

for the poor. More recently, large corporate law firms and mass-market entities for middle-class legal services have experienced phenomenal growth in size and revenues (Galanter and Palay 1991, 46–48).[6] The practice organization—its marketing and budget-enhancing power, its system of rewards, its style of professional development—has become a central feature in the landscape of the legal profession.

The emergence of larger and stronger organizations has been accompanied by significant change in the character of these institutions: they are more economically self-conscious, responding to the financial or budgetary goals of their ownership or funding sources; private-sector organizations aggressively compete in a rather volatile and unstable marketplace for both clients and lawyers; and people within contemporary practice organizations think of themselves (and are treated) less as independent professionals and more as instruments or employees of the organization.

Two different reactions or stories, one accepting, one critical, have emerged as explanations of these changes in the contemporary legal profession. On the one hand, change is seen as conventional. The story is of a profession being renovated and improved, with obvious benefits accruing from the importation of business management styles and technologies into the notoriously disorganized world of lawyers. The vocabulary of this story includes terms like planning, accountability, budgets, streamlined (i.e., more pyramidal) governance structures, marketing, and lateral and vertical opportunities for advancement rather than traditional professional terms like calling, service, self-regulation, and noblesse oblige.

A decidedly more upbeat, even breathless and celebratory, version of the story of the improvement of the profession originates from the new legal journalism, and particularly the voice of its most prominent leader, Stephen Brill of the *American Lawyer* group of newspapers. While the analytic component of these publications, such as rankings of the most profitable and largest law firms, have had major impact on the traditionally closed world of practice organizations,

---

in 1970 to almost 55,000 in 1980, a 40 percent increase for this period. Almost half of these were employed by Fortune 500 or Fortune 50 companies in selected industries (Curran et al. 1985, 19). A further 22 percent increase occurred between 1980 and 1988 (Curran and Carson 1991, 4).

6. "In 1968 the largest firm in the United States had 169 lawyers and the twentieth largest had 106 lawyers. In 1988, the largest firm had 962 lawyers and there were 149 firms larger than the largest firm in 1968" (Galanter and Palay 1991, 46).

the new journalism projects a style akin to the business literature of the turn of the twentieth century, which produced hagiographical profiles of Andrew Carnegie, Henry Ford, and other titans of industry. The late-twentieth-century equivalents of those early celebrations of great Americans are *American Lawyer*-style articles about the deal makers and rainmakers and brilliant strategists in various American law practices. The overall effect is to beat the drum in celebration of the transformation of American law practice and the emergence of top-tier firms, great leaders, brash young lawyers who are magnets for business, and the general excitement of it all. These stories have a distinct flavor of social Darwinism: we read not only about winners, but investigative journalism's choice of losers, profiles of chump firms that do not understand what is happening to the profession.

A different, more critical account of change in the legal profession is a story told with some emotion about a decline in values, the triumph of greed, the transformation of law from a public good to a marketplace commodity and a "profession" degenerating into a mere "business." In an issue of the *Journal of the American Bar Association* that touts a manufacturing-style retooling of law practice, there also appears an article reciting stories of dissatisfied lawyers and describing a "malaise" in the profession, "occasional oases of contentment" contrasting with the "bill-until-you-drop syndrome," and the "cancer of nastiness spreading through the profession's soul" (Jefferson 1991).

These two stories or reactions are deeply contradictory accounts of the legal profession. They share common ground in two respects. First, they agree that the legal profession *is* undergoing rapid transformation, but the metaphors for change are worlds apart: loss and destruction versus growth and fulfillment. Second, both stories claim to be about professional values—the decline of professional values or the rise of a new form of professional value. Both stories represent important insights about the contemporary profession but suffer from serious defects of style. A tone of pious self-righteousness usually pervades the story of loss, and an insufferable aura of self-congratulation often suffuses the story of gain.[7]

---

7. After writing about the two stories, I discovered this passage in James Clifford's *The Predicament of Culture*: "[M]odern ethnographic histories are perhaps condemned to oscillate between two meta narratives: one of homogenization, the other of emergence; one of loss, the other of invention. In most specific conjunctures, both narratives are relevant, each undermining the other's claim to 'tell the whole story' . . ." (1988, 17).

Leaders of state, local, and national bar associations have initiated efforts to respond to or harness the transformation of law practice. In the mid-1980s the American Bar Association created a Commission on Professionalism, which issued an eighty-page document, subtitled *Blueprint for the Rekindling of Lawyer Professionalism*, calling on the law schools and the practicing bar and judiciary to take steps to promote public service and "resist the temptation to make the acquisition of wealth a primary goal of law practice" (American Bar Association 1986, 15). In 1991, the ABA issued a report entitled *At the Breaking Point: The Emerging Crisis in the Quality of Lawyers' Health and Lives—Its Impact on Law Firms and Client Services*. Groups within the ABA and local bar associations, as well as the federal and state judiciary, have promoted documents like a *Lawyer's Creed of Professionalism* or local codes of conduct designed to promote more civility and candor and discourage venality in litigation. The federal courts have adopted the controversial Rule 11 of the Federal Rules of Civil Procedure imposing sanctions on lawyers for inappropriate conduct in the use of the courts. Ethical rules of the profession that were codified in 1970 were completely revised by the ABA in the 1980s and generated extensive debate within the profession: new model rules of professional conduct have been considered and amended and adopted by the supreme courts of most states. The American Law Institute is engaged in a substantial project to revise and organize the law of lawyering.

This book is not an account of the contemporary legal profession that attempts to decide whether the profession is in decline or revival. A case can be made for both perspectives. One could argue that there are many indications that the law is not serving our society well: legal services are poorly distributed and increasingly inaccessible to larger portions of the population; the costs and complexities and delays of litigation and much transactional law are formidable societal burdens and matters of deep resentment by clients; and lawyers express great dissatisfaction over the conditions of work within the profession. On the other hand, the legal profession in the United States has never been more diverse, prosperous, competitive, or influential in the economic life of the nation.

Regardless of whether the perspective of the profession is critical or celebratory, analysis of the profession and prescriptions for change are often premised on a flawed understanding of the meaning of professionalism in contemporary law practice. This book is an effort to bring insight to the debate over the contemporary legal profession by illuminating a different way of thinking about professionalism—one more germane to the problems and realities of modern law practice.

Profession, professional, and *professionalism* are words that come easily to lawyers, and they resonate with a number of meanings, which can be grouped in the following ways:[8]

> appropriate behavior, doing things well, effectiveness, or good appearance (as in the professionalism of a document, or professional behavior, professional dress);[9]
> expertise (as in marketing professional, a professionally designed information system);[10]

---

8. The use of *profession* to refer to the collective body of legal practitioners is clear enough, and leads to no confusions of which I am aware. Similarly, the use of *professional* and *professionalism* to refer to doing something for gain in contrast to amateur and amateurism is not a distinction that raises problems. One final use of *profession* is also largely unproblematic: the idea of the assumed role or mannerism, as in professional patriot or professional do-gooder.

9. Some examples:

The partner had intended to fire the associate . . . in a humane and professional fashion by providing him with one year to find another position. (Bellon 1991, 38)

Consider showing staff video tapes on topics such as professional telephone etiquette, professionalism in the law office and client relations. (Booth and Raridon 1991)

A clothier visited the associate at his office, advised him on professional dressing and made him three suits. Since then, the young lawyer's reputation within the firm has improved. (Kaitz 1991)

A grammar and style checker, usually a separate program, will add to the professionalism of many documents. (Geary 1991, S1)

10. Examples:

Almost every major firm in the country hired a non lawyer executive director in the 1980's to run its operations. . . . They are professional managers who are brought in to help you and build a business. (Orey 1991, 3)

The outside law firm is . . . more often than not armed with a box of marketing tools designed by marketing professionals. (Escher 1991, S1)

With a professionally prepared, formal announcement, San Francisco–based Brobeck, Phleger & Harrison in May announced hiring Margaret Block as director of practice support. . . . In addition, information-systems professionals are coming out of the computer room and into the mainstream of the law firm to discuss information needs with lawyers and clients. (Novachicik 1991, 20)

dispassionate, no-nonsense, objective, nonpolitical behavior (as
in professional demeanor, or professionalizing the prosecutor's
office);[11]

the idea of a career, a life of work (as in professional development);[12]

work itself, work skills, or the ability to be skillful (as in improving professional service);[13]

There is also a tax department . . . staffed by five nonlawyer tax professionals.
(Clarke 1991, 60)

[H]ave the nameless legal assistants, case clerks, secretaries and word processors,
once again, been relegated to the back cave, never to be seen or mentioned[?]
We have respect for our profession. (Sitzman 1991, 7)
11. Examples:
His career has focused on government, but he has made partner in a major
firm. He is not, in short, an Ed Meese or Dick Thornburgh. A period of pure
professionalism could be a welcome relief. ("Enter Mr. Barr" 1991, 12)

Mary, a 29 year-old lawyer is a rising star at a large downtown firm. She has
developed a tough, uncompromising professional demeanor that has earned her
a reputation, despite her youth, as a formidable adversary and a hard negotiator.
(Sells 1991, 30)

The focus of his seven-point campaign platform was a promise to professionalize
the D.A.'s office and free it from its close ties with the sheriff's department.
(Ainsworth 1991, 1)
12. Examples:
In any profession, the pattern of assignments you work on is the professional
development process—you just have to learn how to manage it. (Maister
1991, 32)

[A] 75-lawyer firm in Denver . . . conducted a confidential survey of partners'
attitudes about work load, stress, professional satisfaction, fairness of the compensation system, perception of the quality of the firm's work and firm environment. (Studley 1991b, 45)

Evaluation is one segment of professional development . . . well-managed firms
use the process of evaluation hand-in-hand with individual performance reviews
to motivate, develop and reward their superstars and solid performers. (Wehmann 1991, 39)
13. Examples:
It's depressing to realize that timesheets could be the principal archives of one's
professional contribution. (LeVan 1991 S2)

Many firms seek to merge with or acquire a small group or groups of attorneys
because they expect size and a better balance of skills and client base to provide
them with improved professional service and long-term economic advantage.
(Rose 1991a, 1)

a personnel category referring to someone trained as a lawyer (as in contract professional, or professional time);[14]

appropriate values and integrity (as in professional vision, declining professionalism or impropriety or lack of professionalism);[15]

learning and understanding (as in professional growth);[16]

autonomy (as in regulation eroding professionalism);[17]

ethical rules (as in state variations in this form of professionalism);[18]

the business or occupation of law (as in professional success, professional reward, or professional service for customers).[19]

[A]s far as the quality of the work that each of them puts out, I think they're equally professional. (Orenstein 1991, 1)

14. Examples:

Among the many hiring strategies available to both law firms and corporations is the use of a flexible pool of contract professionals to augment a smaller core of permanent attorneys. (Bellon 1991, 38)

Every law firm tracks professional time; now, according to the survey, almost half of all major law departments track attorney time as well. (Bellis and Morrison 1991, S4)

[T]he firm should have a business plan that requires each professional to be more actively involved in elements of business development. (Grossbard 1991, 24)

15. Examples:

[T]he fastest way to become a second-rate business with second-rate revenues is to do anything that even hints of impropriety or lack of professionalism. (Mestel 1991, 46)

She said the healthy firms share . . . [c]ommitment to a common professional vision for the firm. . . . Initially, lawyers went into practice in partnership because it reflected the way they view themselves professionally. (Dahl 1991, 33)

[L]awyers have sacrificed their professionalism on the altar of mammon. . . . He tries to isolate the causes of what's seen as declining professionalism. (Kornstein 1991, 2)

16. "For professional growth, this can be done by attending continuing legal education seminars or meetings sponsored by outside groups" (Rose 1991b, 4).

17. "The delegates apparently were persuaded that ancillary business will lead to the erosion of professionalism, self-regulation and independent judgment" (Saniborn and Lavelle 1991, 3).

18. "This area of professionalism ["marketing ethics"] is replete with state variations causing confusion, dominated by perceptions and emotions, and hindered by lack of widespread knowledge" (Haserot 1991, 15).

19. Examples:

A number of commentators now use the expression "professional services business."

Although law firms are likely to shed few tears over recently impoverished
recruiters, such trends do reflect the changing nature of the legal profession as
a whole. An understanding of what really happened to the business this past
year can be instructive for recruiters and law firms alike. (Mestel 1991, 46)

Customers service, service to clients, whether it's professional, whether it's selling
Oreos, depends on relationships. ("The AM Law 100" 1991, 6)

The recession may be very helpful to the legal profession in this regard, because
the legal profession—I think more so than publishing or accounting—has in the
past been a profession where if you're a bright overachieving young man or
woman, you get on a track in college and you make a decision to go to
school . . . going into the profession of law today is a lot like going into any
other profession, which means it's not enough to be bright and overachieving.
(Henning 1991, 1)

Today, I see in terms of our firm's client base—lenders, developers, financial
institutions, mid-and-small-size-companies—that in-house general counsel are
also cutting back. . . . They are feeling the same pressure the professional service
organizations are. (Rubenstein 1991)

"To be at the top of your profession requires an awful lot more than just handling
cases," says Gitlin. "All of this [activity in professional organizations] helps build
your presence in the marketplace, and that helps your firm." (Heller 1991, 1)

It's professionally correct these days to harp on the fundamentals. . . . Somehow
or other those notions [of law as a business] have become less professional.
(Brill 1991b, 6)

J. Thomas Lenhart . . . acknowledges that the experience will give the firm a
boost in developing a food-and-drug litigation practice. "We view this [a contract
to monitor the FDA] as an opportunity to do something that is, frankly, professionally rewarding," says Lenhart. "Obviously, it gives us a chance to learn
more about a substantial area of legal work." (Kaplan 1991, 1)

It is no secret that the professional services business is getting more competitive
every day. . . . Professionals are marketing and selling all the time, whether they
realize it or not. . . . The term "professional" here refers to the individual who is
licensed to provide the professional service being sold—in this case, the attorney.
The term "non-professional" refers to others who are involved in the marketing
or selling process, but who do not have the license to deliver the professional
service involved—even though they are professionals in the marketing or selling
of professional services. (David 1991, 40)

There are still partners who bristle at having the legal profession called a business
or referring to clients as customers. However, when it comes to billing and
collection, the firm is very much a business, and when the client receives your
bill, he or she regards you as a vendor. (Hildebrandt 1991a, 20)

[C]onsultants . . . still do not understand there is a difference between corporate
strategic planning and planning for a professional service business. (Hildebrandt
1991b, 46)

Illustrations of how various are the nuances in the use of the word *profession* and its adjectival and ideological form abound in the popular legal press. Usually the meaning can be deciphered from context, but often the precise meaning is obscure. Here, for example, are some suggestions as to meaning (interposed within brackets) to the following passage by a columnist writing in the *Manhattan Lawyer:*

> Helping associates identify their existing and potential professional [i.e., business] network is Holland & Hart's first lesson in business development.... Another strategy is to emphasize business development as a route to increasing control of one's professional [i.e., career] destiny. Lawyers with loyal clients and specialists in high-demand fields have autonomy, clout, visibility, and mobility that can help them achieve professional [work or career or values] satisfaction. (Studley 1991a, 36)

The ambiguity of meaning of "professional satisfaction" in this passage is fundamental to understanding why the profession family of words is so popular among lawyers. The words have an almost incantatory function, combined with the special utility of so many meanings that listeners or readers can take what they want from them, ranging roughly from concepts of business acumen to high moral principle to proficiency and lofty standards of quality. And they have one other quality that is invaluable: favorable resonance. In whatever mode of meaning, they generate agreeable vibrations or responses from the reader or listener.

Nowhere is the profession family of words more adroitly used than in efforts by lawyers to convince each other. The firm brochure is a document describing a law-practice organization.[20] Law firms, corporate law departments, and public agencies submit these brochures to law school placement offices to paint an attractive picture of their organization to students who are prospective new lawyers for the firm or agency. At first glance, firm brochures display an almost anesthetizing similarity in touting characteristics of the practice: the high quality of work and personnel doing the work, the

---

20. Firm brochures are also used to impress prospective or existing clients. Sometimes the same document is used for both client and law-student audiences.

interesting nature and diversity and importance of the clients, the
fine training and career-development opportunities for new lawyers
(including pro bono and public-service activities), the fairness of the
evaluation system for junior lawyers, and the splendid resources such
as computers and libraries and secretarial and paralegal staff.

What is more interesting about this literature of uniformity are
the marginal cases where organizations broach characteristics of difference. *Professional development* is a phrase typically used to denote
the kind of training and exposure a young lawyer can expect from
a practice or organization. Large firms argue that the most sophisticated professional development occurs in an environment of major
clients posing legal problems of great complexity and moment. Small
firms argue that the finest form of professional growth and training
takes place in the bureaucracy-free environment of a small group of
colleagues learning from each other.

Firms thus disagree strongly about the structural relationships
for an associate that best promote professionalism and professional
development for the junior lawyer. The range of answers varies
strikingly:

> [W]e have tried to avoid the rigid departmentalization and bu-
> reaucratization of many large firms. . . . We do not measure suc-
> cess in billable hours (we have no minimum requirement) or rely
> on any other single criterion for evaluating an associate's pro-
> gress. In general, we have sought to eliminate those internal pres-
> sures and rivalries within the firm that can seriously detract from
> the enjoyment of practicing law. (Wiggin and Dana 1991, 1)

> The work assignment philosophy is uniform across all depart-
> ments. After selecting a department, the associate can select to
> work, over a period of time, with many of the partners in the
> department, for a wide variety of clients, and in virtually all
> areas of the department's work. . . . We believe that our system,
> through concurrent work with different clients, gives associates
> at an early stage of professional development a broader view of
> our practice, clients, and firm. At the same time we believe our
> system trains associates more thoroughly and effectively than
> other systems. It combines the intensity of closely supervised
> work with the fastest possible exposure to the breadth of our

practice and to a large number of partners in each area of practice. (Davis, Polk, and Wardwell 1990, 10–11)

Because of the diverse and evolving nature of our practice, the firm has a flexible, non-departmentalized structure that accommodates both generalists and specialists. The firm maintains a collegial atmosphere reflecting a common basis of mutual respect and shared values. . . . Ordinarily . . . associates prefer to have assignments in several different areas during their early years. Like many of our partners, many of these associates choose to remain generalists, moving to new cases and projects as their interest, the law, and the firm's needs change. (Covington and Burling 1991, 9)

Young and aggressive, the Firm is committed to establishing the first national law firm practicing exclusively in the field of complex litigation and dispute resolution. . . . The Firm's associates are among the highest paid in the United States. Each associate has the opportunity to work on sophisticated cases in an environment that encourages rapid professional development. In-house training, a team oriented approach to litigation, and the opportunity for rotation through the Dallas, New York, and Chicago offices are all designed to accelerate each attorney's professional growth. . . . The nature of the Firm's practice and its plans for growth require that the Firm hire attorneys who possess the talent and drive that enables them to assume substantial responsibility for major cases . . . [and] who thrive on the intensity and challenge of "bet your business" litigation. (Bickel and Brewer 1991, 1)

Each attorney in the firm, including associates, is expected to participate in practice development efforts not only to obtain new clients but also to retain and expand the scope of services rendered to existing clients. . . . New associates are expected to focus their efforts on developing the legal skills necessary to serve existing clients in a thorough and timely manner. More experienced associates often serve as faculty for legal education seminars or participate in various public service and community enterprises to begin building the professional and personal relationships

necessary for effective practice development. Each year associates
with three or more years of experience work with a practice development coordinator to formulate and implement individual practice development plans, which are later considered during the
evaluation process. (Dorsey and Whitney 1991, 11–12)

Although there are obvious difficulties in generalizing from a
form of unregulated advertising, these brochures illustrate current
understandings and confusions about the idea of professionalism. The
conformity, the relentless similarity of the material, suggests the existence of some conventional ideas about what it means to be professional. Conventional professionalism (whether conceived of as a
satisfactory career, values, business, or work) arises from serving
clients, the supervised learning on the job that constitutes training
in the practice, public service and pro bono gestures, and a supportive
environment in terms of colleagues and support staff and facilities.
These ideas might appropriately be termed the standard conception
of lawyer ideals or expectations of the goods and duties of practice.

On the other hand, the uniformity of the brochures gives rise to
a certain skepticism. The brochures are a means to authenticate the
organization and thereby attract young lawyers. It is hard to escape
the inference that the organizations that author these brochures see
the standard conception of lawyer ideals in largely instrumental
terms. The organization uses the ideal of professionalism to describe
or rationalize practices of the organization ranging from intense specialization to support for the generalist, from collegial to competitive
atmospheres, from training new lawyers sheltered from business to
strong encouragement to cultivate clients. From what is said and left
unsaid, one can develop a sense of a firm or agency personality
behind the recitations about exciting clients, superb training and work
opportunities, supportive environments, and public service. Beneath
the marketing façade stands the reality of organizations, which
embody widely differing understandings of professionalism.

The appropriation of concepts of professionalism for organizational purposes creates fundamental problems for the legal profession,
one that leaders of the bar have difficulty acknowledging. To the
extent the professional ideal is a marketing decision, a construct or
a justification of the organization to its clients, lawyers, and future
recruits, it is fruitless to appeal to common understandings or core

concepts of professionalism to convince lawyers, in the words of the ABA Commission on Professionalism, to "resist temptation."

The practice organization is the center of temptation. It is the arena for working out pressures of competition for clients, internal tensions over compensation, and delicate balances between the costs and benefits of supervision and practice quality, teaching and public service, collegial decision making and focused directions for the growth of the practice. The standard conception of lawyer ideals does not include the most fundamental trade-offs an organization makes between decisions about business and decisions about professional identity. Professionalism is not an abstraction in an organization. It is forged in every decision of the practice. This *vertical* conception of professionalism works in different ways from the *horizontal* or standard conception of professional ideals.[21] The organization draws on an array of different understandings of the concept of the professional to fashion a set of house norms or rationales for the structures of the practice. Standard concepts of professionalism are transformed by the readings and rationalizations and compromises developed within the practice organization.

The meaning of professional values is now so malleable that the terms *professional* and *professionalism* are now well-nigh useless. No commonly accepted definition of profession exists. The ABA Committee on Professionalism lists five elements of professionalism: (1) special privileges from the state, (2) substantial prerequisite intellectual training, (3) the client's trust due to an inability to evaluate the professional's work, (4) the client's trust premised on the professional's devotion to serving the client's interest and the public good, and (5) self-regulation (American Bar Association 1986, 10 n. 7). This is a sociologist's definition, and even if we were to concede that under certain circumstances such a definition may work for purposes of distinguishing how law or medicine differs from some other activity,[22] it does not begin to capture the ideas or ideals that inform lawyers' views of themselves, the way they respond to the competing pressures of clients, colleagues, the business of law, and (in the words of the professionalism report) the "public good."

Robert Gordon has identified a relatively coherent concept of professionalism in the elite New York bar of the late nineteenth

---

21. I am indebted to Robert Post for this metaphor of the axes of professionalism.
22. But see Metzger 1975 who cogently criticizes such list making.

century (1984). The leaders of the bar conceived of themselves as reformers, not unlike Tocqueville's lawyer-aristocrats. They were committed to the scientific understanding of the law and political action to restore a framework of predictable and impartial application of the law, freed from special interests. Gordon argues that this ideal of professionalism unraveled in the early twentieth century under pressures of the great expansion of corporate clients, skepticism about legal science, and more institutionalized law-firm structures serving the needs of corporations. Rayman L. Solomon reviews the changing themes of lawyer professionalism through the speeches of bar leaders in response to what he describes as certain "crises" for the twentieth-century legal profession: Prohibition, the Great Depression, expansion of federal regulation during the New Deal including the court-packing plan of 1937, McCarthyism, and the debates over creating legal services for the poor beginning in the 1950s (Solomon 1992). Solomon's study concludes that professionalism is a kind of talismanic weapon to be used to buttress the political or social views of the particular bar leader.[23]

Practicing lawyers are *never* opposed to professionalism. Professionalism is the law's apple pie and motherhood. It is a kind of incantation, or blessing, conveniently large enough to serve as the antidote for an enormous array of discontents, from billable-hour regimens to excessive partisanship, from abuse of discovery to acquisitiveness. Or professionalism is used to rationalize new business practices and department structures—or lack thereof—by law firms who use their particular house brand of professionalism as a tool for recruiting new associates or lateral hires. No common, coherent concept of professionalism informs the actions of twentieth-century lawyers in the United States because of the deep confusion between the horizontal and the vertical cultures of professionalism. The organization uses or reinvents common understandings of professionalism for its own purposes.

We need to begin a reconstruction of our understanding of the profession. The whole idea of profession originated in a medieval, and therefore largely religious, sense of a calling, a taking of vows to uphold certain principles and solemn commitment in the eyes of

---

23. In fairness to Solomon, I should point out he does allude to several continuities: anticommercialism, independence, opposition to lay encroachment, and advocacy of the "public interest" (Solomon 1992, 2).

God. In the course of secularizing these ideas, the concept of profession became a creature of the sociologists, whose interests focused primarily on differentiating professions from bureaucracies. This obsession with the distinction between bureaucratic and professional forms of organizing work is increasingly problematic, as the lessons of Japanese industrial experience appear to suggest that the more successful the bureaucracy, the more it treats its workers like professionals. Traditional theorists of professionalism did not account for business and organizational values, which they viewed as inherently destructive of professional values and inimical to true professionalism.[24] Under today's conditions their logic would require the conclusion that the professions no longer exist, or are so transformed as to be inappropriately categorized as professions.

We need an understanding of the profession that both frees itself from the rather useless typological debate over bureaucratic and professional forms of organization and accounts for the dramatic changes occurring in the profession as a result of strong economic enterprises emerging as the dominant form of professional organization. During this transitional time, when our understanding of the profession is inadequate to account for the radical transformation of professional life in our culture, the words *profession* and *professional* and *professionalism* become detached from any clear tradition or coherence.

The disintegration of the concept of professionalism parallels what Donald Schon describes as an "urgent dilemma of rigor and relevance" facing the contemporary practitioner (Schon 1987, 241). The dilemma, according to Schon, derives from a deeply embedded set of assumptions about professional knowledge that dominates education of professionals at American universities. These assumptions of "technical rationality" are derived from nineteenth-century positivist understandings of science, knowledge, and meaning. An underlying discipline or basic science is assumed to be the foundation for an applied or procedural problem-solving component; and performance skills and attitudes deploy both this basic and applied knowledge (Schon 1987, 243).

The problem with technical rationality, according to Schon, is that it does not accord with the realities of professionals actually coping with "messy, indeterminate, problematic situations," where

---

24. I refer to Durkheim and popularizers like Flexner, modern sociologists like Parsons, and legal philosophers like Lon Fuller.

professional artistry is required to frame the problem to be solved
and cope with uncertainty, complexity, and uniqueness (Schon 1987,
245). The dilemma is that the creativity of the professional does not
seem to follow describable procedures and therefore seems unrigorous.
Practitioners develop different strategies for avoiding this sense of
lack of rigor. One strategy is to narrow the reach of the practice to
highly technical specialties, where the problems come predefined and
therefore are less relevant to actual practice (245–46).[25] Another is to
become "selectively inattentive to data" incongruent with professional
theories and techniques and therefore provide poor service to the
client. Schon argues that a kind of knowing and reflection in action,
or artistry, or on-the-spot experimentation not unlike a good conversation, characterizes a first-rate professional's approach to real
problems. This artistry can be described, taught, or coached, provided we are "attentive to differences in the framing of problematic
situations and to the rare episodes of frame-reflective discourse in
which practitioners sometimes coordinate and transform their conflicting ways of making sense of confusing predicaments" (Schon
1987, 245).

Standard conceptions of lawyers' professionalism, such as those
espoused by the organized bar, are analogous to Schon's technical
rationality. The presentations in firm brochures capture this official
ideology rather well: first-rate professionalism includes serving clients
well, learning and growing in knowledge and skills, working with
helpful colleagues, providing public service to the community, and
earning a good living. Like technical rationality, the standard conception of professionalism simply does not account for the reality of
professional life today, where the vertical dimension of organizational
culture transforms the meaning of professionalism.

The breakdown of technical rationality is not the death of the
professional ideal: Schon offers a challenging description of the meaning of professional practice. Similarly, the breakdown of standard
ideals of professionalism does not necessarily entail abandoning *any*
ideal. Rather we need to describe ways in which creative lawyers
engage in what Schon might call "reflective discourse" to make sense
of the confusing predicaments of contemporary professionalism.

---

25. In law, this strategy is often described in different terms as the distinction
between client-responsive billing partners or rainmakers, who attract clients, and
technical specialists to whom the billing partner refers work in a large firm.

Our first priority is to understand, in some depth, what is happening to the profession. And this requires going beyond understandings of the economic or social hierarchy of the profession and looking at the internal dynamics of practice organizations. The leaders of the organized bar are not the only lawyers concerned about changes in the profession. Lawyers in firms and departments and agencies work through this challenge on an almost daily basis. Understanding the character of different organizations of practice, their texture, their acoustics, or the way participants work within them—their unique culture—is indispensable to understanding the nature of change in the contemporary profession and the extraordinary heterogeneity of professional values within various types of practice organizations. We are all amateur evolutionists watching the adaption of lawyers to the changing environment of practice. We need to resist predicting too quickly the typology of the surviving species. There is a range of creativity and complexity in adaptive behavior by lawyers in practice organizations. We need to examine closely the elements within organizations that affect their transformation.

Global concepts of professionalism are refracted, if not replaced, by the day-to-day struggles over clients and governance and incentives within the practice organization. We can no longer define professional values independently of specific organizational settings and cultures,[26] not because lawyers are oblivious to general professional ideals or understandings of the economics of the profession, but because the particular configuration or relationship between economic and other professional values is worked out within each organization and emerges in the form of a distinct professional culture. The landscape of the profession has become more kaleidoscopic, confused, and variegated as elements of a common professional culture fragment into thousands of professional cultures.

I am not suggesting that we cannot deepen our understanding of the legal profession by studying the economics or the sociology of the private firm and other forms of practice organization. But it would be a mistake to assume that all boutiques, or legal-aid bureaus, or large corporate law firms are the same. For example, lateral movement of partners between large law firms, now commonplace, could be cited as an illustration of sameness. The evidence, however, including the

26. Robert Post helped me to arrive at this formulation of my thesis, a more modest and plausible account than I was initially inclined to present.

story of the McKinnon firm in chapter 2, reveals how hard it is to integrate new people, to make a merger or new practice group a success for both entities. Cultural differences between law practices are palpable, not ephemeral, phenomena. Corporate culture is such a significant theme in the literature of business that it is rare to find credible generalities about the sameness of all organizations in a particular industry. Leaders of different organizations confront similar economic circumstances and markets in different ways, treat their employees differently, establish varied systems of internal and external communication—in short, create a unique organizational character that affects the way people in the organizations see themselves and approach the challenges of their industry.

The premise of this book is that the culture or house norms of the agency, department, or firm play a dominant role in the way a lawyer practices. The organization profoundly affects the lives of lawyers: from styles of dealing with clients to relationships with colleagues and coworkers; from the choice of legal work itself to connections with civic and community life; from the social status of the practice to the sense of professionalism; from lawyers' incomes to feelings of satisfaction and fulfillment in a career. Practice organizations now by and large constitute the legal profession(s). Many lawyers and legal educators maintain that a coherent understanding of the practice of law requires a grasp of the ethical rules of the profession, as well as the meaning of professionalism—the law of lawyering, as some call it. I am convinced that another proposition is at least as fundamental: no coherent account of professionalism, legal ethics, or the contemporary legal profession is possible without understanding the workings of practice organizations.

I have chosen to explore the contemporary legal profession through close looks at several different law practices, to make the professional organization emerge more vividly, as the epigraph from Fernando Pessoa would have it, by describing it well. My medium is the story, or the organizational biography, which captures or reveals some of the contours of practice culture. The practices in these stories are varied enough to reflect major forms of professional practice: large corporate firm, medium-sized firm, corporate law department, public agency, and small firm. But these are not typical or representative practices, if only because the search for the typical is a delusion in the contemporary world of law practice. There are no iron laws of professional evolution that bind lawyers to certain types or styles of organization. If there is a message to be drawn from these stories, it is that the institutions of practice have a limitless range of futures, each a function of the ability, imagination, and aspirations of the lawyers who constitute the practice.

These stories should be of interest to several audiences:

lawyers and judges seeking to understand the transformation in the profession and their own practices and courtrooms;

people thinking about a career in law and the range of options in law practice;

law students concerned about understanding and "reading" organizations accurately, and more carefully evaluating their employment options;

lawyers and law-practice administrators encountering challenges of personal development within their practice organization; and

people outside the legal profession interested in the law, professions in general, or organizational change.

The purpose of these stories is to capture the real frontier of professionalism and legal ethics, to attempt to describe the domain that worries lawyers because it most deeply affects the character of their professional lives. This is not a world of the flashy case or the melodramatic client, but the day-in, day-out struggle to build a life in the profession that resolves the competing demands of economic stability and values of colleagueship, craftsmanship, and professional statesmanship.

Part of the reason for the neglect of these issues is the culture of legal academia. A large number of law professors are refugees from the practice world, who arrived in teaching disaffected by the economics of private practice and largely unsympathetic to, if not contemptuous of, examining how lawyers respond to the economic pressures on their organizations. Understanding of the profession is further impoverished by the pervasive disinterest by American law professors in empirical studies of the justice system or the profession.[27]

---

27. There are a number of notable exceptions to this generalization. See for example, Galanter and Palay 1991.

It is not surprising, therefore, that law students emerge from their schooling with a profound naïveté about the organizations of practice. They set out, like Tertius Lydgate in the epigraph from *Middlemarch*, on a largely unexplored terrain, ill-prepared to cope with the pressures and challenges, let alone the subtleties and realities of practicing in organizational settings. The practice organization is by and large missing from the American law school. It is my hope that this book will stimulate law students and professors to join lawyers in thinking about the character of the organizations that constitute the practice of law.

One way to approach this book is simply to enjoy the stories about lawyers in their organizational setting. But my ambition is that these stories move readers—to paraphrase the epigraph from Goethe—to attend more deeply to the profession, form their own convictions, and use these stories to enliven their thinking about the legal profession in American society. Part 1 of the book will suffice for those who simply want to read some nonfictional stories about the legal profession and to derive their own conclusions.

Part 2 of the book is what I make of these stories, a gesture responsive (in words of the epigraph from Isabel Colgate) to the need to test these stories against such truths as I can lay my hands on to uncover continuities in the effort to understand. In the first chapter of part 2, I consider each of the stories and provide some reflections on their significance. The final chapter of part 2 constitutes my thinking about connections between telling these stories, the stories themselves, and my views of the contemporary legal profession. Finally, in the Afterword, I describe how I came to write the stories and ruminate on this process.

Parts 1 and 2 may be viewed as two different but closely related books. Each part is written in a different voice. In part 1, a historian seeks to describe the nature of five law practices through the narrative device of the practices speaking for themselves. In part 2, a student of the profession talks about what he learns about the profession from them. Part 1 is the book I set out to write. Part 2 was the book I was forced to write by colleagues who kept asking the question, what do *you* think? Both parts derive from an instinct to understand better the contemporary legal profession and a desire to engage the profession, including its academics, in a livelier and more richly contextualized debate about the current and future course of the legal profession in this country.

Law practice has always been a bundle of mixed values that do not lie in comfortable relationship with each other: values of serving clients' needs, values of colleagueship and support, values of craftsmanship and practice standards, values of earning a living, and values of an independent professional role. The emergence of organizations as powerful forces in the accommodation of these incommensurate values has, during the past decade, accentuated conflicts that previously lay relatively dormant. The stories in this book are about lawyers struggling over these values. The setting for the struggle is the organization, which experiences tensions associated with powerful competitive pressures that lead it to develop mechanisms of control and direction over the lawyers who make up the practice. The subtext of each story is the question, what holds this practice together? What motivates these lawyers to function as a group? The organization has become the mediating force between lawyer, clients, and the community at large. The culture of the organization has become a crucial determinant of the quality of professional life.

Part 1.
Stories of Law Practice

Chapter 2

Playing in the Big Leagues at McKinnon, Moreland, and Fox

Analyzing the Doctrine of Cravatheat Emptor

It is such a disaster for associates, for the profession, and the profession's relations with clients that it would have been worth taking up a collection from lawyers around the country—say a hundred dollars a head—and donating the money to Cravath just to buy them off and help them achieve their objectives. They have jerked the profession on a chain fighting over one hundred or so warm bodies that inhabit the law reviews of top schools. It's nuts.

This rather testy assessment comes from Frederick Marx,[1] a senior tax attorney at McKinnon, Moreland, and Fox, a fast-growing and, in the words of a local reporter on legal affairs, "hot" Bay Area law firm.[2] Marx's anger is addressed to "the ripple effect" of salary increases for starting associates, necessary to keep pace with the major, "almost predatory" ("The AM Law 100" 1986, 1) 25 percent increase in associate salaries announced by the Wall Street firm of Cravath, Swaine, and Moore in April 1986. In October 1986, salaries for new associates at Cravath started at $65,000 per year and ranged close to $100,000 for those with high-prestige judicial clerkship experience.[3]

While the Cravath public announcement was framed in terms of meeting the competition with the investment-banking industry and

---

1. The specific references to institutions in this story, as all the names and places in chapters 2, 3, 4, and 6, are fictitious.

2. "Bay Area" is a large metropolitan area outside of New York City.

3. In 1992, the starting salary for a first-year associate at Cravath was $83,000.

the problem of high housing costs in New York City, no one—least
of all McKinnon lawyers—finds those explanations credible. A number of lawyers at McKinnon would not be surprised by statements
in a 1986 issue of the *American Lawyer*:

> Cravath suffers in the recruiting wars . . . because it has a rep-
> utation as a sweatshop, in the sense not only of working people
> hard but also of not being particularly nice to them. In addition,
> students—who seem increasingly savvy about relative business
> opportunities at different firms and in different areas of practice—
> are wary of a firm that makes so few partners. ("The AM Law
> 100" 1986, 24)

One in ten associates become Cravath partners. Cravath's problem
was that the attrition among associates—one-fourth of the 170 regular
associates left in 1985—was so severe that the senior ranks of experienced associates, who are far more efficient and valuable than new
associates and can be billed at rates highly profitable to the firm,
were growing slim. According to sources in the firm quoted by the
American Lawyer, if the new salary increases for Cravath associates,
projected to cost $3 million a year, lead to increasing associates'
average length of stay by one year, the firm would generate an
additional $4 million a year in gross revenues (1986, 24).

Bay Area firms freely acknowledge that New York City is a
different game altogether, that is, that they will never be able to
compete head-to-head for legal talent attracted by the allure and
excitement of the nation's financial center. But newly graduated lawyers with doubts about New York—and there are scores of talented
people in that category—might find an initial $20,000 to $25,000
salary differential a rather strong reason to resolve doubts in favor
of the Big Apple. The major Bay Area firms have tended to lag about
$10,000 behind Wall Street. The ripple of the Cravath decision, based
on the announced intentions of some of the leading Bay Area firms,
runs to about a $10,000 to $15,000 increase for entry-level lawyers.
The ripple, however, makes real waves within the salary structure
of a firm because associates with more seniority require commensurate raises—not on the heroic scale of the new associates grateful
for the profitability, foresight, and aggressiveness of Cravath, but
sufficient bumps up the scale to create at least a modest progression.

McKinnon is, in the words of one partner, the "upstart" or newcomer. It is the only first-generation firm among large Bay Area firms; it has built itself through skillful acquisitions and mergers— the "rape and pillage" method, as one associate laughingly puts it— into a firm of 135, with 57 partners. Reputation and self-image coincide to a large extent: young (its leaders are in their early fifties), aggressive, hard-working, talented business advisors and transactional lawyers, with an expanding client base of entrepreneurs and, more recently, some establishment business and financial institutions. Performance is appropriately rewarded at McKinnon, a factor that accounts in part for success in attracting high-level talent to the expanding firm. The performance and reward ethos may be the primary reason some partners at McKinnon are so galled at the prospect of forking up an additional $10,000 to $15,000 to recent graduates untried in the world of practice.

The *American Lawyer* annually ranks America's highest-grossing law firms. McKinnon has a consistent profile in these rankings. Information is given for several categories, including profits per partner (the average income of the owners of the firm, the equity partners). The *American Lawyer* profitability index is the ratio of profits per partner to revenues per lawyer,[4] a rough measure of how the profit margin of the firm and its leverage, or ratio of lawyers to partners, "combine to make the proceeds flow to the bottom line" (Brill 1985, 15), namely profits for the partner-owners. McKinnon's rankings in these two categories are significantly higher than its overall gross revenues ranking. McKinnon's profits per partner put it in the top half of the other large Bay Area firms in the *American Lawyer* listings.[5] In business terms this is a remarkable performance for a firm first formed in the late 1960s as a thirty-person corporate boutique that has grown primarily through strategic acquisitions of talent from other law firms.

While McKinnon views itself as a highly successful and profitable firm (and is widely perceived as such in the Bay Area), comparisons

---

4. Another way to express this is the profit margin (the ratio of net revenues to gross revenues) times leverage (the ratio of all lawyers to partners). See "The AM Law 100" 1985, 14.

5. This statement is accurate for the 1985 through 1993 rankings. See pull-out management reports in the annual summer issue of the *American Lawyer*. In 1985, fifty firms were ranked and in 1986, seventy-five firms were rated. Since 1986, the survey has covered one hundred firms.

with Cravath are instructive. Cravath's revenues per lawyer are about twice that of McKinnon, and its profits per partner are over three times that of McKinnon.[6] New York billing rates and Wall Street clientele are major reasons for this difference. One other difference between the two is their relative reliance on leverage, the extent to which the profits of the firm are based on the excess of billings over costs of associates and nonequity partners. A firm with a high ratio of lawyers to partners is usually (but not invariably) far more profitable for partners than less leveraged firms.[7] For example, two Bay Area firms in the listing with the highest per-partner profits have lawyer to partner ratios in excess of other firms in the area. The Bay Area mean is about three lawyers per partner. The Cravath ratio is over four to one.[8]

Many of the McKinnon partners share name partner Jack McKinnon's view that lawyers are at risk of repeating the folly of the sports team owners, who have allowed labor costs to increase faster than their ability to pass them on to consumers. Alice Zorn, cochair of the bankruptcy department, believes that large firms, in order to remain competitive for talent, will end up with starting salaries that increase overhead to such an extent that they risk losing business to some of the better smaller firms that charge lower fees. Al McGill, who chairs the corporate department, expresses the view— widely shared in large firms—that nine out of ten first- and second-year associates do not justify (in terms of revenues they generate) what they are paid.

Despite the distaste of some partners and concern of most, the decision to go along with a salary increase was viewed in the firm as almost inevitable. The firm had determinedly made tough, often risky, decisions in the past to grow in order to join the ranks of the "majors." It could not now shrink from the implications of staying in the big leagues after working hard to get there. The decision at Cravath, Swaine, and Moore was a calculated business decision to address an internal structural problem—high attrition of valuable associates—that, if successful, would pay for itself over time. In

---

6. This statement is accurate for 1985 through 1993.

7. One of the most consistently profitable firms on the *American Lawyer* charts is Wachtell Lipton, which is structured by and large without leverage and specializes in highly profitable merger and acquisition work.

8. This statement is accurate for 1985 through 1993.

contrast, McKinnon must respond to an external structural problem of how to keep pace with what are perceived to be peer firms, and to stay abreast of the competition in recruiting able law school graduates. The fundamental issue the firm faces is how to pay for this decision.

Tom McHugh, a senior associate unenthused about his pending salary increase generated by the effect of higher entry-level salaries, sees the other side: the stakes are raised through increased pressure for billable hours. According to McHugh's analysis, if the firm decides to match Bay Area competition, it must either increase billing rates, take the funds out of partners' pockets, or put pressure on the associates. He is experienced enough to know that there is intense resistance from clients to higher billing rates, and resistance from partners to taking what one of them calls a "big hit." The scale of the hit for the equity partners, the total annual cost to the firm of the salary increases at McKinnon, is in the neighborhood of $650,000; this figure does not include adjustments for so-called nonequity partners, who do not share automatically in partnership profits. Although he has some confidence he will be made partner, McHugh sees an end result of fewer associates becoming partners.

A majority of the eleven-person executive committee of the firm cites the pressure of the Cravath ripple as the single biggest problem facing McKinnon.[9] The scale of the hit, which represents somewhat over 2 percent of gross revenues,[10] does not upset some people so much as the implications of paying for it. The consensus in the firm, extending well beyond the leadership group and largely in agreement with McHugh's analysis, is that the money will have to be recovered in several ways: greater expectations of associates and partners for billable hours, lengthening the time it takes to become an equity partner, flattening the upward curve of pay increases for associates and nonequity partners, and increased scrutiny of the productivity of lawyers at all levels. This productivity focus may lead to a process of weeding out associates performing poorly at an earlier stage in

---

9. Some executive committee members view this as a far more tractable problem than figuring out how to train a younger generation of lawyers to develop the professional and entrepreneurial abilities that characterize the leaders of the firm.

10. The $3 million "hit" at Cravath is about 3 percent of its $97 million gross revenue. The higher percentage at Cravath is a function of a larger number and percentage of associates, a higher salary base, and perhaps greater increases in associate pay based on years of experience.

their careers, extending associate status for marginal associates capable of handling average work, and asking some partners to seek opportunities elsewhere.

Lawyers throughout the firm express emphatic agreement with McHugh's perception that clients will not tolerate an increase in hourly rates. Abe Fox, one of the two preeminent leaders of the firm and its biggest rainmaker, muses how much he might like (i.e., how great it would be for business) to take out advertising in every business publication in the Bay Area announcing that the firm was *not* increasing associates' pay. A number of people express the view that while the Cravaths of the world with large Fortune 500 clients can afford to pass their costs on to clients, McKinnon is limited by its substantial base of somewhat smaller, more entrepreneurial and fee-sensitive clients, who are more prone to "shop around."[11]

John Lubber, chairman of the tax department, wonders whether one couldn't put choices to incoming associates (assuming the quality of work of each associate is equal): "If you want to earn, say, $60,000 a year, we expect twenty-two hundred hours from you; for $50,000 we want eighteen hundred hours; and for $40,000 we expect fifteen to sixteen hundred hours." Lubber, however, shares the general feeling that such a differentiated system would not work, if only because everyone would opt for the high achievers' numbers. He also worries that any significant change in the odds of making partner—say, four out of twenty making it instead of twelve out of twenty—would create a different atmosphere of cooperation in the firm. One of the attributes crucial to the tax department is the willingness of people to criticize freely and improve the work of others. The fabled dog-eat-dog culture said to exist in some New York firms encourages people to withhold help or undercut the work of associate compet-

---

11. This may be a naïve viewpoint, since most major institutional clients come with large in-house law departments that can be as resistant to rate increases as many of the entrepreneurial corporate clients McKinnon, Moreland, and Fox serves. The advantage of some corporate law firms is the high percentage of "premium" work, that is, the ability to charge at a much higher hourly rate or to charge a fee not tied directly to hours spent on the project. One well-known form of premium work rarely associated with large corporate firms is contingent-fee plaintiff's personal-injury litigation. For corporate firms, merger and acquisition, securities, and syndication work are often billed at a premium. Moreland, who shares a major leadership role with Fox, expresses the view that New York law-firm largess to associates is a function of the extraordinary, but transitory, phenomenon of the immense profitability of merger and acquisition work.

itors. Actions like that would be a serious blow to the morale and quality of work of his department.

Numbers have begun to circulate. The firm has established the minimal number of annual billable hours expected of associates as eighteen hundred to two thousand hours. There is now talk of raising the minimum another two hundred hours, a not-insubstantial increase, since the figure amounts to twenty-five eight-hour days. A number of partners feel there is some room to increase hours, based on internal analyses showing associates in some departments averaging somewhat above seventeen hundred hours annually. A Price Waterhouse blind study comparing a number of different statistics from Bay Area law firms indicates that McKinnon is second highest among large Bay Area firms in the average number of hours billed by associates. Al McGill, chair of the corporate department, is highly skeptical that making some people work harder will make a significant difference. The four- to six-year associates in his department are working now at the top level of their capacities. He sees no alternative to the hit coming off the profits of the top levels of the partnership.

A number of partners express concern about the firm's becoming a sweatshop. Bay Area lawyers enjoy using that shorthand to refer to the preposterous demands large New York firms make upon the time of their associates. A non-McKinnon Bay Area lawyer unashamed of *his* firm's sweatshop reputation argues that McKinnon is already a sweatshop, "and what is wrong with that? The long hours come easily if there is exciting, adrenalin-generating work with the pressure of deadlines for putting together deals." Many McKinnon lawyers, however, view a significant increase in pressure for billable hours not as an extension, but as a "change in lifestyle." Fox, for one, recognizes a contradiction in strictly business terms. To the extent lawyers are spending all their work time chalking up the hours, they are not active in the community establishing reputations and building the connections that often attract more business to the firm.

The normal human reaction to an increased emphasis on billable hours is recognized by a number of partners. Mark Gardner, a senior partner in the litigation department, worries about "dumping" hours[12] and suggests that management will need to focus increasingly on

---

12. Gardner is referring to working hours on an account that are not strictly necessary. No one at McKinnon, Moreland, and Fox suggested there was a possibility of billing for nonexistent hours.

meaningful hours. The billing partner will be under even more pressure than he or she already is to use careful judgment and to discount (i.e., reduce) bills loaded with unproductive hours. Associates are acutely conscious that billable hours are the "lifeline of the firm," and that, to the extent more emphasis is placed on total hours, work will be more stressful. "Values are caught up in the time sheet," remarks Rick Stone, an associate who recently joined McKinnon by way of a merger with a litigation boutique firm he joined out of law school. Before the merger, his superiors did not want him to be too conscious of billable hours: "The idea was to learn to practice law, and if it took an extra five hours to do it right and learn something, that was OK." To Stone, billing is more of a dilemma at McKinnon because part of being professional is being scrupulously honest about the necessary evil of time sheets, whether it is avoiding "eating" hours and giving incorrect information to partners, or resisting the padding of hours that is unfair to clients.

"The tragedy of it is the false expectations of the kids," argues George DeVane, head of the environmental department. He does not like the added pressure on billable hours because it will require him to change his management style. People will have to specialize earlier and be managed more tightly. It will be hard to broaden the experience of an associate. A more serious management challenge is working with those new associates who have the strongest social consciousness, the highest concepts of professionalism. These are typically people who underbill, and it takes three or four years to acclimate them to appropriate and accurate billing. There is danger of destroying the illusions of extremely valuable lawyers by pressing them too quickly with the business side of the practice.

DeVane believes that the actions of the firm will cause some damage to esprit de corps that probably cannot be prevented. There will be a tendency on the part of everyone to think twice before adding people to deal with expanding business opportunities. A cost-benefit analysis will need to be applied to spending time: is the legal advice for the client of sufficient economic value to justify its cost? He predicts that within a year or two the ultimate result will be a decrease in partners' profits.

The Cravath decision also generated a lot of talk about tiers. The *American Lawyer* is typical, describing the event as "the final shake-out":

We're headed now for a swift transformation. Where there has been a large, blurred top tier of as many as hundred firms defined only by size and prior reputation, within a few years there will be a new, smaller elite of just a few firms that are paying top, top dollar for the most prized associates and luring away their weaker competition's best partners with promises of more money and better support for their practices. (Adler and Baer 1986, 1)

Steve Sacks, a senior partner who works with headhunters in search of top-level talent to add to McKinnon, agrees that Cravath's decision has changed the game. Only a few firms will be able to play. He leaves no doubt that he expects McKinnon to grow and play the game in the major leagues, not the new minor league AAA or AA levels into which many large firms will settle. It will be a tougher game, in which it will be a lot harder to become an equity partner. People will be weeded out faster. A shorter maturation period will be expected of associates. If they are paying for associates at the same rate as other major Bay Area firms, they should be able to expect the same quality level. He, for one, does not intend to lower his income or increase his hours to pay for the increase.

Howard Moreland, one of the managers of the firm, is convinced that the future of corporate law lies with the specialized transaction-oriented megafirm, something like the Big Six accounting firms. Many of his partners do not share this view, but all would agree that McKinnon adopted a business plan in the early 1970s to grow larger in a manner most likely to achieve large or megafirm status. They believed that the small firm could no longer afford to service sophisticated clients who need a broad range of specialty practices. In the 1970s a firm under forty attorneys was small. Today, small is less than 100, and in a few years the 250-person firm may be considered small. A major merger with another firm is not out of the question for McKinnon, but the business sense and direction must be clear. As an alternative to a major merger, McKinnon may pursue the acquisition of small specialty firms or practices or individual practitioners whose portfolio meets McKinnon's plans. All this will involve a change in lifestyle: more demands on hours billed, more nonequity partners, nominal bonuses for associates coming in at high initial salaries (except for "superstars"), a more performance-oriented, up-or-out flow of people and their futures.

Tom McHugh sees the whole process of reacting to Cravath as taking the "New York route." And he adds, wistfully, "I sure would prefer to keep this place more like California."

Viewing a Merger

Dorothy Monheit was musing about the transformation in her circumstances. In the summer of 1983 she had joined the twenty-person litigation firm of O'Connor, Markham, and Flynn under an arrangement where she worked about two-thirds time, skipping lunch and leaving each day at about 3:30 P.M. in order to care for her small child. She had another child early in 1985 and was delighted with the firm's continued support of her part-time lawyering. She liked the environment of O'Connor. To say there was a sense of family about the place was too strong, but it had warmth. The training at O'Connor was excellent, better than her first job at a firm prior to having her first child. O'Connor had character. Partners' offices reflected their individualism. There was pride in the high quality of their work, their clients, their excellent support staff, and the fact that people were treated well.

Early in 1986 Monheit's work world took a dramatic turn. O'Connor decided to merge with the then 120-person firm McKinnon, Moreland, and Fox. Jack Markham and his partners felt that business concerns necessitated the merger with a larger group. Monheit sensed the firm leadership was primarily interested in practicing law and tiring of the growing burden of administration in a firm beginning to approach 30 lawyers. They resented, for example, having to struggle over the appropriate capitalization of the firm and the capital demands they needed to make of new partners.

One look at the offices of McKinnon was enough to make Monheit apprehensive about the move into a firm over five times larger than her own. According to Monheit, "decor makes a statement," and the statement made by the ultramodern, off-white, chrome-trimmed environs of McKinnon studded with modern abstract paintings was definitely not warmth. It had all the charm of a large bank: exceedingly tasteful but austerely functional—it was all business. (This aseptic decor led one O'Connor associate to crack, "Not a bad place if you don't mind practicing out of a hospital room.") Monheit explained why she was troubled with the merger: She was not so worried about McKinnon's reputation for aggressiveness as she was concerned whether the large firm would tolerate her special part-time arrangement. And during the hectic months of transition, she could not get a reading on her special case, since there were so many other important matters to negotiate.

After her first six months, Monheit began to relax. She was reviewed by her new superiors in the litigation department and everyone was amazed at how well things had worked out. She liked the feedback and guidance she was getting in the new firm, which had a mentor system that paired partners and associates. But the bureaucracy annoyed her. There were forms that had to be filled out for everything and countless memos on every conceivable topic. The word-processing system required relearning. She also detected one cultural difference. She had been taught at O'Connor that aggressive "ego beating" tactics were only justified as a defense: if someone does it to you—you only do what you have to do, picking the right time and place to respond to ugly moves by an opponent. At McKinnon she discovered that litigators were much more likely to initiate hostile behavior against an opponent.

Before the merger took place, McKinnon hosted a reception for female lawyers at both firms that, by all accounts, was a success. Monheit takes pride in the fact that a third of the partners in the merged firm are women. She has no perception of discrimination against women at McKinnon. Indeed, she finds herself so busy that she hasn't attended a number of the open houses sponsored by McKinnon to show the new arrivals the ropes. If anything, Monheit claims, the merger is harder on "them" than on "us."

Not all the O'Connor associates are as sanguine about the merger as Dorothy Monheit. Jack Peterson has long been "prejudiced," as he puts it, against the impersonality, overspecialization, and the unfriendly "company" atmosphere of large firms. He had already felt the growth of O'Connor to some thirty lawyers had led it beyond that sense of "common purpose" that he sought in a law firm. But he is pleased to have the resources and training of McKinnon—the emphasis on the practical business side of his work—but doubts that he will need more than two or three years of this training. He particularly dislikes McKinnon's strong emphasis on billable hours. "Billables aren't the only thing: it is important to look at other factors, like quality of work." Another O'Connor associate confirms that although people worked very hard at the old firm, billables were never important. The job was to get things right. A pet peeve of Peterson at the new firm is the red tape. For example, he had made a pact with himself: if he passed the bar, he would undertake his share of pro bono work. But the bureaucracy at McKinnon requires an elaborate permission procedure. "Around this place, you have to sign a statement if you want to go to the bathroom!"

Associate Alan Muser compares the structured, formalized, more businesslike atmosphere of McKinnon with the loose, more casual, less pressured, and less regimented style of the premerger O'Connor firm. Gerry Muller, another associate surprised to find himself in a large firm, describes the O'Connor firm as the proverbial small firm with big-firm clients, a place where the team spirit prevailed, where there was a chance to work intimately with partners. The "downside" at O'Connor was the lack of organization and policies. Because the senior people at the two firms knew each other well, there has been no clash of cultures at the top. In fact, the two firms had complementary practices. After the merger was consummated, the only resistance came from the McKinnon litigation associates, who found themselves in a department with several new former O'Connor partners. Lunchtime at the new firm reminds Miller of high school, where one calculates who is sitting with whom, who carries the conversation, who goes out together. It has been a "rough marriage," and somewhat tough to crack into the third-year associates' clique, but by and large people outside the litigation department have been friendly. At McKinnon there is less of a chance for a second chance: first impressions seem to count for a lot in the larger firm.

The leadership of the O'Connor firm knew they needed to merge with a larger firm due to the "old synergism argument," as one partner puts it. In order to compete in a cutthroat market with trial departments of major law firms around the country, their local complex commercial-litigation firm needed the tax, corporate, and real estate backup of McKinnon's business departments, as well as the litigation business from McKinnon's corporate clients. But strong litigation boutique firms are not uncommon. What precipitated the move was the decision of its dominant figure, Markham, chief rainmaker, supervisor, leader, and best lawyer rolled into one, to slow down due to an ailing wife and some health problems of his own.

Virtually all the new arrivals from O'Connor describe two major features of the new firm: more formality and bureaucracy (infernal paperwork), and a sense of not knowing what is going on, a certain distance from key decision making. The associates are inclined to be more candid about the lack of management and growing pains in the old firm, largely because Jack Markham had no interest in management and systematic business development. Clients were simply attracted to him. Ted McClean, an O'Connor partner, explains the sensation at McKinnon of not feeling like you own the business. He complains about the high cost of the administrative structure at McKinnon, the politics of people protecting their own bailiwick and looking for things to do, people whose entire worth is tied up in picking a word processor.

While the associates from O'Connor are still trying to adjust to a merger, many learned about it only the day before it was publicly announced. Secretaries are openly unhappy with the move. They intensely dislike the regimentation of the new firm, the stronger sense of hierarchy, and the new word-processing system, inferior to the one to which they were accustomed. The O'Connor partners, confident about the long-term business sense of the transfer to McKinnon, are still uncomfortable in their new surroundings. One partner describes this discomfort as the "trauma of selling your business," of having "cashed out without cashing out." There is a felt loss of intimacy and flexibility. O'Connor partner Alice Zorn describes it as "giving up a dream" of making something that was your own and that was a real success—letting go of that something special—for solid business reasons. She also senses her exposure and visibility as a successful woman lawyer in a small firm may well dissipate in the larger-scale firm. But she has made her name, and her future in McKinnon is now entirely up to her.

The O'Connor merger has indeed been hard on McKinnon. O'Connor is a prize catch, a strong firm economically, with lawyers and clients—and a leader like Markham—that would be extraordinary assets to any firm in the country. The premerger trial department of McKinnon was not as strong as the leadership of the firm thought it should be. The O'Connor people have made an adequate department into a strong one. Negotiations with the O'Connor leadership were protracted and spirited. "The deal kept changing," says one partner. McKinnon, for the first time in its long tradition of acquiring lateral talent, paid a significant premium in terms of initial guaranteed draws to key O'Connor partners and to others who were considered by the McKinnon people to be overcompensated. O'Connor did not operate, as does McKinnon, as a meritocracy (i.e., pay based on clients brought in and serviced). A number of McKinnon partners were upset with the generosity of the merger arrangements, although they knew it made excellent sense from a business point of view. There was a minor revolt when some McKinnon partners became aware of a concession made in the negotiation that certain O'Connor partners would command larger offices. The O'Connor people, recognizing that this "juvenile turmoil" might sour a good businesslike deal, did not insist this part of the merger agreement be honored. Markham went on the masthead (McKinnon, Moreland, Fox, and Markham) as well as the executive committee. Several other O'Connor partners were given key positions in the merged firm, including the leadership of the McKinnon litigation department.

A Happy Acquisition

The O'Connor experience contrasts sharply with McKinnon's acquisition of the environmental department of Michaels and Todd some eighteen months earlier. At Michaels and Todd, a large firm with more than one hundred lawyers, George DeVane and Art Soames built one of the two premier environmental departments in the Bay Area. The firm was a politically well-connected and extraordinarily congenial group dominated by trial lawyers. Effective trial work for local industries was nurtured by DeVane into a transactional specialty department that handled private and tax-exempt financing, procurement contracts, as well as federal and state regulatory issues related to installation of pollution-control equipment and environmental cleanups.

DeVane's department was at ease and comfortable at Michaels and Todd, but their business situation was a difficult one. The litigators who led the firm did not consider the transactional work of DeVane's group *real* law practice, a not uncommon attitude within the trial bar. Relative compensation, benefits, perks, and the unpleasantnesses of office relocations reflected the low status of DeVane's department in the Michaels and Todd pecking order. Governance at the firm did not lend itself to predictability. Politics within the executive committee involved fierce battles over partnership decisions

(DeVane had lost some of these for his practice group), and rumors were rife of people breaking away to form their own practices. One former Michaels associate, Irv Mendelson, described its leadership as "an oligarchy dominated by dinosaurs who didn't appreciate what they had." Mendelson, who was an associate in DeVane's department, describes how the Michaels firm seemed to change its partnership structure almost annually: after five and a half years of work there, he determined he was as far from making partner (real partner, not the new joke position of junior partner) as when he started. Two months before McKinnon approached DeVane about a merger, Mendelson left the firm to become an environmental consultant.

McKinnon knew it could use a group in environmental law, a specialty of importance to its industrial and real estate clients. When first approached, DeVane indicated that he did not want to move. Even after talking with emissaries from McKinnon, he hoped he would not have to make a decision. McKinnon offered significant upgrades in compensation (one former Michaels lawyer estimated increases ranged from 25 to 75 percent for the lawyers of the environmental group) and opportunities for growth and better servicing of clients through association with McKinnon's strong transactional departments like tax, real estate, and corporate finance. DeVane was offered a position as department head of an autonomous environmental unit, and a place on the executive committee. His department would come as a group and stay as a group—presumably as insurance that they would move as a group if things did not work out.

DeVane was apprehensive about the move for a number of reasons. His people generally had lower academic pedigrees than the McKinnon lawyers. They would become, under the McKinnon system, a profit center and have to play the productivity game with the rest of the firm. The cultural stereotypes that separated Michaels and Todd from McKinnon, Moreland, and Fox were enormous. The caricature of a Michaels attorney is the fun-loving, clannish softball enthusiast; of a McKinnon, the hustling, whining highbrow. Once word leaked out that DeVane's group was interested in leaving, "everyone called." The decision to go with McKinnon emerged from a combination of excellent financial terms, the strength brought by association with McKinnon's transactional practice (the money and the synergy), the autonomy they would enjoy, and McKinnon's track record of success in acquiring other practices. The clincher, however, was negative actions by Michaels and Todd, who felt that considering a move was a form of betrayal. The atmosphere became so hostile that DeVane and Soames knew they had to move quickly. A number of their associates decided to stay with Michaels and Todd, but as they saw the environmental clients move with the two partners, most straggled into McKinnon within a week or two after the two partners left.

DeVane muses on the reasons why the litigators of Michaels and Todd—and litigators in general—react so badly to defections: "They are more combative people. The world is more black and white. Negotiation is not necessarily their forte. They take rejection—whether by a jury or by other lawyers—badly." He believes that litigation is the most depersonalized of legal specialties. Litigation replaces the client, becomes the client. Trial lawyers often develop a sense of *owning* the litigation. They project this sense of ownership on the world and react to many situations as if something is being taken from them. Perhaps a long history of a lawyer-client relationship with a corporation may lead to some sense of institutional ownership, but the reality is that no one owns the client.

The young lawyers who arrived from Michaels and Todd—apart from the two partners, Soames and DeVane—were traumatized by the suddenness of a transition they had not wanted, the strong sense of rejection and disapproval by their friends at Michaels, and the fact that the reason they were practicing at McKinnon was that they had no other options. Uprooted, they were forced to move because they had no clients. "They [DeVane and Soames] cut a deal and the business was moving: It was out of our hands," comments Fred Murstead, now a McKinnon associate.

McKinnon worked hard to greet their group of almost thirty environmentalists and reduce the cultural barriers perceived by the new people. They sponsored a number of parties and other efforts to make Michaels people feel at home, but these were not generally successful, other than as gestures of welcome. The Michaels people, as one of them puts it, view McKinnon as "more pretentious." The new arrivals did not feel comfortable in their new place and the pressures to integrate were so great and so ineffective (largely because of the perception by Michaels people that it was a one-way absorption into McKinnon) that the McKinnon leadership pulled back and accepted "cultural dichotomy," as one Michaels lawyer describes it.

A minimal degree of socializing continues between the Michaels group and the McKinnon regulars.

As Herb Schnurr, a former Michaels associate, points out, even after eighteen months in the new firm, their group still uses the terms *we* and *they.* The Michaels group is located on a floor with two relatively small McKinnon departments and feels as if the McKinnon people are the newcomers. The group has more of a sense of togetherness and independence at McKinnon than it did at Michaels and Todd. Schnurr's colleague, Jerry Born, talks about how little difference the move ultimately made: he is working at McKinnon on the same things he worked on at Michaels and under the same person, DeVane, a "makes-things-happen" kind of lawyer. Unlike Michaels, where there was always a struggle for resources (word processing and document preparation capacities, meeting rooms, catering, library research, etc.), McKinnon knows how to support people who generate business and provides "a hundred times" better services for its lawyers.

Frederick Murstead and Tom McHugh both enjoyed the Michaels firm, the socializing, the softball. They were more at ease there. At Michaels, there were a number of functions involving spouses; there are virtually none at McKinnon. Their wives enjoyed the other firm more. They were aware of the entirely different personality of McKinnon—more staid, less lively, but more "up front." Al Collins describes McKinnon as more sophisticated, more business-oriented than Michaels, "a lean mean operating machine," a quality he attributes to the younger average age of the top McKinnon leadership. Murstead describes the dramatic differences between the two places in terms of the politics of decision making. It took ten minutes to decide on the ten people proposed for partner at McKinnon last year. A similar decision at Michaels would have taken hours of bloodletting and generated countless rumors. McKinnon is not a rumor mill. Professionally, remarks McHugh, there is no comparison in terms of the support McKinnon provides for a lawyer's practice. McKinnon has an ability to do deals, develop business, network. They have rainmakers. Their style and priority is toward business. Those factors are really the important ones.

McHugh recognizes another difference. Michaels was a democracy. All the partners would sit around for hours and vote on every issue. "I could have seen myself as a factor or force in the Michaels and Todd partnership." McKinnon, on the other hand, is basically run by two people, and this has distinct advantages. Decision making is more rational; everything is less political; departments have more autonomy; if the department does a good job and a lawyer contributes to the profitability of a department, the lawyer is treated properly and gets ahead. "But I don't expect to be part of the ruling class" at McKinnon.

DeVane sums up why the merger with McKinnon has gone well for his department. McKinnon is run as a business meritocracy. Seniority plays only a minor role in the compensation picture. "The key piece is compensation," rewarding those who deserve it. If the firm were ever to move toward equality in the compensation structure, it would disintegrate. The McKinnon people have a sense of the big picture of practice, how business is generated and how cross-fertilization and synergisms take place. The merger has fulfilled all of McKinnon's expectations, but not all of DeVane's. The expansion of the department's business has not occurred by McKinnon bringing clients to the department. DeVane's department has brought clients to other McKinnon departments. The business of the department has expanded largely through its own resources. What makes the merger work for the environmental group ("a typical $1 + 1 = 3$") is the extraordinary increase in their client-servicing capacity made possible by the association with McKinnon.

DeVane explains why the O'Connor merger generated dissension at McKinnon. The O'Connor firm was not run as a business. Regardless of the administrative difficulties of the acquisition, the merger with O'Connor was a good move because of the quality of the lawyers and enthusiasm for them at McKinnon. The "people for whom the deal was done" were pleased with the merger, but then the deal kept changing to cope with a number of overcompensated people. McKinnon "caved in more than is characteristic of us" and some McKinnon people began to wonder, "Why don't you love your own as much as those you are courting?"

Howard Moreland characterizes the differences between the O'Connor and Michaels deals in somewhat different terms. He speaks of the propensity of some of the O'Connor people to "intellectualize everything" compared to the ability of the Michaels people to "accept the package" and feel "they are at the right levels." Moreland feels the firm will not lose what it wants from the O'Connor group. "It is like a corporate merger: they will adjust over time."

The Merger That Didn't Happen

Ashton, Miller, Cartright, and Stein was coming apart at the seams and most of the major firms in town were interested in picking off talent that carried clients with it. A large group of about thirty to fifty lawyers from Ashton Miller was prepared to join McKinnon. Howard Moreland was enthusiastic about adding them to the firm. Abe Fox was supportive. In view of the enormous respect Fox and Moreland enjoy for the business and leadership acumen they have demonstrated in a series of successful decisions significantly increasing the size of the firm, merger with the Ashton Miller group had momentum. But something rare took place at McKinnon: the leadership could not swing the deal. A large number of the senior people in the firm spoke strongly against the merger in a series of meetings of the executive committee and department heads.

A number of factors brought down the Ashton Miller move. There was doubt about the quality of lawyers McKinnon was attracting. No one, least of all Moreland, made the case for the merger primarily on the distinction of the lawyers. The business rationale was the exceptionally fine client base of the lawyers of Ashton Miller. Skepticism was expressed about just how much of Ashton Miller's clientele would move with them. A cultural argument was also at work. Many of the Ashton Miller lawyers, certainly the ones who would bring the clients, were older and did not share the McKinnon "work ethic." They were beginning to lighten up on their hours. This raised real concerns among those in the firm who were worried that the firm did not have the depth of younger talent to staff all this business with the deal-making abilities and business acumen of the senior lawyers. No one had much respect for the way Ashton Miller had let itself go. The firm was dominated for years by Sol Miller, who, as Fred Strong, chair of the pension and retirement group who had practiced at Ashton Miller some years ago, put it: "ran the place like a synagogue with Sol as chief Rabbi." There was a total lack of collegiality, and Sol dealt with threatened defections by simply buying off the threat, a practice that led eventually to an avalanche of defections that brought down the firm.

Two other arguments were particularly persuasive. Rumor had it that a handful of Ashton Miller partners were implicated in an investigation of zoning irregularities in a prominent Bay Area suburb. To their credit, the Ashton Miller people confirmed the reality of the investigation. They hoped, but could not guarantee, it would lead to nothing that implicated their people. Marc Crews, one of the most respected senior people in McKinnon, the man who most lawyers in the firm would probably identify as the firm's conscience, was particularly disturbed about the potential taint of the investigation. McKinnon already had a reputation as an aggressive, hard-nosed group in the local legal and business communities. It might run a significant risk through such a merger of giving its competitors good grounds to charge it with being sleazy. And McKinnon's new arrivals—the O'Connor and Michaels groups—were profoundly unenthusiastic about the merger. As DeVane puts it, about 40 percent of the lawyers of McKinnon, Moreland, Fox, and Markham had been there eighteen months or fewer at the time the Ashton Miller decision was being discussed. Absorbing yet another large group of lawyers at a time when the growing pains of the other mergers were still being worked out appealed neither to the new people nor to many other lawyers in the firm.

Howard Moreland wisely keeps his own counsel about the defeat of the Ashton Miller proposal, but it had to be a matter of deep disappointment to him. He knows that a merger of any substantial group of lawyers is not possible without widespread support within the firm. His vision of the growth of McKinnon to become one of the major firms in the region—and perhaps someday even to become a national firm—ran up against the business judgment of senior people in the firm. They were more risk-averse than he. McKinnon has a long tradition of rejecting (on business principles) offers of merger or lateral transfer. Although McKinnon's reputation is built in large part on spectacular growth through merger, the firm strictly insists on real synergy, without which merger makes no sense. The lure that many firms find in satellite offices in cities elsewhere in the state—or in Washington, D.C., or other major cities—has been resisted by McKinnon, despite many flirtations and near seductions.

To make these work, there must be McKinnon people, people who care about the institution, in the other office.

The Ashton Miller discussion is viewed by many in the firm as a major event. To some, like Marc Crews, it was substantively the right decision, and made the firm stronger and more attractive. Moreland probably viewed it at the time as the wrong move, a reflection of the innate conservatism of lawyers without a true long-range vision. Many people cite the decision as a shining example of the process or the character of the firm. The O'Connor people are pleased with the result. They were amazed at how open, how contentious and vigorous was the discussion, and particularly pleased to know there were no hard feelings in its wake. This tolerance for speaking one's mind, for loyal *open* opposition is obviously accepted and encouraged by the firm leadership.[13] As Graham Simms, a member of the executive committee puts it, Howard Moreland and Abe Fox backed off from the merger after listening to the concerns of their colleagues, as if they had said, "These guys are my partners. I must be wrong."

Leadership

Graham Simms categorizes McKinnon's governance as "oligarchy exercised with democracy." This he compares with the feudal governance systems of some other large firms where monarchs and barons and dukes face uprisings of the serfs if they abuse their people too badly. Simms describes a broad range of styles used to exploit the fact that most people are more responsive to higher-ups, ranging from the frenetic "Do it!" to the cajoling management style he thinks is more characteristic of McKinnon. When lawyers feel part of a

---

13. A senior associate recounts the time he got into a shouting match with Abe Fox at a Christmas party over some issue. He went home wondering if he would have a job at the firm the following year but found out that the incident *never* had an effect on his evaluation or compensation at the firm.

Marc Crews cites the time shortly after he had joined the firm when two people came up for partner. During a two- or three-hour meeting and full discussion in which *everyone* talked without acrimony, both were voted down. He was surprised. At his old firm, people could not talk openly; they invariably broke up into groups to discuss such difficult, major decisions.

growing, vibrant, and successful organization, a cooperative team-work style is not read as directives from management.

Terrence McVey, a former O'Connor partner, believes the insti-tutional personality derives from the personalities of the leaders. McVey says he is still trying to figure out the personalities of Moreland and Fox.

Both Fox and Moreland have grown and evolved with the growth of the firm, according to Frederick Marx. Fox, the acknowledged rainmaker of the firm, is widely respected for his judgment about clients and political relationships. Lately Fox has distanced himself from administration and Moreland has become more like a managing partner. "Vision" is the word Marx uses for Moreland. He is aggressive and will work to force his position on you. It was Moreland's advo-cacy that led to the recent expansion of the executive committee of the firm and the creation of other committees to involve more levels of the partnership in the firm's operation. Both Fox and Moreland have been self-sacrificing, taking less out of the partnership in com-pensation than they could, particularly in down years. Under their leadership, the firm has a strong financial commitment to charitable causes, all made without much fanfare or self-promotion since it is seen as part of client-related business expenses.

Al Perlow describes Fox as the client man, the preeminent busi-ness person, while Moreland is the inside man, the glue that holds the place together. Moreland is bright and aggressive. He deals well with people. He is always well prepared at meetings. He tells you what's on his mind. And he is not afraid to make a mistake: if you don't buy his line of bullshit, it *never* comes back to haunt you in terms of your compensation or progress in the firm. Marx makes the same point about Moreland: he may be sore, but there is no retri-bution. Al McGill describes Howard Moreland as a sensational dreamer. "You often wonder where the hell he came up with his latest idea." Howard enjoys relationships, the human side. He likes being a father figure. Fox is Mr. Follow-through, the no-nonsense person who wants to get the job done. They balance each other.

Richard Johns cites the story of Ashton, Miller, Cartright, and Stein as an example of how fragile law partnerships can be. It requires a lot of work to hold them together. In the ten years he has been with the firm, he has never seen an issue become deeply controversial. The firm has not suffered problems with moving their offices, lateral hires, mergers, or partnership decisions (although these are sometimes tough)—issues that often tear up other firms. Fox and Moreland are involved in every major decision. They operate by trial balloon and consensus.

Jack Mitchner talks of "a lot of energy at the top level." Both Fox and Moreland have excellent judgment. They are very frank with each other. They have no problem disagreeing. They are able to assert a view and not have major "ego risk" in the outcome. The cadre of ten or twenty senior people—the group with whom Moreland and Fox test ideas and work to achieve consensus—are not dissimilar to their leaders. They are not dependent for their success on the approval of their peers. Because they have significant clients and achievement, "They deserve their hunk." They rely very little on "vertical approval." Their extra energy can be devoted to the common weal.

Moreland and Fox sit on the eleven-member McKinnon executive committee. It is the "unicameral legislature" for the major decisions of the firm such as offers of partnership, the decision to move to new space, the pension plan,[14] lateral hires and mergers, etc. A variety of committees makes recommendations to the executive committee. Their jurisdiction ranges from hiring, summer associates, health insurance, billing/finance, and legal opinions to library and files, liability insurance, benefits, pro bono service,[15] and business referral. Marc Crews heads the important goals and standards committee, comprised chiefly of department heads who focus on hiring standards, training issues, and lawyer morale. Goals and standards is a deliberate attempt, according to Mark Gardner, to put professional issues higher on the priorities of the firm. But neither the executive nor goals and standards committees are at the top of the hierarchy of governance in the firm. Everyone recognizes that the compensation committee, composed of Moreland, Fox, and another senior partner named Robert Nance, is the most important committee in the firm.

"Money holds it all together." That is the view of partner Richard Stoller, who describes the end of March as a troubling time each year

14. Since McKinnon has no written partnership agreement, the retirement and pension system is a fundamental document in which vesting is timed and structured, according to one partner, as a "golden handcuffs" arrangement to discourage partnership defections.

15. Little emphasis is given to pro bono activities although a number of lawyers are active in bar association work and McKinnon participates in major pro bono projects of the Bay Area when other large firms are also involved.

when people are awaiting the decision of the compensation committee. Financial data on the performance of the firm for the prior calendar year is available, so there is some rough sense of how good the year was and the general scale of compensation increases. But there is a sense of uncertainty promoted by the highly discretionary structure of the compensation system, which Abe Fox describes as "the old-fashioned way."

Two of the main differences, Abe Fox notes, between a corporation and a law firm is that every partner is virtually a permanent fixture and considers himself or herself a highly educated executive. The challenge is to balance running the firm as a business in a way that motivates and satisfies most people while at the same time maintaining a professional atmosphere for people who are not going to be able to change that much. McKinnon has maintained an environment of informality and open interaction and uses its compensation system as a means of motivating people. Lawyers know that they can grow on their own merits. Even the people who do not grow feel they have the chance to do so at McKinnon.

A lawyer's compensation at McKinnon comprises two elements, the basic "draw" and the bonus pool. The draw or compensation base is decided by the compensation committee once every two years. Although the decision with respect to draw is calculated from the lawyer's past performance, it operates prospectively regardless of actual performance during the subsequent two years. The decision on bonus, on the other hand, operates as a division of profits based on the performance of the firm (and the lawyer) during the previous year. Roughly 65 percent of a partner's compensation is in the form of draw,[16] although this percentage varies greatly from partner to partner. (The leaders of the firm are more dependent on bonus income than the junior people.) The system is driven by the distribution of the bonus pool, which is deliberately designed to "lower the comfort level" and reward what the lawyer actually contributed to the financial performance of the firm. Lawyers who—as the euphemisms go— "fall asleep" or are "on the fast track" find their relative status can change quickly in such a system.

16. Abe Fox gives a typical example: a junior partner at a major law firm is given points (i.e., a percentage share of total partner profits) that lead in a given year to compensation of $150,000. The partner comes to expect that that is his or her income level. In the McKinnon system, the draw would only be $100,000 to $120,000 and the remaining $30,000 is not the partner's unless he or she earns it.

Moreland and Fox are well aware of how treacherous is the terrain the compensation committee must negotiate. Abe Fox describes the compensation system as the major business problem of the firm. His and Moreland's leadership and reputation depend on these decisions being perceived as equitable, "objective," and defensible in terms of a business analysis of lawyer performance. They strive to avoid "politics" or playing either personal or departmental favorites, and they are perceived by and large as playing by these rules. They spend considerable time making these decisions, typically meeting with every partner in an attempt to permit each partner to argue his or her case and give the impression that the committee attends carefully to each partner's situation and performance. As the firm grows larger, the compensation interview is not always a convincing act to younger partners who are well aware that their leaders are not agonizing over salary decisions at their level.

Compensation is one area in which the normally aggressive and self-confident leadership treads with extreme care. The top dozen lawyers are not a major problem: they expect to suffer if the firm as a whole does not do well. These senior people are given a preview of decisions in order to generate a loose form of consensus within the leadership before anything formal is announced. But the "next twenty" are more difficult. These are the people on whom the growth of the firm is most dependent, the group that the leadership needs to protect and satisfy even in a lean year. The special tensions of salary setting for this group derive from the need to avoid "disrupting the fabric of the whole firm" while rewarding adequately people who compare themselves to their perceived equals or lessers inside and outside the firm.

If compensation is the major business problem of McKinnon, Moreland, and Fox, another less tractable issue is the departmental structure of the business and the role departments play in the "balance" (as Fox puts it) between the operation of a business and the maintenance of an atmosphere of professionalism. According to Alice Zorn, the firm treats departments as a series of "businesses within the business" that operate with their own training and evaluation styles, social functions, and mechanisms of quality control. Department leaders deal with each other at the executive level. Firm-wide committees and functions provide a sense of belonging to the firm as a whole, but the department is the fundamental organizational element. George

DeVane describes the firm as a "confederation of autonomous units." Steve Sacks calls McKinnon a "collection of boutiques." Many people are troubled by the implications of this structure. Marc Crews, for example, has been trying to organize firm-wide training programs that cross departmental lines. John Surtee, another leader in the corporate department, has lobbied hard to organize a cross-department work assignment system to broaden the experience of associates. But the memoranda and meetings and entreaties to develop associates with the broad-based business law understanding of the top leaders of the firm have not affected or reduced the dominant role of the department in the career development of associates and junior partners.[17] Neither Fox nor Moreland has been active in these moves.

A senior associate, Victor Stahl, was attracted to join the firm by the incentive systems of McKinnon. It is a young firm, a growing firm, where associates can move faster to develop clients. Other large firms pay associates in "lockstep" for at least three years, but at McKinnon there are significant compensation differences in the same class of associates after eighteen months. After two and one-half years Stahl was being paid as much as $8,000 a year more than some of his classmates. The minuses of the firm, Stahl adds, are simply the bottom side of the pluses: there is little tolerance for people who don't do well. It is easy for partners as well as associates to feel insecure and stressed in a firm that prides itself on a "lower comfort level."

Younger members of the firm have no illusions about the incentive structure of the firm. Every ambitious associate wants his or her own clients. Rick Stone, one of the senior associates brought over from the O'Connor firm, is delighted with the foothold he is developing in a variety of different practice areas, primarily because he views it as making him a more valuable business counselor, attractive to clients. Having clients brings more control of your financial future and your work environment. It is one thing to meet the deadlines negotiated between you and your client, but quite another to meet the deadline of the lawyer responsible for the client. "The name of the game," comments Gerry Muller, "is having your own clients; the people who cut the pie are the ones who bring in the pie." Muller thinks that is the way the firm *should* be run. McKinnon is no different

---

17. One lawyer suggested that Surtee's efforts could be read as an attempt by the corporate department to hold on to its dominance or leadership role in the firm.

than any other firm in this respect. "If you don't want to be an employee partner, then you have to attract your own clients." Twenty percent of the partners bring in 90 percent of the business, and Muller wants to be in the business-attracting 20 percent. Muller sees the majority of McKinnon partners as employee partners, and he wants nothing of it:

> I'm working harder than I thought I ever could. When you consider the time I put in, the night work ending on occasion at 1:30 A.M., the responsibility I assume, the stress, the lack of feedback, if I am not advancing beyond employee-partner status by the time I am in my late thirties, then it might be better to go teach somewhere. Of course the up side is the respect and prestige and job security of being a partner, and $125,000 a year is nothing to sneeze at. And I'll have kids by then and may feel trapped. After all, it is in my control: if I have not established a client base and brought in enough business to advance beyond employee partner to real partnership status, it might be better to go in-house[18] and get home to the family each night at 5:00 P.M.

One partner describes the leaders of the firm as "driven and upward mobile," a phrase that captures some features of the work ethic of Gerry Muller and many of his colleagues. Now and then another feature crops up in conversations with lawyers whose sense of excitement over the growth and dynamism of the firm does not assuage their consciousness of how hard they work. Partner Harold Reich talks about the "hassle" of working on demand, not knowing when one will have to work late, and a mixed sense of job satisfaction when the client indicates "nice job" for something expected of you without any sense of how you had to bust your ass to overcome the difficulties of the assignment. He has no hobbies. He likes being with his family. He wonders whether he will be a lawyer the rest of his life. Partner Everett Gans swears he would quit tomorrow if he could make a living from his photography. Graham Simms muses about a teaching career one of these days, and a number of lawyers indicate that the next move will be out of law.

Jerry Born, an associate in George DeVane's department who is

---

18. Work in a law department of a corporation rather than a private law firm.

enormously pleased with his exposure and advancement in the firm, knows that McKinnon "works you to death and pays you oodles of money." He has been well rewarded in the firm and is pleased and flattered at the business coming in, but he puts in lots of hours. He wishes he could be home with his two kids "at a time in life when they still like you. I like to think I can get out of it, that one day I'll say I've had enough. When I think of the hours George DeVane puts in, I don't want to work that hard." DeVane is proud of his department and his extraordinary work routine. He says of his former firm, "The great mistake of the Michaels lawyers was their equating professionalism with a fraternity."

Chapter 3

The Close-Knit Family of
Mahoney, Bourne, and Thiemes

Founder

Brian Mahoney came from a desperately poor Irish family of eight children, worked his way through local Catholic schools and Canisius College with a fine record, and did brilliantly at the law school at SUNY Buffalo while completing his Ph.D. in English there. One of the finest large firms in town hired him in the mid-1950s, no doubt the first shanty Irish lawyer in the history of that blue blood firm.

Mahoney was a brilliant natural speaker, a great, indeed phenomenal wit, and a person of enormous warmth and magnanimity. His high energy and boundless goodwill were all the more amazing because he suffered daily from serious migraine headaches. He was something of a young wonder professionally and politically: elected to the New York Assembly at age twenty-three, he was close to the then mayor of Buffalo, whose son he helped through college and law school. When Francis X. Flynn, for thirty years the attorney for the archdiocese of Buffalo, died in the late fifties, the archbishop called Mahoney and asked him to represent the church on a substantial real estate matter. For Mahoney's work, the firm billed and was paid an amount extraordinary for the time. In gratitude for his efforts he received a $250 bonus from the law firm. Mahoney, who by that time had two children, began to think about starting his own firm.

In 1961, Mahoney opened practice with a college friend, Frank Bourne, a general practitioner, and their clientele consisted mostly of a constellation of Roman Catholic institutions—hospitals, religious orders, Catholic Charities, as well as the archdiocese itself. Mahoney served as the treasurer to a successful liberal Democrat running for Congress in 1964 and in the following year merged with the congress-

man's old firm in the expectation that some referral business would be
generated from the congressman. Mahoney and Ben Spevack, the
eighty-year-old doyen of the merged firm, were a classic odd couple.
Spevack—able, hardworking, meticulous, and cost conscious—left
notes on the doors of lawyers whose lights were on unnecessarily.
The free-spirited Mahoney was generous to a fault, and heedless of
the financial implications of throwing himself into a new cause or
campaign.

By 1967, Mahoney was at the top of his form. He was a prominent backer and organizer for Robert Kennedy, a close and intimate
advisor of both the mayor and the archbishop, and a leading reformer
mentioned as a possibility for governor.

Christopher Schultz, Mahoney's successor, recalls his first meeting with Mahoney in the late 1960s. He entered an office deluged
with papers and books. Mahoney's tie was stained from the fallout
of a tuna sandwich he was eating and offered to share with Schultz,
a third-year law student answering an ad for a job. After welcoming
him, Mahoney reopened the book he was reading and proceeded to
recite some poetry of Yeats, over which he marveled. Mahoney then
ruminated about the inestimable value of people like Yeats for the
betterment of the world. Schultz was completely taken with Mahoney
and confessed his disinterest in law practice and real ambition to
travel to Africa and pursue a career in public service. By the end of
the interview, Mahoney had convinced Schultz to visit a powerful
committee chairman in the legislature to see about working in a staff
position on one of the committees on which Mahoney served as an
assemblyman. From that day, Mahoney treated Schultz as a colleague,
peer, and friend.

The merged firm soon came unhinged; Mahoney and Bourne
split from the Spevak group, and added to the masthead Mahoney's
protégé, Jack O'Malley, a bright and hardworking associate. But by
1971 the firm, which Schultz had joined as one of three associates,
was experiencing real tensions. O'Malley, the talented business lawyer
with a growing family, saw a dim future for the business prospects
of the firm. Mahoney was accessible to everyone regardless of their
status. Congressmen, dissident nuns, and janitors all received equal
time. Mahoney, Bourne, and O'Malley was a kind of second legal-
aid society spread among Vietnam dissidents, political campaigns,
and assorted worthy causes brought in by religious clients—all taken

regardless of the costs, particularly the costs of Mahoney's absences from the firm. For Schultz, these were heady times as Mahoney's right hand, but Mahoney could not articulate, or even engage in a serious discussion over, an economic plan for the firm. O'Malley left to work for a real estate developer but within months joined a large firm with which he has had a distinguished career.

Fred Thiemes, a lawyer then in his early sixties with a practice representing successful real estate developers, joined the firm the same year that O'Malley left. Thiemes indicated he wanted to begin his retirement and would like to develop a responsible method of putting his practice in good hands. (Thiemes, now in his late seventies, has never retired and is still practicing in the firm.) Within a month, Thiemes realized that Mahoney would not be a business lawyer, and Chris Schultz was designated to fill that role and learn from Thiemes, an excellent teacher.

In December 1971, Schultz was weighing an attractive offer to take a position in the local redevelopment authority but relented at the personal appeal of Mahoney, who asked him to stay at the firm. Within sixty days, Brian Mahoney was dead of a sudden and massive heart attack at age forty-four. To this day Chris Schultz speaks movingly of the trauma of Mahoney's death, an event that affected him as deeply as the death of his own father. Mahoney mourners filled the cathedral and spilled out into the street. Brian's brother Kevin, a priest, gave the eulogy, the text of which is framed in Chris Schultz's office. It reads in part:

> What he loved most about people was the chance to befriend them in their need, to ease their pain even though it magnified his own—that pain which he never outwitted but which he held in heroic contempt. By the alchemy of his boundless drive, resourcefulness, generosity and availability, he transmuted his own sufferings into a soothing medicine for countless others.

One can still pick up comments in Buffalo about the tragedy of Brian Mahoney's untimely death.

The Successor

Chris Schultz describes returning to the office after Mahoney's burial early in 1972 and working with Brian's longtime secretary to answer letters, send out bills, and finish the work found in the chaos of his office. This process of stabilizing existing client relationships lasted two and one-half years. Chris not only took over much of Brian's business, dividing the archdiocesan work with Bourne, but within a week he began to manage personnel, pressed the firm to collect fees, created new billing processes, and moved to control expenses. In effect, the firm had its first management. He immediately realized the extent of Brian's disdain for the business side of practice. The firm had a negative net worth. The most Mahoney had drawn from the firm in any one year was $33,000. Mahoney had no assets in the firm, indeed had borrowed from the firm. The retainer agreements with the archdiocese and other Catholic institutions were so unrealistic that they were liabilities to the firm.

The archbishop began to call on Schultz for assistance, which ripened into the loyalty of a client. The archbishop eventually authorized a press release about his intentions to continue using Mahoney, Bourne, and Thiemes. There were scores of offers to merge with other law firms, which interested no one. Schultz and Bourne successfully renegotiated the retainer agreements with the Catholic groups and replaced Mahoney on various boards, Schultz taking Mahoney's seat on the board of one of the largest banks in the area. Schultz also began to look for additional help, since the firm had a substantial client base. A key acquisition, suggested by Fred Thiemes, was Ed Dawkins from the attorney general's office—"a teddy bear inside the office, but a grizzly in litigation, the kind of lawyer opponents really don't like when they are trying a case against him." Dawkins's successful trial work for the firm's clientele, together with his handling of plaintiffs' cases that found their way to the office, greatly strengthened the earning capacity of the firm.

With the firm on a reasonable financial keel, Schultz sought to bring into the firm someone who wanted to make money and shared his commitment to keep Brian Mahoney's work going—the political activism in liberal Democratic politics and, as Chris puts it, the "do-gooder public service" ethic. Ron Isaacs, a key aide to the mayor, joined the firm in 1974 after a lengthy wooing by Schultz. The understanding with Isaacs was that he would spend part of his time building his own real estate development company. Together they began to build a business plan for the law firm. Since the firm was already representing several hospitals and developers, they both saw and worked hard to realize the potential of a more sophisticated real estate and health care practice. Isaacs, drawing on his reputation in the mayor's office, brought in a new real estate development client, as well as business from his own company. Both actively recruited talented younger lawyers to work and develop health care and real estate concentrations in the office.

Schultz and Isaacs began to conduct firm meetings in order to build a constituency for looking at the practice differently. The initial meetings were, from Schultz's point of view, exercises in frustration. As he puts it, "It is hard to get professionals to change—no one is taught to appreciate management issues since lawyers tend to think the only thing that is important is their individual judgment." Schultz and Isaacs finally concluded that the process was ineffective. They met with each of the partners and obtained their agreement to become managers of the firm. This arrangement, which improved the atmosphere of the firm, gave Schultz and Isaacs a free hand to develop the practice. Each had great respect for the analytical and strategic talents of the other. Isaacs, whose interests lay in creating a real estate development organization, was happy to have Schultz serve as the sole managing partner. The firm prospered, doubling in size from nine lawyers in 1981 to twenty lawyers and an equal number of support staff by the mid-1980s. As Schultz puts it, "We knew we could make money and still do what Brian Mahoney did." Both Schultz and Isaacs were active in successful local political campaigns, as well as Catholic and Jewish philanthropic work. Isaacs's increasing attention to his development company, which enjoyed success and attenuated the care he was able to give to law practice, led to a series of discussions between Schultz and Isaacs during 1985 that resulted in Isaacs's formal transfer from partnership to "of counsel" status with an office in the firm. Schultz and Isaacs continue to seek each other's advice on a variety of issues. Mahoney, Bourne, and Thiemes carries on under what many people in the firm describe as the "benign dictatorship" of Chris Schultz.

The Firm as a Cooperative Community

People at Mahoney, Bourne, and Thiemes are quick to cite something special about the working atmosphere of the place—a special spirit of cooperation. Secretaries talk about the informality and lack of rules, the absence of clock watching, the feeling of never being looked down upon, of being treated as equals. Young associates refer to an atmosphere of "real caring," virtually no internal competition, the sense of a support network, and the openness of communications with people willing to sit down and discuss a problem.

The senior person in the office, Fred Thiemes, reflects what seems to be an office consensus when he states that there is no better working environment anywhere—a fact that is important to him and everyone at the Mahoney firm. He talks about the youth of the firm and consequently the need of young lawyers to learn. Part of the reason they have learned so well is that they operate as a team. Thiemes has no hesitation asking for help because his relationship with the other lawyers is everything he could want. Indeed, he insists on having one or two young lawyers back him up for each of his clients, so that several different people in the office know and can relate to his clients. He does not withhold any information from the young people. They can provide continuity of service. At the age of seventy-eight, he still looks forward to coming into the office each day. Schultz views Thiemes's loyalty, the affection and respect he is accorded at the firm, and his obvious delight in practicing at the firm as not insignificant factors in the chemistry of the organization.

Isaac Rothstein, a partner whose popularity with some church-group clients has earned him the office nickname, "the monsignor," attributes this "collegial way" of practice—from the first-name style of the place to the willingness of everyone to pitch in to help in a crunch or to talk over a problem—to the fact that compensation is not tied to what people are billing. "No one is looking at the hours." There are no minimum hours at Mahoney. "Pride drives us to work hard." Joe Magee, who was recruited to the firm by Brian Mahoney and is now a partner specializing in real estate, points out that firm profits at the end of the year are divided equally among all the partners, so that if one person does well, all do well. As Al Jackson, a partner who services many of Mahoney's major business clients, puts it, leveraging out one's compensation to the maximum is "not the game" at Mahoney. "The moment you worry, or even begin to think about whether others should be making more or less than you, you create tensions that aren't here now. The security, the respect, the fine clients, the fun that comes with association with this firm are part of the compensation, which in my case is good, has increased each year, and exceeds all my projections of what I could be making at my age."

Schultz utilizes a number of nonhierarchical gestures to underscore the importance of the we're-all-in-this-together spirit. All partners and associates have offices of the same size. The letterhead and other features of office life make no distinction between partners and associates. (The partnership meets as such only quarterly.) Virtually all of the many social events sponsored by the firm—such as the theater parties, the annual dinner and show in Toronto—are open to everyone, including spouses. Secretaries have somewhat better access to the firm box at Bills football games than do the lawyers.

Schultz makes it clear that lawyers at Mahoney are accountable for their behavior toward other people in the firm. "At so many large firms," Schultz argues, "there are numbers of aberrant personalities, people with intense needs to demonstrate that they are bright and doing better than their peers, who satisfy their needs by beating up on associates and secretaries." This form of destructive behavior is not tolerated at Mahoney. If a young lawyer or a secretary is legitimately distressed at the actions of a lawyer, Schultz will be in the offending lawyer's office immediately to discuss the need for changed behavior, and a note goes in the lawyer's folder for another mention at the annual review. A young partner confirms the effectiveness of Schultz's enforcement techniques: mistreating a secretary runs the risk of having a long period cut out of your work day while Schultz preaches to you the value of cooperativeness and the special character of the office. "It's not worth the cost, but keep in mind no one here treats secretaries well because they fear Schultz's sermon. We *believe* in it and have found it silly to work in places were the persons without the degrees are treated as inferiors." Associates invariably report that their reviews include conduct toward others in the firm. And an identical process for support staff is the responsibility of Christine Shue, the office manager.

Schultz is careful to avoid another evil he associates with large firms, the destructive internal competition over who bills the most or who is the most valuable to the firm. In his view, such an environment is costly to a firm because it weeds out sensitive and reasonable people. One technique he uses to foster cooperation includes absolute secrecy about the number of hours billed by anyone in the firm. Obviously attorneys can keep their own records about the number of hours they bill, although few seem to do so, and billing procedures provide some general sense of the activity of other members of the firm, but none of the information distributed to partners about compensation includes hours, or responsibility for clients, or the profitability of work for a given client. "I don't want," says Schultz, "anyone feeling that work for some Catholic Charities group is less valuable to the firm than real estate syndications." Schultz also deliberately attempts to avoid departmentalization and foster cooperation by clustering or grouping lawyers to serve the major clients of the firm. He moves new lawyers—to the extent it is safe and effective for the client and firm—into as much direct client contact as they want. Partners and associates become billing attorneys overseeing charges to clients as soon as it is clear they are the primary contact with the client for a set of transactions. Schultz believes it is critical to reduce the distinction between partner and associate in terms of both client relations and interactions between lawyers in the firm.

Schultz is conscious of the power of his own example. It is clear the long hours he spends at the firm are an important influence on its work ethic. He is an equally powerful influence on the firm's play ethic. Despite his slightly paunchy appearance, Schultz has always been an avid jock, and much of the extensive partying of the firm is like a family picnic, centered around softball or volleyball or basketball with beer-and-soft-drinks informality. Some people in the office almost never participate in firm social events, some come to virtually everything, and most attend the affairs they enjoy most.

It is hard to quantify the strong sense expressed by people in the Mahoney firm that it is a hardworking place, and that *everybody* works hard. Lawyers report weeks that normally run between fifty and sixty-five hours, of which forty or fifty are billable. Secretaries and lawyers alike express the view that the needs of clients often generate extraordinary hours in evenings and on weekends, and everybody is expected (and willing) to pitch in and help. Schultz reports that average billable hours for attorneys range from 165 hours a month (or about 2,000 hours a year), to 100 a month (about 1,200 a year), but in view of the extensive nonbillable pro bono activities of the firm, it is hard to assess these figures.

Public Service

One of the Mahoney partners, Joanne Abraham DiVicenzo, laughingly describes the difference between Jewish guilt, which she saw firsthand in a small firm earlier in her career, and Catholic guilt, which is the Mahoney style. Jewish guilt tests your loyalty and love for individuals and the family, and Catholic guilt questions your devotion to mankind.

Working for mankind plays a substantial role in the pride lawyers, paralegals, and secretaries take in describing what is unique about Mahoney, Bourne, and Thiemes. Mahoney people rarely cite their "doing good." But, to a person, they express confidence that the extent and range of activity and organizational commitment to community activities distinguishes them from most law practices. Arthur Laughlin, a young partner, compares Mahoney pro bono practice with the "grand tradition" represented by a leader at his old firm, a man who led many law-reform efforts in the state and served on the Council of the American Law Institute. In the grand tradition, law was not a commodity to be bought and sold, but a form of public service. Mahoney carries this further, according to Laughlin. "Here, public service is on an equal footing with, and sometimes even prevails over, economics." Herb Giesen, a senior associate, expresses the view that, although he works by and large in banking transactions, he feels much better knowing he is, in effect, subsidizing the firm's public-interest work. Joe Magee calls it Brian Mahoney's presence, Mahoney's spirit of doing everything he could to help people, his inability to say no. The product of an Irish blue-collar neighborhood, Magee works for his old neighborhood Lions Club as well as a small church-sponsored group rehabilitating houses in the black community.

Like most other features of the practice, encouragement of public service is part of management. The Mahoney firm is the only law practice in Buffalo to receive an award the mayor occasionally gives to businesses for outstanding community service. Schultz reports that he brings up public service at performance reviews of lawyers in the firm. His policy is that people in the firm should participate in some form of community service, which he calls (with some self-deprecation) "do-gooder" activity. He is personally involved in a wide range of such work, serving on boards of poverty organizations active in housing, neighborhood development, legal services, and care for the elderly. He has recently been deeply engaged in a program promoting Christian-Jewish dialogue and raised money to support nuclear arms control groups. Schultz periodically gets knee-deep in political campaigns; owing to his reputation as a political strategist and advisor. (He claims, half in jest, that one can equate Democratic politics with the Good.) Schultz will sometimes suggest an idea or an opening on a board to a junior person, but his philosophy is to urge people to find their own projects.

A few people in the firm are not actively involved in public-service work but share in the satisfaction often expressed in the office over the extensive work of the firm devoted to nonprofit, charitable, and religious organizations. It "lends a flavor to everything," as Dawkins puts it. Dawkins talks of his pleasure in successfully defending a lawsuit brought by neighboring businesses against a soup kitchen for street people established by the archdiocese in downtown Buffalo. For some lawyers this poverty clientele makes all the difference, enabling them to do good *and* well. Joanne Abraham DiVicenzo finds it satisfying to unravel problems for a struggling center for retarded people and thereby advance a societal interest rather than be a hired gun for a major business corporation. Other lawyers in the office are less enthralled with the Catholic clientele and see little that is unique in it except prestige for the office or "an interesting client mix." "We're not holier than other lawyers," insists Fred Thiemes.

One of the staples of the office repertoire of stories is Joe Magee's Sunday afternoon at the office working on a real estate development project when a call came in from a client. A Jehovah's Witness needing a Caesarian section who had been denied admission to another hospital had arrived at the client hospital, still adamantly refusing to accept a transfusion. Magee rounded up another Mahoney partner with some health law experience, and within an hour a hearing was held before a local judge at the woman's bedside. The judge rejected the hospital's position that house physicians have the right to order a transfusion against the will of the mother in order to save her life. The case was appealed to the appellate division, which dismissed the case as moot, but the law firm was generally given high marks for its prompt and responsible handling of the process and its advocacy for the hospital. (The mother had a safe delivery without transfusion.)

The public-service ethos is not limited to lawyers. Joan McTeague, Schultz's secretary, points out that many members of the clerical staff are active in political, or church, or local community affairs and feel the way many of the lawyers do, that an important ingredient of the firm is its clientele of church-related and nonprofit enterprises. Kathleen Malone, a part-time paralegal who handles much of the

adoption and real estate transfer work for the archdiocese, notes that
the recent growth of the firm and development of a stronger business
base has not been marked by any diminution in its service to nonprofit
clients.

A few Mahoney lawyers feel that the atmosphere and reputation
of the firm for pro bono work somehow make them more willing
than most lawyers to restrain a client and convince a client to restruc-
ture a transaction to avoid an out-and-out sham. Most of the lawyers
in the firm, however, do not feel that the heavy dose of nonprofit
and religious clients affects the manner or style with which Mahoney
lawyers deal with clients. They argue that they would practice no
differently in another law firm. A leader at one of the firm's corporate
clients suggests otherwise. He alludes to the remarkably easy transition from serving community groups to serving private clients.
Public service at Mahoney informs or affects their unusually sophisticated thinking about service to their private clients. Public and
private work fit together, because serving others is different from
"being an expert," which seems to be the ethos of the large firms his
business also employs. According to Schultz, it is the service ethos
that drives the firm. Regardless of whether it is a paying or nonpaying
client, strong, consistent service generates what is most satisfactory
and valuable about the practice of law—the confidence and loyalty
of clients.

Hiring

Schultz describes the hiring process at Mahoney, Bourne, and Thiemes
as "painful" and "outrageously cautious." After initial screening by
two members of the recruitment committee, prospective lawyers are
interviewed by most of the twenty lawyers in the firm, a lengthy
process that reflects an obsessive preoccupation with finding people
who "fit in." The Mahoney firm interviews on campus only at SUNY
Buffalo and reviews résumés of people from other law schools. They
found that recruiting trips in the past to Ithaca, New York City,
Boston, or New Haven were a waste of resources, chiefly because
people from elite schools, if they are interested in Buffalo, are drawn
naturally to the large firms. If these graduates know the town and
have some sophistication about the Buffalo legal community, they
will find the Mahoney firm by themselves.

Schultz never passes up the opportunity to stress how much Mahoney differs from large firms. Hiring is no exception. In addition to the qualities that a large firm looks for (a good head, integrity, and a record that indicates a commitment to hard work), Mahoney insists on another quality—character, the willingness to work well with others and treat people at all levels in the organization with equal respect. The firm tries to avoid what Schultz calls "the vertical personality," loosely defined as the kind of person who shows respect to everyone above him or herself in the pecking order, has uneasy competitive relationships with peers, and treats everyone below "like shit." The vertical personality will thrive on the internal competition fostered in large firms, where only a few of each class of incoming associates survive to become partners. Such personalities will jump through every educational hurdle to work in a "Holy Grail" firm and will fight their way up at great personal expense—even the expense of their peers—to become partner. "That is *not* the way of life we want at Mahoney."

Schultz tells the story of a young man, more mature than most law students, at the top of his class at SUNY and a lead editor of the law review, who was eager to join the Mahoney firm despite the several offers he had from larger, better-paying firms. He was attracted to Mahoney at least in part due to the cooperative atmosphere of the place. Virtually every firm in the city considered him a prime catch. The Mahoney interviewers noticed that whenever Schultz and another lawyer were in the room, the young man spoke only to Schultz; whenever a lawyer and a paralegal were doing the interviewing, he spoke to the lawyer. He *always* addressed himself to the more senior person and ignored the apparently less-important person. They came to the conclusion that they were dealing with an unconscious "vertical personality" and declined to hire him. "He went to one of the big firms," comments Schultz, "where he will do well."

Not all hiring is at the entry level. A few lateral entries have added to the partnership and associate ranks. Schultz acknowledges that every lateral entry creates problems for the firm because there is an element of injustice about it. The young people servicing clients have a natural concern about bringing in someone at a higher level. Schultz takes pains to offset these concerns. New hires and lateral entries are discussed in depth before decisions are made, so that a consensus emerges in support of the decision. A person hired at the partnership level explains that Schultz promised to "take care" of any resentment that might arise. Since he experienced no trace of a problem, he assumes Schultz was capable of delivering on his promise.

The firm long ago reached consensus on the need for a tax expert. Mahoney's real estate and corporate clients need specialized tax advice. Because it had no internal tax specialist, the firm maintained excellent relationships with a few tax accountants and tax lawyers in other law firms. But its inability to be a full-service provider was a nagging problem, if only due to fear that clients might migrate to large firms, which are eager to reinforce client concerns over the limited range of small-firm services. After several years of searching for a tax partner, the firm finally found someone who fit their criteria of sufficient experience and sophistication for their clients and compatibility with the Mahoney cooperative work environment. The difficulties of the search reveal much about the firm. The market for first-rate tax people is extremely competitive, and Mahoney could not offer the satisfactions of specialization and professional collegiality—and remuneration—of large-firm tax departments. Mahoney lawyers were particularly wary of this lateral hire, because they know of examples in other firms of talented tax lawyers who insinuated themselves into every major transaction and eventually came to dominate the clients and the business of the firm. One younger member of the firm, half tongue-in-cheek, put the main reason for the difficulty of connecting with a tax specialist somewhat more succinctly: "They are all assholes."

One of the main themes of the Mahoney hiring process is the specter of the large firm as a negative model, and a number of the more recent recruits have had some form of experience in large firms.

Stan Skulski, a new associate, spent six years in the Air Force prior to Law School in charge of a group of navigators for B–52s carrying nuclear weapons. During the summer after his first year at SUNY Law School he worked for a government agency in Washington. Both his military and government experience convinced him to avoid a situation in which people were "depersonalized and treated as numbers." The "horror stories" he had heard about large firms that are reluctant to give junior people responsibility led to an application for a student clerkship at the Mahoney firm, which led to his permanent position.

June Smith, a senior associate soon to be made partner, began

her career in a Cleveland law firm and moved with her husband to
Buffalo, where she took a job in the office of the city attorney. She
first submitted her résumé to Mahoney in the spring, had interviews
in late summer and early fall, and an offer came in December.
Although the long delays between contacts bothered her, she liked
the extensive meetings with everyone in the firm, their candor, and
the thought they gave to what she would do and with whom she
would work. She was not "just hired."

Smith's civil rights orientation dates from her law school days.
Her Cleveland firm was about the same size as Mahoney, with a fine
reputation for high-quality practice and pro bono work. The good
liberals who constituted the firm did not like to bill and were poor
business people, thus vulnerable to a new partner who emerged in
the late 1970s to dominate the firm and move it to become intensely
money motivated. Smith saw this as a corrupting process that strained
personal relations, eliminated pro bono work, and created a culture
of mistreatment of secretaries and junior people.

Aileen Carney, a new associate, was a summer associate at a
large firm in Hartford, where she was a student at the University of
Connecticut Law School. She did not like the experience. There were
a few parties, none of which included spouses or people outside of
the firm. In fact, they were structured gatherings without spontaneity
or fun, where it was clearly understood that law clerks were to
demonstrate their social skills. The male-oriented firm had difficulty
keeping its handful of women associates. People in the firm combined
rigidity with a high opinion of themselves. Carney's most telling
indictment of the firm was the problem of "reality and façade." She
learned quite by chance at the end of the summer that the firm was
dominated by one person, and fierce internal politics made it essential
to "buddy up" to influential people. "Things were not what they
seemed to be." She had relatives in Buffalo and applied to Mahoney
due to her interest in health care law. She was particularly pleased
that her second set of interviews included clients. She was also
impressed with the sense that people felt they had something very
special at the firm, as if it were "a treasure they will share with
certain people."

Arthur Laughlin, a new partner, is another large-firm refugee.
His first experience as a summer associate with the large firm brought
him under the tutelage of an outspoken senior litigator who subsequently became a judge. He took a job with the same firm, like most

students at the top of his class at SUNY, because he "had an offer." Being the litigator's protégé turned out to be politically disadvantageous, because the senior lawyer was not well liked.

Laughlin compared Mahoney with his old firm. Both try to maintain high professional standards. The old firm had more facilities, such as a good library, and it was easier to be educated there because people with expertise could be consulted and thus a lawyer could reduce his sense of exposure. Luck was important in the big firm. A new lawyer's supervisor was crucial to success in a firm riddled with poor interpersonal relations and politics. Unlike Mahoney, the old firm was disingenuous about involvement in social or civic causes. What they said did not translate into action or encouragement for the associates to engage in such activities. Laughlin compared meetings of the associates of the old firm to a session of the postwar Supreme Soviet. These meetings were characterized by "doublespeak" from the leadership of the firm about compensation policies and the odds of making partner—all falsehoods that anyone who probed would find to be untrue.

Jane Mateo, a graduate of SUNY in her late twenties, joined the firm after taking the bar. Over a year ago, Schultz encouraged her to "grab the brass ring" and become a summer associate with a large Buffalo firm although he predicted to her that she would not like it. Schultz waged a campaign to recruit her by inviting her to join the Mahoney softball games that same summer and making her feel that "we are the people you'd like to be with." She ended up with offers from both firms, except that the large firm offered about $12,000 more a year than Mahoney paid. Her peers told her to go with the big firm. She began to wonder whether that advice was not part of the "put-another-plug-on-your-résumé" syndrome, since no one suggested she stay at a large firm more than two years before doing what she *really* wanted to do. She felt the formality of the big firm: "imagine, a *catered* barbecue!" She noticed and took an aversion to the imaginary badges that people wore around the place labeled partner, just-made-partner, senior associate, junior associate, and staff—each group ready to dump on the group lower down the ladder.

Clients

The Mahoney firm is as careful about selecting clients as it is about recruiting new members of the firm. The small base of a dozen institutional clients is a major value-creating asset of the Mahoney organization. Isaac Rothstein points out that the firm rejects as clients people with whom they feel they cannot have a good association. Theirs is a personal practice. It is important to like one's clients. "Our clients set the tone of the law firm," according to Al Jackson. Limited capacity is also an important criteria for judging whether to take on a new client. Except for wills and estates work and litigation, the firm severely limits the intake of new business and frequently finds itself turning down potentially lucrative clients because it is fully committed to controlling growth to serve its existing institutional and business clients.

A number of partners allude to a relentless policy of the firm to build the "relationship client." The relationship client, according to Arthur Laughlin, makes life better because one knows and enjoys the people for (and with) whom one is working. These clients sometimes create stress or emotional tension, almost like a marriage. The commitment to (and to an extent, a dependence on) the client requires certain compromises, such as endless patience when they yell at you, and a willingness to be there—anywhere and anytime—when the going gets rough. The relationship with the client is so close, mutual respect is so high, that several people in the firm mention they have no doubt Mahoney lawyers would stand up, or say no, to a client if necessary, and their clients would respect them for it.[1] The top people in client organizations, according to Schultz, know that you are no different in skill from other good firms. It is therefore crucial to avoid communicating to people throughout the organization that sense that you are doing only what is asked of you. The lawyer should never lecture the client, but be a creative problem solver. The lawyer must convey the message, "I care about you and want you to succeed—you can count on me for all kinds of support." If you can genuinely mean and convey this message, you receive tremendous loyalty in return.

Al Jackson refers to the pleasure, in dealing with the relationship client, of being a "full-blown counselor" who "brainstorms" with the

---

1. This situation rarely, if ever, arises with major clients, probably because they are organizations that in some respects were chosen by Mahoney as clients unlikely to be interested in sharp practices. The close affinity between lawyer and client leads to a natural inclination to respond favorably to the advice of the lawyer on close questions.

functioning levels of client organizations. He was so intimately involved in the development of one of their fast-growing clients that he knows more about them, and their numerous affiliated corporations, than most of the several hundred new business people in the client organization. "The episodic client rents your heart, because the call only comes when there is a problem." The relationship client calls in advance, and work proceeds as if it were a joint venture. "We share in the successes. We're at the openings and Christmas parties, and understand, perhaps better than most others, how they achieved their goals. We're not undertakers." To Jackson this is a lawyer's heaven, the chance to work with interesting, smart, dynamic people while having an opportunity to do some good and grow from it.

The limited number of clients has important internal consequences. A client is viewed as "our" (the firm's) not "my" (the individual lawyer's) client. Several Mahoney lawyers are familiar with the organization of each client and are prepared to step in to do their work. Accepting a new client is a decision by the firm, not an individual attorney. One lawyer who left the firm expresses the same admiration as every other lawyer in the firm for the quality of Mahoney clients, but found heavy focus on the "our" aspect of all clients somewhat heavy-handed, almost "crushing." She realized she did not have a single client of her own after her departure from the firm.

Clients are sensitive to their special status at Mahoney. Jack Bergin, head of a nursing-home health care group, describes how Mahoney works for a small number of clients with whom they have close ties. They don't serve everyone who comes through the door. They give priority in directing their recent growth to servicing what they have, rather than taking on new clients. Both business and nonprofit clients report being involved in interviewing prospective entry-level and lateral hires, and appreciate having their views and reactions taken into consideration by the firm as it increases its legal staff. A number of clients mention that Mahoney brings them opportunities, such as business for their organization or suggestions for excellent additions to their boards of directors or advisors.

Other special characteristics of Mahoney are not unnoticed by their clients. Rick Jones of Catholic Charities admiringly describes Schultz as someone who inspires people by charity and personal dedication and sees the firm as a group committed to public service, personal satisfaction, and a sense of integrity about what they are doing. Jack Bergin likes the "philosophical matchup" with his health care group, which has goals beyond that of increasing their net worth. Sister Isabelle Marie, the CEO of St. Adrian's Hospital, admires the excellent business judgment of the firm, its reasonable cost, accessibility, and meticulous invoices. She especially admires the fact the firm is "social minded" and "out to help people"—they have a "belief in what they do." "Some lawyers work hard at a stuffed-shirt image," says Dr. John Ruth, CEO at Wilson Heights Hospital. But Mahoney is different. Ruth has involved the firm extensively in the affairs of his organization, which is compatible with Mahoney's culture of informality, down-to-earth attitudes, and openness. Ruth feels that Mahoney is "almost like a family" in the way it nurtures its young people. Wilson Heights has been through at least two major shifts of the lead Mahoney attorney servicing their needs. In each case they were approached by Schultz, who said "trust me," and in each case the move worked out splendidly. Joane Fort, a leader of a real estate development client, refers to a number of unusual qualities of Mahoney: its internal lack of competitiveness compared to the usual fixation on billables, the emphasis on a community spirit, civic mindedness, "incredible egalitarianism," and the extent to which the firm is an extension of one person's personality and style.

One of the strengths of the firm is its ability to advise generally on corporate and organizational problems and overall business or project strategies. Schultz is often cited by the firm's clients as their "big picture" advisor, the person to whom they most readily turn for planning or political insight. The people at Wilson Heights Hospital, a new venture created from a former government hospital, particularly valued the Mahoney firm's strategic advice and help with creative thinking in the intensely competitive environment of modern health care. A number of clients admire the business judgment of Mahoney lawyers. They mention an "entrepreneurial spirit," a mentality of getting a deal done and not being overly legalistic, a "broad perspective," an ability to grasp and negotiate internal organizational politics, the priority on understanding the business sense of the transaction and how the client thinks rather than "being a lawyer."

Many of Mahoney's business clients regularly use other law firms, often large ones, and thus have some comparative perspective. Bergin's health care group chose Mahoney in an effort to duplicate an experience they once had with a junior partner of a large firm, with whom they were so close that he was virtually part of the team, a principal. For a variety of reasons, chief of which may be the maturity of their own organization, that old intimacy has not reoccurred, but they are still pleased with Mahoney's legal support. Bergin sees Mahoney as a "less complicated" environment than a large firm:

> Often, the large firm environment causes a situation where, even on a relatively straightforward matter, two partners and two associates are at work. At Mahoney, it is likely that one person will be assigned, resulting in a more efficient handling of the matter, as well as the probability of fewer hours charged at a somewhat lower rate.

George Hughes, an officer at Mahoney's banking client, finds large firms more complacent and expensive, but often useful in specialized areas such as tax law. Another client feels that for major transactions, like an SEC filing, Mahoney cannot compete with the technical skills and machinery of the large firm that can throw numbers of associates into a crash program. But for day-to-day service, Mahoney is superior to the larger, more bureaucratic organizations. Another client says he prefers Mahoney billing rates to "New York City" rates. Joane Fort characterizes the Mahoney business people as extraordinarily young. They must decline important work because their lawyers do not have the breadth of experience or maturity in practice to undertake major projects. She finds that Mahoney is not less expensive than large firms. The big firms have two advantages over Mahoney—size and Wall Street hours. Large firms have greater capacity to put a number of people to work on major projects with tight deadlines; and their older, business-wise attorneys can solve a problem in a phone call for which a young Mahoney lawyer would generate a lengthy opinion.

Mahoney lawyers are sensitive to the extremely competitive environment in which they operate and are acutely aware of the fact that they have a clientele that by virtue of size, entrepreneurial activity, and sophistication would typically be served by large firms. Schultz will on occasion sit down with a billing or lead lawyer for a client and strategize activities appropriate to remind the client of the value and capabilities of the firm. He actively solicits client feedback. Joane Fort reports that Schultz invests heavily in soliciting reactions to her experience with the firm and communicating an Avis, we-try-harder attitude. Schultz also prides himself on the fact that communications are so open with clients, and relationships so close, that clients will on their own initiative alert the firm to a problem.

Most Mahoney lawyers consider small size a positive and important characteristic of their practice, but the firm is growing as part of an agreed policy to respond to the needs of its clients. Many of the Catholic institutions have grown in size and complexity, and three business clients in particular have experienced exponential growth. The firm has found itself on occasion suggesting to clients that they need to find other law firms to assist them. Growth has therefore occurred as a defense against putting client relationships at risk. One advantage of growing to meet clients' needs has been a greater sophistication in the practice. Mahoney lawyers are proud of their expertise with novel financing schemes that are at the cutting edge in their fields.

People at the firm cite various figures for projected maximum size[2]—perhaps twenty-five to thirty—but many are skeptical about the realism of such ceilings. No growth plan has been created, nor has there been any detailed discussion of the ideal size of the firm. Although a fair amount of worrying occurs about the consequences of growth in terms of loosening the sense of collegiality and informality ("in the old days you could see a third of the firm at the urinal"), the consensus is that reasonable, carefully controlled growth is inevitable and is being handled well thus far. Fred Thiemes regrets that the annual outing for the office support staff on his boat, "where we wine and dine in style," will fall victim to the limits of his deck. There are many signs of Schultz adjusting to larger size. He now delegates more of the administrative and finance details to Christine Shue, the office manager, including evaluation sessions with each secretary. A number of eyebrows were raised when he had Isaac Rothstein sit in on his evaluations of the younger lawyers, perhaps as prelude to delegating some responsibilities in this area.

Al Jackson worries about his ability to respond to another facet of growth, the transition from being a one-on-one lawyer directly accountable to a client to a supervisory role with several other real

---

2. The firm includes twenty support staff, including secretarial and paralegal positions, the office manager, and word-processing and bookkeeping support.

estate finance lawyers. The management skills of dealing with associates and delegating work effectively do not come easily for him.

Economics

Fee-generating clients, or as Al Jackson puts it, the firm's rock solid economic base, fall generally into two broad categories, each accounting for close to half of the gross revenues of the firm. One sector comprises the archdiocese and related institutions such as Catholic Charities, hospitals, colleges, and a variety of church-affiliated institutions—the traditional base which by and large Schultz has built from the Mahoney legacy. The other sector includes many clients drawn to the firm by Ron Isaacs, such as Isaacs's own development firm and another large multistate housing developer, a fast-growing nursing-home conglomerate, a contractor, and the bank of which Schultz is a member of the board. Most of the revenues of the Mahoney firm are generated by about a dozen major clients.

During the fall, Schultz and Christine Shue work carefully on a monthly expense budget for the next calendar year. A monthly income budget is also formulated, based on projections of new people, new rates, and monthly cash income estimates derived from historical billing experience. If Schultz feels there are questionable matters in the budget, or something that he thinks might be challenged such as the projected draws for each partner, he "talks to a few people" to get their advice and reactions. In mid-November Schultz circulates the budget with a memorandum to the partners asking them to look at it and setting a meeting where he reviews the basic assumptions and goes over every line of the expense side. He and Christine Shue prepare carefully. Schultz reports that the partners have never taken issue with the budget after such a presentation.

One of the most unusual features of the Mahoney financial picture is its negligible receivables. Bills unpaid after sixty days are rare, typically amounting to no more than $35,000, usually on the understanding from the firm that there are reasons for the delay relating to a closing or financing. The firm attributes this performance to the strong loyalty of its clients and to its unusually prompt and detailed bills.

Schultz has devised a ritual known as "billing night," a once a month meeting of partners and billing associates that transforms the chore of billing and the strict efficiency of assuring prompt billing into a firmwide celebration. Several lawyers report that they look forward each month to the moveable feast of billing night. The evening begins in a conference room in the firm about 6:00 P.M. The lawyers sit around the table, editing the printouts of their bills chargeable to various clients, the accumulation from daily time sheets totaled by the firm financial administrator. Mahoney presents to each client detailed descriptions of the work, so that each lawyer must review (and, if necessary discuss with the group) hours and amounts being charged to clients and the text of "work performed." The session also serves as a forum to discuss the activities of the firm, new undertakings, projections of upcoming heavy time demands or overloads, war stories, firm management, or other issues of importance. After the totals for each client are assembled, Schultz reports on the total projected billing for that month and how this figure, along with income and expenses for the prior month, relates to budgeted targets. Following the editing session, the lawyers proceed at about 8:30 P.M. to an old-fashioned pub, where everyone in the firm is invited to join them for dinner and an evening of socializing. The administrative and word-processing staff members work late revising the edited bills so they are ready for signature the following morning. They join the crowd at the pub for drinks later in the evening.

Gross revenues of Mahoney, Bourne, and Thiemes, which were $1.9 million in 1984, increased an average of about $500,000 a year to $5.5 million in 1992. Average revenues per lawyer, which were $165,000 in 1985 and grew to $220,000 in 1989, dropped to $183,000 in 1990 and rose to $243,000 in 1992. Expenses, including all associate and staff salaries, were $1.3 million in 1985 (56 percent of gross) and $3.2 million in 1992 (57 percent). About 75 to 80 percent of net revenues are distributed to the partners as an initial draw, i.e. regular take-home pay, graduated so that the highest-paid partner takes about twice the draw of the lowest paid. The bonus, or supplementary draw funds, is split equally among the partners, so that total incomes of partners range from $140,000 to $270,000 in 1992. Undistributed net income of partners is used for partnership expenses, such as health care benefits and charitable donations (which were a little over 4 percent of net revenues in 1989, rising to over 7 percent in 1992); the rest contributes to the firm's working capital in accounts allocable to each partner.

If we examine the universe to which Mahoney chooses to compare itself—the large corporate-practice firm—Mahoney's numbers come more sharply into focus. The firm would, of course, not come close to qualifying for the annual tally of the one hundred largest-grossing law firms in the nation: the last firm to qualify for top one hundred in 1992 grossed $71 million, and the top firm on the list just over $500 million ("The AM Law 100" 1993). The median law firm of the largest one hundred in terms of revenue per lawyer was about $365,000, significantly higher than that of Mahoney. But this figure is somewhat misleading. One of the most striking features of the one hundred largest firms is the profound impact of geography, that is, the marketplace, on the numbers. New York City dominates the list in terms of the number of large law firms and their profitability. The median New York firm in terms of revenue per lawyer registers $465,000. For Los Angeles the figure is $445,000, but San Francisco and Washington, D.C., median firms record numbers about $75,000 to $95,000 less than New York or Los Angeles. The Chicago median is at $315,000, and probably the best metropolitan area for purposes of comparison with Mahoney is Cleveland at $285,000. The firms at the bottom of the listing are located in regional metropolitan areas, not major money markets, and their revenues per lawyer are $20,000 to $30,000 higher than, but generally comparable to, Mahoney's figure. Of course, gross revenues and numbers of lawyers are not necessarily good indicators of business viability, and no doubt scores of other law firms around the country would compare even more favorably in business terms to the large firms in the list on the basis of revenues per lawyer. Nevertheless, it seems fair to say, at least compared with the published numbers of large law firms in similar marketplaces, that Mahoney must be considered a financially sound and successful practice.

The figures also reveal what is unusual about the Mahoney firm. The rankings of the top one hundred firms in terms of profits per partner (i.e., the division of net revenues among the equity partners or owners of the firm) reveal an enormous difference between the Mahoney numbers and those large firms from regional centers that generally register at the low end of the list. Profits per partner at Mahoney in 1992 equaled the lowest ranked AM Law 100 firm, but were about 25 percent lower than the median Cleveland firm. Accordingly, Mahoney's profitability index (the ratio of profits per partner to revenues per lawyer), which indicates how well the firm generates profits for its partner-owners, is abysmal by comparison to most large firms. The median profitability index of the one hundred largest is 1.03, the highest 2.04. Mahoney's 0.74 is comparable to the ninety-fourth firm on the AM Law 100 list.

Mahoney's profit margin, the ratio of net revenues (gross revenues less expenses) to gross revenues, was 0.426 in 1992, and this is comparable to many of the largest grossing firms. But ordinarily a small firm like Mahoney should be expected to have a significantly higher profit margin because its overhead expenses should be lower than a large firm that must maintain a large library and various support operations like accounting, automation, personnel, marketing, or even food services. Since the offices and living style of the Mahoney firm display no evidence of conspicuous consumption, the explanation for this peculiarly low profit margin must be generous treatment of the compensation of support staff and nonpartner lawyers. Low margin numbers usually accompany high leverage, the ratio of all lawyers to partners, since it means the firm is supporting as an expense a large number of employee lawyers who are generating profits for a small number of owner lawyers, the partners. But Mahoney's leverage is 1.6, which is also a figure off the charts, well below any law firm among the top one hundred.[3] In other words, the numbers indicate that Mahoney treats its nonpartner lawyers differently than large firms: they are compensated more generously (not in absolute terms but compared to the highest-paid partners) and have far better access to becoming equity partners.

One other feature of Mahoney economics differentiates it from large firms: the extraordinarily compressed structure of its compensation scheme. While the income of the younger partners at Mahoney

---

3. Wachtell, Lipton, Rosen, and Katz has one of the lowest leverages of any firm in the top one hundred, at 1.9. It is also the smallest of the firms and has the highest profit margin of 0.66. Apart from the idiosyncratic Wachtell Lipton, there appears to be a rather clear correlation between leverage and the profitability and profits per partner of large law firms ("The AM Law 100" 1993, 59–63). Profitability of these practices is also greatly dependent on revenues per lawyer, a function of type of practice and acceptable billing rates in the local professional culture. Leverage, too, reflects local marketplace expectations of the rates at which associates are made partner. Revenues per lawyer and leverage tend to be lower in regional centers outside of large money centers like New York City, Los Angeles, Philadelphia, and Chicago. The other firms with comparable leverage to Wachtell Lipton of the one hundred largest are located in Minneapolis, Milwaukee, and Cleveland.

matches that of their peers in Buffalo large firms, senior partners like Schultz and Dawkins earn significantly lower incomes than their big-firm counterparts. The ratio of Mahoney's highest-compensated to its lowest-compensated partners is less than two to one, and the ratio of highest-compensated partner to lowest-compensated associate is about four to one. These ratios would be considered preposterous in large firms, where rainmakers (the lawyers who attract sizeable clients) and senior people in the firms claim very substantial shares of the profits of the enterprise. The comparisons with large law firms underscore the fact that the articulated ethos of building the firm and creating an environment of equal treatment of people carries over to the economics of the firm. Generosity to maturing associates, younger partners, and support staff takes clear precedence at Mahoney over profitability to partners, at least in comparison with the profitability leaders among large firms.

Leadership

The Mahoney partnership agreement describes the duties of managing partner as "the development and implementation of all operating policies." The duties of the executive committee, composed solely of Schultz after the move of Isaacs to of-counsel status, include conduct of the overall management of the firm, including setting annual draws for partners and compensation for all other employees.

The dominant status of Schultz as managing partner under the partnership agreement does not fully reflect his leadership role. Jack Warner, a new associate, puts it bluntly: "Chris Schultz is not just crucial to the firm, he *is* our firm. He tries to make this place the way he is—nonhierarchical, friendly, good to people at all levels, realizing that law isn't the only thing, hardworking, fun loving. He pushes himself too hard. He does nothing halfway." Absent the tone of hero worship, other lawyers in the firm confirm the dominant role of Schultz in every aspect of the practice. Schultz is variously described as "the umbrella man," the "controlling" person, "irreplaceable," a "one-man show," a "monarchy," the person "who has made the firm what it is," the "heart of the firm," the one who "chose the other nineteen."

Chief among the assets Schultz brings to his role as managing partner is a clear vision of the Mahoney organization. It begins with a strong critique of the contemporary world of law practice. Leaders of law firms, he argues, by and large fit into one of three categories: the biggest rainmaker, the best lawyer, or the strongest personality. Firm leaders are almost never the people with the greatest management skills, or the best vision for the firm, or clearly articulated goals for the enterprise. Law school doesn't teach law-firm management, and practicing law doesn't seem to produce these skills. Lawyers either have innate management skills or learn them somewhere else. The big money earned at large firms is rarely sufficient reason for people to feel good about life there. Managers at these firms don't know how to deal with the root causes of ennui and poor morale. They don't worry about the behavior of their people. Some think they can attack these problems by sponsoring picnics and handing out softball shirts. Holed up in their big corner offices, they see most people bringing them problems, not opportunities to serve. Often the best response they can give to a difficult problem is, "If you don't like it, leave." Those who fall by the wayside in this process are often in fact the sensible ones. For the most part, law-firm leaders have neither the support of partners nor personal interest in attacking their real problems of unending anxiety and pressure, behavioral problems, and the need for more and more hours to produce more and more money. Somewhere, the firm must articulate a common purpose and sense of group well-being that is not centered solely on fees and money.

Schultz believes lawyers willing to state and live out their values and moderate their income can build the firms they want. He considers himself supremely lucky to have stumbled across a leader like Brian Mahoney, who had a sense of vision and purpose. Schultz describes the goals of the firm in these terms:

1. a sense of common purpose and firm loyalty, which includes the next four goals;
2. a spirit of cooperation and mutual support within the firm, including secretaries and paralegals;
3. a valid, not a gestural, reputation for public service;
4. a valid reputation for quality lawyering and effective client service;
5. steady economic growth; and

6. slow but steady growth in size, which is the most feasible way to achieve goal number 5.

The long-term problem of the firm, in Schultz's view, is holding and nourishing the distinctive quality of the firm amid the transforming pressures of growth. In the mid-1980s Schultz prepared a seven-page single-spaced memorandum for all attorneys in the firm, entitled "General Notion of Firm Growth." The document elaborated the goals of the firm, analyzed the reasons for growth (the needs of existing clients), described the tensions growth causes with "the more treasured values" of internal community and public service, and mentioned the need for (and extraordinary precautions the firm should take in approaching) additional lateral hires.

The Schultz style of leadership is characterized by people in the firm as nondirective, attentive, analytical, and above all, fair. He attempts to reach consensus on all major issues but will act without it when he determines it is necessary. One partner describes the firm's operating procedures as exposition and discussion of an issue, followed by the "hearing-no-objection-the-motion-carries" move. Schultz prefers agreement, the sense of "common purpose." He talks "endlessly" (his term) about the issues and ideas that affect the firm at sessions like billing night and the firm's social and business occasions. He does not like dissonance or pretension, says a staff member. Schultz places great stock in telling stories about other lawyers or about Brian Mahoney, or anything that illustrates his themes and ideas. Schultz obviously enjoys what he does. Shaping people's lives and helping them grow and see their future are matters of enormous importance and pleasure to him. One observer of the firm describes him as a controlling leader, effective in part because of his explicit disavowal of many of the obvious techniques of control. He is self-effacing and has little need for public or private recognition of his achievements or his control of the firm.

Another characteristic of Schultz's style repeatedly mentioned by members of the firm is his penchant for follow-through. When a matter is brought to his attention—matters of office procedures, personnel, lawyer assignment, or client unhappiness—Schultz almost never lets it hang but deals with it promptly and, by and large, effectively, in the view of the firm. He has a reputation of reacting quickly to remove support staff whom he and others in the firm perceive not to be working out, while Isaac Rothstein, the firm expert in employee-relations matters, would be far more accommodating in his approach. So strong is his reputation for never letting issues hang that lawyers give him the benefit of assuming that unaddressed questions brought to his attention are weighing heavily on Schultz's mind.

Schultz believes strongly in giving feedback to the younger people, distributing pats on the back, encouragement, or criticism. He gets obvious pleasure from developing people. The formal evaluations with each of the associates are carefully structured to address legal skills, maturity with clients and office colleagues, and progress on the time line toward partnership. He encourages periodic educational sessions on new developments or changes in regulatory agencies in various practice areas in the office, such as real estate, finance, health care, or personnel and labor law. Schultz has begun periodic meetings with young lawyers in the firm, in which he discusses his mistakes and failures and how he dealt with them. Part of the lesson of these discussions is to provide an antidote to what Schultz feels is the penchant in large firms to talk constantly of success, thus making people feel terrible when the inevitable miscalculations and mistakes occur. He has also begun talking more about client contact and management, so that younger lawyers understand both that they are expected to assume this role and why senior lawyers need to be involved in the client relationship on "big picture" occasions. Schultz is eager to avoid the often "heavy-handed" and "herky jerky" actions of members of large firms who use authority to maintain control of the client.

Because of his strong antibureaucratic bias, Schultz has avoided creating written policies for the firm. There is nothing in writing about benefits or sick days. "They trust people here," says Aileen Carney: "There is no attitude of what can I get away with." As the firm expands, this too may have to change. One younger lawyer thinks it would be helpful to have some guidelines for routine matters without having to consult Schultz or ask around for answers.

Schultz pays almost obsessive attention to detail and nuance. He arranges to stop by to say hello at any important meeting with a client inside the office. Joanne Abraham DiVicenzo describes the advice he once gave her when she sought to become a part-time partner. He urged her to have lunch individually with every partner in the firm to discuss objections they might have. The consensus achieved, the partnership decision was a perfunctory one. An experienced political campaign manager and strategist, Schultz leaves almost nothing to chance. The stories of his concern for people in the firm are legion and are universally accepted as the genuine article. One rule of the firm is that a lawyer working with a secretary on overtime must make sure the secretary gets home safely, at the least walking her to a taxi. His informal policies include generous maternity leave, and support for family emergencies.

Schultz's share of partnership profits is outrageously low by almost any standard. He is the managing partner, chief rainmaker, most valuable asset, architect of the financial success of the firm, and supervisor and strategist in the substantive work of many of the young lawyers in the practice. Yet he takes less than twice what the most junior partner receives from the firm. A person of his stature in a young firm could command a substantially higher draw, in the range of three or five times the draw of the most junior lawyer, or higher. It is not uncommon for effective institution builders to take less from the firm than their prominence and control position might entail,[4] but Schultz's magnanimity to his professional family is extraordinary. A strong believer in leading by example, Schultz often expresses the opinion that money, while not unimportant, is not the most important motivator for a professional.

The satisfaction universally expressed in the firm with the quality of Schultz's leadership is tempered by concern about it. Since Schultz is now the age at which his mentor, Mahoney, suffered a fatal heart attack, colleagues often remark that Schultz goes too hard, works at an excessive pace. Schultz was out of the office with a protracted illness and generated large concerns around the firm. As Aileen Carney was evaluating the pros and cons of joining the firm, she was told by

---

4. "The leaders—senior partners who have taken on leadership roles—of almost every successful firm that I have seen, have 'bought' their leadership role in part by sacrificing personal income for the sake of building the institution" (Steven Brill, quoted in Gilson and Mnookin 1985, 388). Gilson and Mnookin go on to state, "[F]irm-specific capital and a strong firm culture are necessary for a sharing model to succeed. . . . The puzzle was: How can a firm develop such capital and culture if they do not already exist? . . . We suspect that those newer firms that have developed along the lines of the sharing model were able to do so because dominant lawyers both set an example and in essence transformed what could have been their individual capital into firm-specific capital" (1985, 389).

a competing firm that Schultz's one-man rule was an organizational disadvantage of Mahoney, Bourne, and Thiemes.

Schultz is sensitive to the problem of one-man rule, and has worked to see that his style and ambitions for the firm become an assumed part of its culture. Members of the firm have a declining sense of being led and a strong sense of a firm momentum toward the shared goals of the group. Recently, a committee of partners sponsored a successful long-range planning program for the firm. Schultz played a negligible role. Virtually all strategies now emerge from group discussion and interaction, not from the managing partner on high.

A prominent lawyer, with a fine clientele and excellent reputation for integrity and public service, approached Mahoney about joining it, along with a few lawyers from his firm. The quality of practice and people fit Mahoney criteria, but after an abbreviated interview process, younger members of the firm objected to the addition. They were disturbed about a merger's precipitating too-rapid growth, thus upsetting the supportive environment so carefully cultivated at the firm. Schultz believed the lawyer would uphold and strengthen the ethics and values of the firm. He favored the move, which he felt would bring to the firm a rather significant rainmaker and substantially broaden the base of the firm's clients, but as he reflected later, "I had to take their objections *very seriously.*" True to his consensus style, he did not pursue the matter. One knowledgeable observer of the firm notes the narrow limits of its tolerance for deviation in behavior, related perhaps to a certain lack of both diversity in outlook and entrepreneurial thinking. It is unclear whether this incident reflects these characteristics of the firm. The younger lawyers may fail to grasp the crucial role of Schultz and Isaacs in the firm's success, the business they attract, and the way they enable younger lawyers to work directly with major clients. Or Schultz may have been too strong a teacher. By serving so brilliantly as the generous parent inculcating values, he may have underplayed the economic basis of the family's fortune.

No heir apparent to Schultz has been designated by the firm. Schultz remains healthy and active. The succession is not an urgent matter and will not be until there arises an attractive opportunity in government for a man of his age, talent, connections, and public-service inclinations. Bourne, a name partner, has not been concerned with the managerial side. Dawkins, the senior lawyer contributing substantially to the financial base of the firm and the person whom Schultz relies on most for support in difficult decisions, is completely supportive of Schultz and little interested in managing the firm. A number of committees have been formed for substantive issues such as retirement, insurance, and conflicts, but there is no evidence of any enthusiasm by Schultz for a more structured committee system. Opinions as to what would happen to the firm if Schultz were suddenly to leave range from a conviction the place would fall apart to a belief that they would all pull together and manage the firm in some way. Even the optimists about the post-Schultz law firm have concerns about holding some clients over the long run, and no one offers predictions as to who or what group would run the firm. Schultz's most obvious first step in signaling greater sharing of management and a structure of succession is likely to be reconstituting the executive committee. It is an example of a problem needing attention that everyone knows is on his mind. For Schultz, the issue is compounded by his own high standards for a transition. "The real challenge," as Schultz sees it, "is to ease people into leadership who *personify* the place, who personally *feel* its values. You cannot discount the fact that a firm in important respects is a reflection of its leadership."

Chapter 4

Corporate and Professional Life at Standish Development Company

A Small Matter of Fees

Robert McGill and his senior management group in the Legal Division of Standish Development Company were incensed. They had just received a bill for legal services for the previous seven months for $580,000. The text of the bill ran about six single-spaced pages, listing in finely crafted detail various activities and discussions ("it probably took an associate two days to write this thing!"). The bill contained no mention of a date of service, who in the law firm worked on the matter, how much time the person spent, or the billing rates for those who did work. McGill and his colleagues felt the bill offered no useful information to evaluate the basis of a charge in excess of half a million dollars. The bill was sent from the firm of Butler Stern Wellington and Yeats for their services to the First Midwest National Bank and Trust Company, permanent lender on a ninety-million-dollar office complex being developed by Standish Development Company. All loan commitments by Midwest, as is customary at financial institutions nationwide, require the borrower to pay the lender's legal fees in connection with the negotiations, drafting of documents, and other matters related to the permanent financing. Midwest always used the Butler firm. Their relationship dated back decades to the origins of both the bank and the law firm.

The Butler bill was the latest in a series of bills over three years that totaled close to $1 million. Worse, there was no end in sight. The deal was not closed. Standish was paying close to $20,000 a day in interest costs for their construction loan, which they had taken out when interest rates were astronomical. The office complex was built and open, and still the lawyers from Butler were haggling over permanent loan documents. The lawyers for Standish knew the Butler lawyers were aware of how desperate Standish was to close the permanent financing. The company was over a barrel, and the Butler lawyers were in control of the roll.

The deal was extraordinarily complicated, involving a renewal project in which county government, a state financing agency, and a nonprofit development corporation had important interests, amplified by lawyers and bankers associated with each of these groups. Initially the most difficult party had been the county or, to put it more accurately, the lawyer representing the county, Jack Ericson, a cigar-chomping Jimmy Cagney type said to be very close to the county executive. Ericson insisted on drafting the entire agreement between the county and Standish, which led to a tough set of negotiations because Ericson was not an experienced real estate lawyer nor, to say the least, an artful draftsman. During those rocky early negotiations, lawyers for Standish considered the possibility of going over Ericson's head to the county executive, but the pressure to close the deal took precedence. They knew, however, there would be a reckoning when the documents reached Angus Hawkins, a younger partner at Butler Stern Wellington and Yeats who did most of the real estate financing work for Midwest.

Hawkins was notorious. He was a compulsive nitpicker in whom stubbornness, a volatile temper, and general insecurity in understanding complicated deals combined to make negotiations with a lender carrying the clout of Midwest preposterously difficult. The young business people at Midwest who cut the original deal with Standish had no interest in supervising Hawkins. They were generally inexperienced, "hotshot MBAs" working at the bank to gain experience in order to move up or out to greener pastures. During the time between the initial commitment and the final settlement on the financing there were three complete turnovers in the Midwest personnel who dealt with Standish. More important, the business people had no muscle. They knew that senior lawyers of Butler had long-standing and close relationships with the senior officers of Midwest, and in effect had higher rank than they did in the bank. Hawkins spoke for Midwest. For all practical purposes he was Midwest, and he was impossible.

The concern among the lawyers for Standish—that Hawkins

might have difficulty with the Ericson-drafted documents—soon ripened into a reality worse than their fears. Relations between Ericson and Hawkins—Jimmy Cagney battling with David Niven—grew so acrimonious that Standish lawyers and the outside law firm representing the company were reduced to serving as arbitrating go-betweens. Niven and Cagney refused to meet in the same room together.

The Butler firm was well aware of Standish's unhappiness, because the company had refused to pay the bills. Receipt of a Butler bill marked the commencement of a small ritual. Standish lawyers would request backup information about hourly rates and hours spent by lawyers who worked on the matter. The Butler firm would refuse to provide the information because it was "against firm policy" to do so. Time would pass, and Butler would press for payment and Standish would refuse to do so in the absence of backup documentation. Butler would agree to provide the information as to hours spent to their client, Midwest. Midwest business people would promptly relay the information to Standish. Billing rates for various people, despite Butler's policy against providing such information, could eventually be obtained, and thus Standish could piece together the basis for the billing. After reviewing the bill, the project lawyer, and eventually McGill, would express outrage to Midwest about both the size of the bill and the horrendous costs being run up as a result of Hawkins's behavior. Finally, Standish would wait until some partial closing when Butler would demand payment, and Standish would negotiate payment of the cumulative interim bill less a discount of $100,000 or so.

Meanwhile, in a separate ring, another bout was taking place between Butler and Standish. The company's development of an industrial building in another city led to negotiations with Midwest over permanent financing. On the basis of its prior experience, Standish insisted they would not deal with Midwest unless there was a cap placed on the cost of Butler's legal work. Agreement was reached on a $100,000 "upset" figure for the Midwest legal fee related to the $35 million financing.[1] However, the deal for the industrial building had to be recast for crucial tax reasons, and Standish acknowledged that it was appropriate for the cap to be taken off. Once the cap

---

1. An *upset* price is a ceiling price.

was off, the flood began, and midway through the industrial building project legal bills from Butler had accumulated to a total of $450,000. The ritual resumed.

After consultation with his senior management group and the officers of Standish, McGill finally precipitated what he describes as a summit meeting with the head of the Midwest Real Estate Department, the in-house general counsel of Midwest, and the Butler partners in charge of the Midwest account. He argued that Standish was being victimized by overlawyering, ineffective negotiating, and outlandish costs in view of the size of the projects being financed by Midwest. To illustrate the company's position, he pointed to the fact that Butler had thus far billed $125,000 for the utterly ineffective work of one junior associate on the industrial building financing for which the total legal work was originally meant to cost no more than $100,000. Charges for secretarial work on the office complex financing documents had already reached $140,000.[2] The Butler pattern of charges was in sharp contrast with those of another firm of comparable quality that represented Standish during the complex negotiations and transactions with all of the parties to the office development. And the hourly rates for the Butler lawyers were exceptionally high, rising over a three-year period from an *average* of $212 to $282 per hour for partners, $143 to $182 for associates, and $25 to $45 for legal assistants.[3] McGill also alluded to the major bank that issued the construction financing for the office development. This bank used a small, highly capable specialty firm charging $165 an hour for partners and $100 for associates, but more important, their lawyers knew what they were doing and engaged in no overlawyering, so that the total charges to Standish were less than $250,000. Finally, McGill insisted they would pay no more than $1.3 million for the office development legal work.

Ultimately, permanent financing with Midwest was settled, and Butler received a 1.3 percent fee on the eventual $100 million transaction after discounting bills by a total of $300,000. The Butler firm never budged from their position that their fees were completely

---

2. Traditionally, lawyers' billing rates include overhead costs, which include secretarial services. The unbundling of these costs through separate categories of billing is a method of increasing fees.

3. These are 1986 figures.

appropriate given the complexity of the transactions and the importance of protecting Midwest's interests.

Stories of the Butler fracas are not uncommon around Standish Development Company. A business person characterizes the incident as a "legal root canal." Jack Newman, a senior real estate partner in the large Pittsburgh law firm that handles more of the outside real estate work for the company than any other firm, knows the story of the Butler fee dispute and hopes that it will be put on record, because of his feelings that vultures like Butler give responsible corporate law firms (such as his) a bad name.

Like most popular stories in an organizational setting, the telling is a parable. Although the numbers are not widely known or generally cited, it seems clear that the memory of Butler is vivid because Butler actions hurt—hurt where it counts—by escalating, along with a number of other factors, the capital costs of the office development project close to unprofitable heights. Thus the story is often told with sequels to illustrate how the company learned from the disaster and took steps to prevent its recurrence.

After settlement of the permanent financing and paying off Butler, McGill and the chief financial officer of the company paid a visit to Midwest to state that the company would never do another financing with them if they used Butler in the deal. They argued that the costs of using Butler, in terms of rates, charges, and delays they cause, alter the economics of a project so significantly that the company could not afford to finance through Midwest. Midwest agreed not to use Butler for future Standish projects. They chose a boutique real estate firm for Standish loans, never informing Butler of their decision.

The successful skirmish with Midwest has spread to a larger front. Legal fees, due to the practices of law firms like Butler, have now become an element in negotiations over every major Standish financing. McGill describes a recent equity financing in which the bank insisted on using a law firm with the same policy of nondisclosure of backup information for bills as Butler. McGill demanded an upset price for the bank's legal fees payable by his company. He thought this would be totally unacceptable to the law firm, but to his surprise, they agreed to the cap. The bank's business person managed the law firm so successfully that the fee came in $10,000 under the upset price. McGill attributes this unusual event to a remarkably astute businessperson in the bank, and more intense competition in the investment-banking business. And he predicts that financing negotiations will eventually take the form of giving the banks an extra percentage of a point in return for their assuming the costs of their own lawyers.

One way to underscore a policy of concern about legal fees is to bureaucratize it. McGill has now developed a three-page retention and billing policy that is routinely sent to bank counsel and calls for preapproval of all hourly rates, projection of an initial budget, the disallowance of separate charges for secretarial and other support services, and a format for bills specifying the people, rates, and hours spent on the transaction.

The most important lesson conveyed by stories of the billing shenanigans of Butler comes from deeper, almost intangible ideas about what it means to be a good lawyer. One of the striking features about the discourse of the lawyers of the Legal Division is that they rarely refer to Standish, or divisions of the company, or individuals in the company: they talk in terms of "the client." The use of "client" has been a constant theme of McGill, so much so that it has become a natural way of talking in the Legal Division. McGill views this as a way of emphasizing the distinction between the lawyers and the business people, reminding the lawyers that the client is the principal and "we are here to serve them," and keeping the lawyers in touch with their ethical responsibilities.

The orientation of Legal Division lawyers toward the client has an old-fashioned flavor to it. One of the attractions of working for Standish mentioned by virtually every lawyer in the division is a special closeness with the business people. They talk of unincumbered exchanges that break down barriers between lawyer and client. The client is, after all, a coemployee or peer, relating to the lawyer without the baggage and tension generated by the omnipresent clock measuring billable-hour expenses of the relationship. There is less distrust, because the lawyer and client *are* literally on the same team.

The lawyer plays a central role with the client. Close relationships are one factor. Another is the lawyer's knowledge of the company. Owing to Standish's philosophy of a team approach to developing projects and the centrality of the networks of legal structures and agreements that create real estate values, the lawyer inevitably becomes knowledgeable about design, space planning, construction, marketing, financing, leasing, and other aspects of development. A lawyer with any experience becomes a generalist with a deep understanding of the business. As one lawyer puts it, "You are not a plumber called to fix a leak but someone who understands the water pressure of the whole system." Lawyers in the division express a clear sense that they have more influence, more leverage over the client than the average private practitioner. To a person they feel it is easier for them to say no to their client than it is for an outside lawyer. They have a connection of trust with the client that enables the client to accept what he or she may not want to hear, without misunderstanding or hard feelings.

Standish considers the Butler story as an example of lawyers who misuse their controls over a client for their own purposes. McGill expresses amazement over the arrogance of the senior people at Butler, who showed absolutely no desire to be responsive to complaints and thereby precipitated a major business confrontation for their client. The scathing terms with which lawyers in the Legal Division sometimes refer to Butler and their ilk carry more than a sense of being burned by an excessive fee or poor service. There is a touch of righteousness in the way Standish lawyers view the relationship with the client as a full commitment of work, understanding, and preventive care.

Company lawyers run across Angus Hawkins from time to time on the periphery of deals with which Midwest is involved. McGill reports that everyone at first noticed an extraordinary change in his style after the blowup with Midwest. He became polite and cooperative almost to the point of fawning. Lately, however, they recognize the old Angus.

The Organization of the Legal Division

McGill inherited a Legal Division in the early 1970s in considerable disarray. His immediate predecessor had lasted a relatively short time and had been asked to leave as a result of a confrontational style that to this day generates interesting stories. Thomas Mullan (now CEO) had earlier been head of the Legal Division and recruited lawyers of significant talent to the division. Before McGill's arrival, they had successfully organized themselves into functional areas. Addressing their morale and compensation problems was one of

McGill's first priorities. Whereas Mullan's style as general counsel
was presidential, focusing on broad policy issues, budget, and personnel recruitment, McGill brought an organizational bent to the job,
paying particular attention to the nuts and bolts of support staffing
and automation and productivity. The company benefited from both
styles. Between 1972 and 1974 the company went through a formative crisis in responding to a severe downturn in the real estate
industry. Many people in the company today credit Mullan with
saving it at that time because he was chiefly responsible for the
systematic—and painful—reduction in overhead by paring down the
number of employees in the parent company from about 1,100 to
450. The Legal Division when McGill took over consisted of twenty-
five lawyers. After exponential increases in the company's business
in the late 1970s and 1980s, the division consists of seventeen lawyers. The lessons of the early 1970s is heard repeatedly at Standish
Development: stay lean. And McGill, whose early years in the company were the tough, indeed agonizing, days of the early 1970s, is
a believer from experience.

The division is divided into three administrative units called
groups. These correspond to the three major line divisions of the
company. McGill and one other lawyer form a small fourth group
that specializes in corporate-level organization and finance. Each of
the three groups is headed by a vice president and associate general
counsel called a group head, who supervises the work of the group.
The three group heads meet with McGill regularly and form a management committee for the division.

Several people describe the division as well managed. One lawyer
characterized McGill as a "benevolent dictator" who does not manage
by committee. He is tolerant of different styles but does not like
confrontation. He is formal, well organized, and thorough. McGill
is in fact something of an anomaly among division lawyers, many
of whom pride themselves by identifying with their clients as deal
makers. McGill has a prominent role in the company as a senior vice
president and one of a handful of corporate officers who constitute
an executive management committee. His substantive legal work (the
personnel and public relations functions report to him and occupy
about 20 percent of his time) focuses on the Board of Directors, for
which he and one other member of the legal staff provide in-house
corporate and securities support. The other lawyers in the division

operate more directly in the real estate business. The unstated premise is that McGill, by temperament and background, is not a deal maker. One of the lawyers in the division describes McGill as the "conscience of the company," a man who is not content with what is legally permissible but concerned with what is the best thing for Standish to do. This characterization of McGill seems widely shared and is not likely to endear him to a crowd of deal makers.

Since McGill concentrates on management and general corporate matters, much of the working character of the division is established by its middle-level leadership, the three group leaders.

Mark Knowles, who heads the development group of four lawyers, started working for Standish while he was still in law school, and has over twenty years of experience in every phase of the legal work of Standish. His tenure with the company predates Mullan's joining it to head the in-house legal department. He is the most senior and experienced lawyer in the division who has never practiced outside the company. Knowles is rather soft-spoken, a steady presence in the division. He leaves younger lawyers mostly on their own but is an accessible and generous resource for questions about all aspects of the company's development business. He takes pride in his reputation in the real estate industry. For a number of years Knowles has taught an advanced real estate course at Duquesne Law School.

Jack Simon, the voluble and articulate head of the operating group of six lawyers, joined Standish from the city attorney's office, where he specialized in redevelopment work. Over the years, along with Knowles, he became a mainstay of the department, widely respected for his encyclopedic knowledge of the company's business. Simon lectures extensively in national continuing legal education programs on real estate development and finance.

Richard Gedmark heads the residential and commercial properties group of four lawyers. He joined the company in 1979. Gedmark had been a middle-level partner in a major Colorado law firm, a real estate specialist. He began to feel restless, to have a sense that "the learning curve had leveled off." Contacted by a head-hunter on behalf of Standish, he did not expect much. He had never heard of Standish. He interviewed for one position with the company but was not interested. When the group leader position opened up, he was flown back to the company again, and McGill was persistent, urging him to bring his wife to Pittsburgh to look over the situation. Gedmark's wife was a key factor in the decision to move. He was reluctant to leave a secure and high-status position in Denver and felt at the time he was burning his bridges. In fact, he has discovered that the Standish position has enhanced his marketability, though he has no interest in returning to private practice. He likes the personable environment of the company, the management attention to work flow and leveraging lawyers' time with legal assistants. The range of new developments and activities at Standish continues to extend him. "I'll stay here as long as it challenges me."

Gedmark likes being part of an entrepreneurial team and developing a depth of knowledge about the business, which contrasts with the way private clients used to turn him off and on for cost-control reasons. McGill gives group leaders lots of room. The hierarchy is less confining than in the private firm. The old attitude of looking down one's nose at the in-house lawyer has now completely reversed: the in-house lawyer in important respects controls the private firm. Unlike private practice, where failure to get along with the client can always be remedied by bringing in another lawyer, at Standish there is a high premium placed on working things out with the client, who expects the lawyer to be the can-do person, the problem solver.

Gedmark has a rather dim view of the future of private practice. He sees law-firm economics growing "tougher," as higher salaries and expenses are imposed on a client work base that cannot expand enough to sustain them. There are tensions between real estate lawyers and litigators, who rack up such sizeable billable hours that they demand substantially larger participation in firm profits.[4] Law firms have turned into unattractive environments, where people must give their pound of flesh, work like dogs, and use their time unproductively trying to respond to the pressures to bring in new business. The long hours of work at Standish equal Gedmark's private-practice hours, but they are more enjoyable and less affected with "artificial pressure."

Gedmark talks of himself, somewhat uneasily, as a "player coach" who allocates about one-third of his time for the new dimension in

---

4. Jack Simon shares these views and adds some additional reasons why real estate lawyers are not in the ascendancy in large corporate firms. Unlike litigation, which faces little "price pressure," real estate is always subject to the threat of "going inside" (i.e., lower-cost in-house counsel). And the commitment of transactional lawyers to modern document-production technology leads some firms to impose a higher overhead load (or lower partnership draw) on the real estate department.

his practice, management. He describes the core of management as evaluation, namely finding the right match between the legal needs of the client and human resources. His one criticism of the office suggests that he also supervises his group members rather closely at times. Law firms, he argues, put more emphasis on research memoranda and the craftsmanship of producing the perfect document, whereas the client at Standish cares more about timeliness than content, as long as the document is adequate. Large firms pay for the high level of professionalism through strained relationships that come from hard editing of the work of associates lower in the hierarchy.

Simon's operating group is largest of the three practice groups in the division. They are funded through an operating budget for all of Standish's properties. McGill can negotiate for an additional lawyer after the number of new operating properties strains the capacities of the operating group. New people on the development side are equally hard to obtain. Development project directors on both the commercial and residential side are highly cost conscious because they are responsible for financing capitalized development costs, including budgeted legal fees. The development group lawyers tend to regard themselves as operating under substantially more pressure than the operating people. Their clients are the high rollers for the company—demanding, deadline-driven negotiators. The operating group enjoys a more diverse and sometimes more inexperienced group of clients who are managers of existing projects. But even the operating group offers opportunities and pressures of deal making: their lawyers participate in the purchase and refinancing of existing buildings, and the expansion or renewal of company office centers.

Litigation is a major activity of the division. The number of lawsuits has not changed significantly since the early 1980s, when there were more than six hundred pending suits. The vast majority of these are slip-and-fall cases or collection matters. What has changed is the number of material lawsuits, matters that have important long- or short-range financial implications for the company, such as antitrust actions or large-scale contract disputes. These major matters are referred outside the division to litigation specialists in large firms. Since an in-house lawyer is charged with the supervision and overall direction of a case being handled by an outside litigator, large lawsuits are a not insignificant drain on valuable time. The simplest measures of the dramatic growth in material litigation are outside counsel fees, up from an annual total of about $600,000 in the late seventies to $4.2 million in the mid-1980s. After discounting this figure by the amount committed to paying lenders' legal costs (about $750,000) and outside counsel handling new development projects that the division is not staffed adequately to handle (about $1.1 million), the litigation budget for outside lawyers roughly quadrupled in seven years.

McGill has devised a form engagement letter for the use of outside counsel. The office also automates the processing of bills received from outside lawyers, so that McGill can keep close track of costs on different projects, as well as analyze cost patterns and trends of using different lawyers in different types of firms.

McGill argues that the Legal Division performs 90 percent of all the legal work of the company on an internal budget of $4.3 million. The 10 percent of legal activity handled by outside law firms (excluding lenders' legal fees) cost $3.45 million or about 45 percent of the $7.75 million total budget for legal services to the company.

The seventeen lawyers of the division and twenty-four legal assistants are supported by an administrator, twenty secretaries, and four word-processing specialists. In the early 1970s, when McGill became general counsel, the division had secretarial staff and one legal assistant called a "documents coordinator" for its twenty-five lawyers. During the next fifteen years McGill completely transformed the staffing structure of the division, reducing the number of lawyers, adding greatly to the number of legal assistants, and providing secretarial or word-processing support for the legal assistants.

The management analysis that underlay these changes emerged from understanding that lease negotiations with tenants in the company's buildings were a relatively routine and massively time-consuming activity for the lawyers of the Legal Division. The company had long ago shifted to a form lease that it insists on using as the basis for negotiations. McGill was an early advocate within the company of word-processing technology as a means of coping with the massive amount of paperwork required by leases deviating from the form. The severe paring back of the company in the mid-1970s provided a combination of exigency and excuse to begin to move legal assistants into the preparation and negotiation of leases. By the late 1970s McGill had succeeded in convincing both those within Standish and those negotiating with it to accept legal assistants in all aspects of lease negotiations. Lawyers review and sign all completed leases, handle particularly difficult issues, and conduct major negotiations that do not fit the pattern of a form lease. The decision to move the leasing away from the lawyers has two important benefits: lawyers are delighted to be relieved of the repetitive work they do not enjoy and are freed to undertake more sophisticated legal work for the company; and the division is prepared to face increases in demand similar to the company's growth in the late 1970s and the 1980s.

A study commissioned by McGill analyzed the effect of the use of legal assistants for the operating group, which generates the majority of leasing work within the division. Leasing work is reflected in two measures, *lease requests* (short summaries of the business terms negotiated by a project manager with a tenant), and *executed leases* (completed lease agreements that produce a tenant). The scale of leasing activity in the company is substantial: for example, in a typical year the Legal Division handles about 4,000 lease requests and produces about 3,000 executed leases. Growth significantly affects the volume of this work. The company added twenty-five new offices and residential complexes in a five-year period in the early 1980s. During the same period, the number of lease requests per project per year increased by 19 percent due to the process of recapturing expired leases and some downsizing, or creating more (i.e., smaller) offices, and stores on the lower floors of office centers. Thus a total of 1,120 more lease requests per year were made of the operating group during a five-year period. The operating group was able to handle this increase in demand by adding a combination of five legal assistants and secretaries. Each legal assistant handled 1.68 lease requests a day at the end of the period compared to 1.2 requests a day at the beginning, a 40 percent increase in productivity. The cost to the Legal Division of each fully negotiated and executed lease was about $60 in 1979, $85 in 1983, and an estimated $160 in 1987, or virtually no increase in cost per lease, adjusting for inflation. The combination of standardizing the lease, automating the preparation process, and assigning negotiations to nonlawyer legal assistants permits the division to close over three thousand deals a year. And the final agreement, a lease, costs the company less than what many private attorneys would charge for one hour of their time.

McGill is eager to explore additional means of improving productivity in the division. He commissioned a study of the operating group to examine the cost effectiveness potential of regional legal offices (answer: none); look in detail at the activities of lawyers within the office to determine if it might be less expensive to export certain activities (answer: no exports justified, except some bankruptcy and commercial collection work that accounts for less than 10 percent of lawyers' time); and focus closely on ways of improving legal assistants' productivity. His consultant recommended three productivity measures:

1. Training sessions in which lawyers and legal assistants meet with project managers to explain to them various clauses in the lease, a front-end education that saves legal assistants hours of wasted time sending out and later negotiating leases that have not been properly explained by the businessperson in the first place.
2. Detailed measures to reduce delays in the elaborate back-end part of leasing after the completion of negotiations—preparing copies for lenders, filming for microfiche filing, and readying executed leases for archival storage, the results of which should end secretarial overtime required to find lost, unprocessed leases.
3. Suggestions for truncating the time-consuming paper flow between legal assistants and secretaries, that is, exploring further automation of the lease negotiation by putting legal assistants on-line in an automated system that can print a finished lease including changes the legal assistants enter into the system.

McGill, convinced of the importance of finding ways to automate, systematize, and streamline work, has eagerly implemented all three suggestions. Office legal assistants are now enthusiastically working with an automated "expert system," under which each legal assistant has an on-line terminal permitting the assistant to make certain preapproved changes in the lease, insert rental and term specifics, and print the final document, ready for execution. McGill believes such a system might eliminate the need to add four secretaries and legal assistants to his staff.

McGill would be the first to argue that the case for more extensive use of technology and nonlawyers has an underlying business rationale, but he is also convinced of the positive human impact of these systems. The effectiveness of these systems is dependent on sound management. Jack Newman complains that he has been unable to duplicate in his private law firm McGill's success in developing a productive cadre of legal assistants. Virginia Carmody, the legal administrator who reports to McGill and serves as the manager most directly responsible for the legal assistant and support staff, gives credit to the environment fostered by McGill. Standish is a more democratic society than the large firm. There is much more bottom-up management in which employees buy in to new ideas through discussion of new moves and initiatives. Luncheon meetings often include nonlawyers. Legal assistants report that Standish is a relatively caring, people-oriented place where management listens carefully. They are treated with respect—like "professionals"—by the lawyers. The result is a sense of ownership and pride in the Legal Division and generally good morale within the secretarial and paralegal group.

The hiring of lawyers is coordinated and effectively controlled by McGill, who discusses with his group leaders needs for additional personnel within existing budget constraints. McGill takes care to involve all lawyers in a group as interviewers so that he has as wide a range of reactions as possible, can gauge whether the individual is compatible with others in the group, and can hire, in effect, by consensus. Several lawyers describe the hiring process as "glacial," with revisits and reference checking and delays that typically drag on for months.

McGill describes why hiring to some extent runs against the grain of his normally crisp and efficient management style. He has an idea of the type of individual he wants. Because the division workload is heavy, he cannot afford to make a poor hire who cannot carry his or her weight. Heavy investment in hiring is a form of preventive management, which can save enormous amounts of time and money spent weeding out a dysfunctional person. McGill therefore treads very carefully in hiring. One of the lawyers in the division thought it would be useful to carry preventive management a step further into better planning. Since the loss of a lawyer creates for an already lean division a significant void that takes months to be

filled, the chronic understaffing could be remedied by creating a junior
staff position to enable McGill to move a relatively experienced lawyer
immediately into a vacant position.[5]

Candidates for a job must meet requirements of real estate or
other relevant legal experience and have "smarts," excellent background, and character, but McGill's chief concern with new recruits
is to figure out "who they are," what are their "value systems, and
professional and personal objectives."[6] He is concerned how their
personal and professional values mesh, what they define as success
and how they rank some of the goods of professional life such as
status, prestige, money, and work environment. He never hires lawyers fresh out of law school because they do not know what is
important to them. "Typically," McGill complains, "all they want is
a good job." He believes strongly that a person aged thirty has different life ambitions than a twenty-five year old in terms of marriage,
family, and outside activities. He is primarily interested in people
who have job experience as a lawyer and have gathered some positive
and negative learning from this experience. He wants people who
choose to work for the company because it reinforces something
positive they want.

McGill says, and staff lawyers confirm, that he is up-front with
lawyers he recruits—they will have a comfortable living but won't
earn top dollar, or as much as they would in private practice. In
fact, with entry-level salaries for lawyers of three-to-four years of
experience ranging from $40,000 to $60,000 in the mid-1980s, he is
able to be reasonably competitive with large law firms in the Pittsburgh area, less so if the comparison is with large Washington and
Philadelphia or New York firms. McGill does not want money to be
a positive or negative factor in the decision to join Standish. If money
is the main motivator, the company is not the right place for a lawyer.

By all accounts McGill is a salesman, too good a salesman for
some staff members, who feel he oversells and leads new recruits to

---

5. McGill views this as obviously a good idea but unrealistic in light of the
heavy budget pressure to minimize staffing.
6. The lawyers in the division come from a variety of law schools: Antioch,
Columbia, Brooklyn, Georgetown, Virginia, Temple, Pitt, Duquesne, West Virginia,
Harvard, and Stanford. Four were editors of law reviews, a number held excellent
federal clerkships, and all but a handful graduated at the top of their classes. They
are predominantly a young group: one in the midfifties, about five in their forties,
and the rest in their thirties and twenties.

an inevitable letdown when they face the demanding workload in the division. McGill is articulate, earnest, and a believer in his company and the professionalism of his division. He unabashedly states his pride in the staff of the division "as human beings and as professionals." He feels there is no schizophrenic life at the company. Professional values at the company are not in tension with the demands of generating income. McGill wants people to live integrated lives, where professional and personal values reinforce each other. He stresses balance but acknowledges there are one or two workaholics in the division.

McGill estimates that in the fifteen years he has been general counsel and head of the Legal Division some twenty lawyers have left the company. Of these, perhaps 60 percent simply "didn't make it." A handful left for better opportunities on the business side of the company or in private practice, and perhaps two or three were unhappy and returned to the law firms from which they came. A handful of lawyers left due to the relocation of a wife or husband. McGill indicates he tries not to cause economic or personal trauma for those whom he advises to leave. He has had good experience with the out-placement consulting firms he has used on a couple of occasions.

"We get headhunted a lot," McGill states with a mixture of dislike and pride in the compliment it represents to the quality of the division. He encourages lawyers in the division to look at other job alternatives, if only to avoid that terrible sense of being trapped. It is healthy, McGill argues, for people to reconsider what they are doing every three to five years and to evaluate what they have at the company.

The People of the Division

The staff of the Legal Division reflect McGill's hiring process, for they are quick to focus on the variety of reasons they have chosen to work for Standish, as well as their strong, generally negative feelings about their experiences in other practice settings.

Julia Adams was a civil litigator in a boutique firm of about thirty lawyers for an extraordinarily demanding man, a "patient and careful teacher" who was a "twelve-to-fifteen-draft" artist on briefs. She had great respect for the firm but concluded, after billing twelve hundred hours in one six-month stretch, that a sweatshop—regardless of its quality—was simply incompatible with the desire of her husband and herself to have a family.

Frank Leyman, a veteran of both the operating and development groups, recalls how unproductive were his three years as an associate at a large firm. He wasn't busy enough, or he was researching "dry holes," so that it seemed the firm spent 99 percent of its time worrying about 1 percent of the real problems of the client.

Jack Spevack, who has been with the company about three years, spent six years in a fast-growing firm of about forty-five lawyers, where he had high billables but a sense of burnout. He came up for partnership at a time when the firm decided to defer partnership decisions due to tighter economic circumstances, the greed of the partners, and the dominance of the firm by one managing partner. His departure—along with another promising associate—led the firm to examine itself with the help of a management consultant. The following year, the firm overreacted and created seven new partners, many of whom were questionable partnership material. In law firms one needs a "rabbi" (a senior mentor and protector). Personality issues are pervasive. There is far less "bullshit" at Standish.

Spevack's former law firm gave no encouragement to his outside activities because they did not have the foresight to see that they would benefit the firm. The lines of communication are seldom open in private law firms. There are strong egos in private practice, without a commitment to common goals or a desire to improve the organization rather than increase compensation. Associates are fungible. Most lawyers he knows want to be doing something else, and they typically get into business ventures with their clients. It is tough in private practice to sustain interest for twenty or thirty years, to see an overall purpose beyond building an estate. And Spevack is pessimistic about the future of many large firms. He senses there will be a big shakeout in the private practice of law.

James Simpson left a medium-sized Washington firm as an associate attached to a partner who set out (unsuccessfully) to form a smaller firm. As Simpson surveyed the possibilities, lateral entry into a private firm seemed uninviting. He did not relish expectations that he must generate business, and he knew he would face the animosity of associates and junior partners below him on the pecking order in any firm he joined.

Paul Philips began practice in the branch office of a large national law firm. He watched an intense political battle that resulted in a takeover by the main office. A partner of inferior quality who accounted for $2 million in business for the firm was put in charge of partners of obviously better quality. His rabbi had his head cut off. The old style of the office, which emphasized first-rate work product and close relationships among attorneys in the office, was replaced by a macho style that encouraged competition among the attorneys, tight departmentalization, and heavy emphasis on billables. It became a sweatshop, with an enforced work ethic in which it was normal to work seventy hours a week. The associate's job was to make money for the partners. In his final year with the firm he had twenty-five to twenty-six hundred hours in billables to clients. He subsequently had an excellent experience in the SEC and had to force himself not to stay there.

The positive attractions of the Legal Division motivate the lawyers as much as their negative experiences in private practice. Jack Spevack contrasts the rather confining atmosphere of the law firm with the conscious efforts of the company to keep everyone informed about goals and issues through group meetings, quarterly departmental meetings, a newsletter, a quarterly corporate luncheon, and a general open-door policy that encourages people to ask questions.

According to James Simpson, Standish is different, *very* different from a law firm. It has much less "baggage." Although the Legal Division operates in a self-contained law-firm fashion, the sense of being part of the Standish organization breaks down the economic tensions and the barriers between lawyer and client characteristic of private practice. Julia Adams has a four-day workweek (for "five days of work"). She considers this arrangement rare in the world of law firms. She appreciates an atmosphere where people are more solicitous about her family responsibilities and reasonable about demands on her time.

Frank Leyman says a lawyer's time is genuinely valued at the company, not just kept and billed. Managers and development directors are about the same age and have many of the same interests as the lawyers, and they defer to the lawyer, appreciate the lawyer. It is OK to take risks if it is explained candidly to the business people: the company respects practical law. Although the hours at Standish are longer, there is less pressure, "no need to show the flag on weekends." The evaluation system in the company doesn't deliver in the way it should, but it is far superior to the haphazard evaluation and compensation structure of the private law firm.

One of the newest recruits to the office is Jane Lynn, who was an associate in Jack Newman's firm and drawn to Standish after she was loaned for a few months for some emergency work. She prefers the company to private practice, largely due to the close interaction with the business people and the feeling that she is part of a team. She misses the sharing of legal issues and problems with her peers at Newman's firm. Staff attorneys in the Legal Division are more like solo practitioners. There is little in the way of continuing education at the company compared with Newman's firm of about 150 lawyers. Supervision is better at the Legal Division, if only because it is smaller. Support staff have excellent knowledge of the documents with which they work and are superior to that of Newman's firm. Work at Standish is more demanding, with more responsibility. The quality of life is better. Clients treat you better. You are more involved with the business aspects of the company. The work is more coherent—not the bits and pieces of projects that come to the associate in the law firm—but a chance to see everything the client does.

Outside Perspectives on the Legal Division

Virtually every outside lawyer who deals with the division comments on how unusual it is. Jack Newman, for example, is blunt in his opinion about the division: it is the best in-house staff of any real estate company in the country. Newman is an alumnus of the Legal Division. The contacts and reputation he built at Standish contributed significantly to his acknowledged success in building a national real estate practice at his law firm. He points to several factors in the creation of the quality law department at Standish. In-house lawyers these days no longer bear the stigma of failed private practitioners; McGill seems to find mature and disciplined lawyers; and Mullan, who founded the division in the late 1960s, has always emphasized that the legal document is the end product of the real estate developer's assembly line. In many companies the lawyer is treated as a necessary evil. Not so at Standish.

Al Birch, an Atlanta lawyer who worked closely on several office building deals with the company, explains that Standish development attorneys are different from many in-house lawyers. They "really do things." Usually inside counsel make excuses, like the need for some committee approval, but Standish is staffed lean and seems to have no bureaucracy, no "stirring of the pot." The lawyers are capable of getting a deal done by themselves. Birch wonders how the company is able to keep the quality of people it has, when its lawyers are so heavily loaded with the pressure of major deals, traveling, and generally "busting their buns."

Jack Greenbaum, a private attorney who counsels the company in securities and corporate matters, considers the Standish legal staff to be one of the more sophisticated, particularly for a company of its size (net earnings of about $45 million on earnings before depreciation of about $500 million a year). He knows a number of companies of similar scale that may have only one or two lawyers, who are barely able to keep up with what is going on. The Standish business people are satisfied with their in-house representation—not a common phenomenon in corporate America. The Legal Division has stature and credibility at Standish.

Philip Moreau, who represents one of the banking lenders Standish uses to finance its projects, argues that the lawyers of the division seem to have a better sense of the business deal than most in-house counsel with whom he works. They know what the client requires, so that they can eliminate nonissues and speak with authority and accuracy. They don't posture and "jerk you around." They are not, like so many in-house lawyers, looking back over their shoulders. They are better than most and as good as any in the business.

Everett Lauder, an outside litigator who handles a number of major lawsuits for Standish, feels that it, more than any other company with which he deals, tries to balance its interests in prevailing in the particular litigation with concern about what is right for all the parties involved, including their adversaries. The Legal Division is proactive, participating in important strategy considerations in a lawsuit. They will review and comment on everything because they "know the facts" and are not just paper pushers and expediters. They actively help in the development of the factual case.

The client of the Legal Division has a clear understanding of the reasons for sponsoring the creation of a strong legal department.

Mullan, the company CEO, describes his goal in founding the Legal Division as cutting down on the indiscriminate and expensive

use of the large law firm then doing most of the major legal work
of the company. Mullan had been a partner in another major firm,
and his first steps after joining were to control the legal work, so
that he could decide in an organized fashion what work was to be
done in-house and out-of-house. He gradually built a staff that could
handle all routine work and much of the complicated transactional
work. They offered the added advantage of avoiding the puffery that
characterizes some outside lawyers. According to Mullan, McGill's
achievement since joining the company as general counsel in the early
1970s has been to create a new level of performance that the people
in the company now take for granted. McGill has been a fanatic in
automating his division and using legal assistants extensively and
creatively.

The great thing about an in-house group, according to Frank
Tuoey, a Standish senior vice president, is that they are "yours." It
is a relief to know that they aren't off in Chicago or somewhere
working on someone else's case. *Your* lawyers' business is not to
generate more business for themselves and see "how many chirping
birds they can feed." They aren't overselling their capabilities. They
meld their capacities to the work at hand. They are deeper inside
the client's head. They have a breadth of exposure and a more exqui-
site grasp of what the company is trying to do. They understand the
company's goals. There is no energy lost in the whole macho syndrome of the outside lawyer. They bring you competence and specialization in *your* scheme of priorities.

For Tuoey, the value of the Legal Division also derives from
strengths of Standish. The lawyers operate in a company culture that
is "tough but not predatory." They are not beholden to the short-
term perspective, so that continuity is important, as are the values
of fair play and substantial justice. Another feature of the company
is the "edifice complex," the special pride in one's work that generates
visible results—a far cry from working in a girdle factory.

Fred Whitney, another senior vice president, explains that the
company needs to vest authority deep in the organization because it
cannot run a project from long distance. It has to have people on
the scene. Having an experienced lawyer as part of the development
group provides crucial continuity and sets up an enormously useful
dialogue.

Rich Francis, an experienced development director in Whitney's division, explains that the company is a "matrix organization," sorted into vertical divisions such as leasing, construction, design, development, and legal, but functions horizontally, with people from all these departments teaming up on a project. It is harder to do all this now with an outside law firm not used to these close working relationships. Francis describes what he means by a responsive lawyer. In the huddle only one guy can call the plays:

> I bear the risk inherent in the development process, not the lawyer. I want the lawyer to do it my way, produce the documents when I want them, tell me how to do what I want to do. I don't need an "agin" lawyer, but I do want someone who knows the realities of risks, not in the abstract. I want to be squeaky clean, no hiding of things: we are up-front around here. Lawyers are crucial to us. Every word of many of these deals is new language. I want someone who is not given to verbosity, who avoids excessively lengthy and obscure documents. There is a special talent to drafting that astoundingly few outside lawyers have. A lawyer should seek to restrain you. It is my lawyer's professional duty to argue with me. If it is a legal point and I feel strongly about it, I may take the argument to Mark Knowles [the head of the Development Division who supervises younger lawyers like Leyman], for whom I have complete respect, but it is more in the style of "run this by him, will you?" With lawyers around the company it is not win-lose, but a win-win, situation.

Standish clients have good things to say about their lawyers. CEO Mullan calls the Legal Division a "terrific" department, an extraordinary legal resource to the company, doing better work than they could get using outside lawyers. Legal Division lawyers are quick, responsive, and fine draftspeople, and their intimate knowledge of the increasingly complex business of the company is crucial to their success. He picks up an exhibit to illustrate his point from his desk, a letter to some major stockholders of the company in the wake of a difficult meeting. He had asked McGill on a Friday afternoon to give him a draft letter that reflected not only the terms of an understanding with the stockholders, but to keep it "soft" and sensitive to the delicacy of the relations with the stockholders. The draft arrived on his desk Monday morning, and it was a superb legal document that also had a warmth and thoughtfulness perfectly crafted to suit the problem. Mullan was convinced no outside firm could have done it.

Frank Tuoey is enthusiastic about the quality of his in-house legal support. He immodestly characterizes his lawyers as having "very sophisticated clients" for whom they do cutting-edge work. The company lawyers are probably as expert as anyone in the country on floating zones, and a recent financing with convertible subordinated securities in the Eurodollar market was handled by the in-house staff. The company's lawyers compare extremely well with many private practitioners, who may be well-known but cannot put a cogent document together. Legal Division people typically gain control of the preparation of documents on deals, a way of controlling the transaction.

Rich Francis, a man fully capable of submitting devastating evaluations to McGill of the lawyers with whom he works, is convinced that the quality of his lawyers has improved enormously. The deals are far more complicated than they were four or five years earlier, and he has in-house people now that are as good as, if not better than, any private lawyer, making it possible for him to put together deals in what might seem impossible time frames. Francis raves about Frank Leyman, who he says can "draft like lightning, understands the dynamics of a deal, and always seems to be able to think six or eight moves ahead." He is taking Leyman out to dinner for the best lobster in town for his absolutely invaluable role in helping him pull off a recent miracle.

The clients are not uncritical of the legal side. One of Tuoey's concerns is costs. Unlike many real estate companies, Standish has chosen to put its development capabilities under one roof, which creates a large fixed overhead. And Tuoey feels the lawyers are expensive, although McGill claims it costs less than going outside. Of course, to the extent the lawyers are hardworking (that is, putting in more than a forty-hour standard workweek), the company may be getting sixty hours of time for the forty-hour basis of allocating costs to a project, a savings to the developer client.

Francis mentions that several years ago "McGill's law firm" had some mediocre people on the development side and was unresponsive as well. "This is a 'no shit, Sherlock' kind of business," says Francis. "I don't have time to wait around, so I'd say, 'Fuck this—let's go get

Jack'" (Newman, formerly of the Legal Division, in private practice). Fred Whitney confirms there was a period in the late 1970s when some of the younger company lawyers were not as client-oriented as outside attorneys. At the same time, Mark Knowles, head of the development group, felt that neither he nor his lawyers were getting clear communications from their clients as to priorities and expectations. In an effort to deal with these mutual concerns, Knowles set up monthly meetings with the business people to work out ninety-day forecasts of needs and deadlines that are fundamental to risk management in the commercial development process.

Thomas Mullan feels the Legal Division is not as well equipped as outside law firms to provide dispassionate advice in major litigation. Company lawyers are by and large transactional lawyers, and there is no substitute for having veteran warriors from the trenches provide sound and deliberate analyses of the possibilities in a lawsuit.

Bill Evans, a development director who left the Legal Division, offers a different perspective on the changes that have occurred in it. One of his reasons for leaving was a growing perception that the lawyers were less in charge. During the 1970s the Legal Division played a greater role in development, both because the business people were less experienced and the Legal Division was a real repository of talent. They were counted on to take charge; documentation lends itself to this. As the deals became more complex and the business people became more experienced and asserted more control of the process, the lawyer took a more professional role, responding more like a lawyer from a large firm to demands made by more sophisticated business people. On the operating side, where the lawyer is involved more with questions of immediate and short duration, division lawyers play a somewhat larger role because of the influx of new business people, an expansion that continued through the 1980s.

Compensation

Despite McGill's care in recruiting people who fit the organization and for whom the bottom line is not the highest professional priority, a general undercurrent of dissatisfaction over compensation is a fact of life in the Legal Division. As one lawyer puts it, there is a natural frustration associated with being in a company where top levels of management, including CEO Mullan and McGill, are making big money. Mullan was paid $900,000 in annual salary and bonus in the early 1990s, plus stock compensation worth approximately $500,000; McGill's annual salary and bonus at the same time was $425,000, with stock compensation valued at $175,000.

The compensation of division lawyers is a mixture of salary, bonus, benefits, and incentive payments. Cash compensation in the early 1990s ran from $70,000 for junior lawyers up to $180,000 for experienced people. The benefits program amounts to an additional 20 percent of salary and is comprised of cafeteria-style, mostly tax-free, programs that the individual can tailor to his or her own needs. McGill argues that the benefits setup is superior to that of most private firms, which tend to distribute higher income but give lower total value because the individual must pay for benefits from after-tax dollars. The company offers a 401k retirement plan, matching a portion of the individual's retirement funds with stock. For a company like Standish, which has experienced growth in the market for its stock, the increased value to the employee can be substantial. Most of the lawyers of the division have access to another incentive compensation program, periodic stock options. According to McGill's calculations, lawyers who receive options under this program have historically added about $12,500 to $15,000 to their annual compensation for each grant of stock options. Lawyers with seniority who have received several stock-option grants have realized a multiple of this value.

Top-level compensation in the company is less disturbing to Legal Division lawyers than are peer comparisons. Lawyers at the company are proud of the challenging nature of the law they practice, its pressure, excitement, and demands on their time, energy, and ingenuity. They feel their practice is superior to what most young partners and many senior partners experience in large corporate law firms. Many of the lawyers in their thirties are acutely aware of the passage to partnership of their friends and law-school classmates. While they acknowledge the pay scale of the company is not out of line with Pittsburgh compensation scales, they feel large firms in the District of Columbia, Cleveland, New York City, or Philadelphia are the more appropriate measure. Compared to their peers in these other cities, they feel underpaid. McGill acknowledges that more experienced lawyers in the division are probably earning between 20 and 30 percent less than their peers in the best major firms, but that the company can compete "on a career basis" through its benefits and stock plans.

When the argument shifts to the perspective of a career with the company, the comparison with colleagues on the business side emerges as an aggravation. A system of quality review applies to all personnel in the company, including the Legal Division. This system is based on defined job levels and individualized objectives agreed upon by subordinate and supervisor. Performance is measured in terms of these objectives at salary-setting time. The range of bonuses varies from year to year, depending on the performance of the company as a whole. This "management by objectives" program works best with quantitative measures, but the Legal Division tries to adapt the system to accommodate quality-of-performance measures. Line personnel such as development-project managers have the potential for higher bonuses (from 20 to 30 percent in good years) than the people of staff departments like the Legal Division (from 15 to 20 percent for outstanding performance). To the management of the company, the rationale for this distribution is that entrepreneurs are the heart of the company, and the people who bear the risks of failure should receive larger bonuses when their work leads to financial success. But the effectiveness of the company's teamwork networks of people from different departments leads staff personnel to conceive of themselves as responsible entrepreneurs, particularly the lawyers who play a crucial role in structuring deals and, in some cases, guiding rather inexperienced business people. The result is that some lawyers in the division feel the potential for higher bonuses of their business peers means the company undervalues their own efforts.

An important factor in the calculus of compensation is the potential for advancement. McGill is a man in his forties. The associate general counsels and group leaders are the same age. The likelihood of members of this management group leaving seems remote to most lawyers in the division. McGill is aware of how constrained are the possibilities of advancement when most of the rungs on the Legal Division corporate ladder are filled. He has recently developed senior attorney and senior assistant general counsel positions in order to justify higher compensation for some of his best people, and to make improvements in supervision and management of the groups. He is also conscious of how difficult and delicate is the task of promoting two or three people from a group of a dozen highly competent and ambitious people. Inevitably, these moves generate the potential of yet another comparison that may seem arbitrary or unjustifiable to division lawyers.

One of the most serious crises of McGill's leadership of the division occurred in the mid-1980s, when the company considered extension of stock-bonus compensation beyond the leadership group to senior-level management. Under this program the company makes restricted stock grants available and provides loans to pay for the stock. The loans are gradually forgiven over a period of time if the individual is still working for the company. The intent of the program is to provide financial incentives to key personnel to stay with Standish, as well as financial disincentives for leaving. McGill argued vigorously that all lawyers in his division should be eligible for these benefits. The initial decision went against him, and after relaying the information to his staff, his senior people, Jack Simon and Mark Knowles, were enraged enough to make moves to leave. Simon received an offer from a large Los Angeles law firm and openly threatened to accept it. Knowles, who had tentative offers from three leading Pittsburgh firms, lobbied his principal development "clients" within the company. Faced with the loss of two experienced real estate lawyers representing over three decades of understanding of the company and its business, senior management agreed to extend the stock bonus plan to the group-leader level of the Legal Division, insuring compensation levels competitive with the private market for senior real estate specialists in private firms. The result, while satisfying the group leaders for the time, added yet another invidious comparison for many of the lawyers in the division.

Except to the extent supervisors are involved in the evaluation of their subordinates, salary information is guarded carefully by the management of the company. But the informal sharing process within the Legal Division is sufficiently widespread that discontent has a factual basis. At division retreats McGill sometimes talks about compensation issues but remains uncomfortable talking salaries or salary policy outside a one-to-one setting. To some extent, McGill and his three group managers have become inured to the insolubility of the problem.

A Different Practice

Whatever may be their complaints about the Legal Division, most lawyers appreciate the difference between their professional lives and those of lawyers in private firms. Lawyers of the division do not consider private practice a desirable option in thinking of possible next steps in their careers. Their feeling of satisfaction involves the professional pride of members of an organization who know they are successful, and a measure of contempt for shoddy work in the profession that they see on a fairly regular basis. But the sense of fulfillment includes a conviction that work at the company is harder, more interesting, more satisfying, and more relevant than that of the best of private practice.

With the exception of a few lawyers who emigrated from notorious sweatshops, most feel that the company commands more hours from them than did private firms. But these hours are different, less burdensome, more "natural," less "artificial." There is not the relentless pressure of the time sheet to record billable hours. Work is driven solely by what is needed to get the job done satisfactorily.

For most lawyers at the company, the pressure to perform is heavier than what they experienced in private practice, if only because most were associates, not responsible billing partners in private law firms. They also perceive that the lean character of the Legal Division precludes the specialist support characteristic of large firms. They may now and then be able to draw on the head of their group for some advice or help in controlling a skeptical client, but essentially they are solo performers on the line with the development or operating team of which they are a part. Part of the tension and exhilaration of this position of responsibility is that negotiating opponents are usually senior real estate partners of major private firms.

McGill seeks to emulate the private law firm in one respect. His concept of professionalism includes the traditional encouragement given to lawyers at many of the best private firms to engage in outside activities, such as community or civic associations, bar associations, and continuing education or law school teaching. A firm believer that he must model what he says if the message is to have any force to it, McGill is active in the Pennsylvania Bar Association, the American Corporate Counsel Association, and boards of civic and community organizations. Several other lawyers engage in similar professional and community activities. Division lawyers feel free to undertake outside activities without explicit counterpressures from the company. In fact, a large number are not active outside of their work and home lives probably due to the demands of their young families, commuting time from their homes in the Pittsburgh area, and their sense of obligation to the company under heavy workloads. McGill expresses regrets about this, wonders whether the group leaders are reinforcing this message sufficiently, and then concludes that all he is in a position to do is to explain by word and example that such activity is encouraged.

Atmosphere or style is a factor often cited by many of the division lawyers as a favorable factor attracting them to the company. They say the division is a good place to work. Although old timers maintain that morale is lower than in previous years (more of a "corporate" atmosphere, they say), the general feeling is that the division is comprised of good, hardworking, and helpful colleagues who engage in virtually none of the internal politics or climbing over backs to get ahead that is said to characterize many law firms.

Most of the Legal Division's recruits were attracted to the company by the nature of the legal work, which they conclude is more challenging than work in private firms. Lawyers and clients within the company allude to the increasing complexity of development activity. One young lawyer keeps a diagram handy of one of his projects, in which there are twelve major corporate and governmental participants, five property owners in addition to the company, three different permanent lenders in addition to a federal Urban Development Action Grant, a score of interlocking long-term leases of land and building levels, and a variety of joint-venture and equity-sharing arrangements. The division lawyers are proud of being at the cutting edge of national real estate practice.

Division lawyers also talk about the variety of their practices. They are close to *being* business people, engaged in a stimulating range of technical development issues of modern real estate practice. They need to be familiar with partnership and joint-venture law, accounting, securities and corporate law, and (in their supervisory as well as preventive law functions) a wide variety of litigation. The sophisticated real estate transaction lawyer must be a generalist to be a successful deal maker in a world of more intricate deals.

Close relationships with the business people are pleasures that most of the division lawyers did not experience in private practice. It is important to the lawyers to have genuinely grateful clients. It is the gratitude of a fellow team member. McGill talks of his "client-driven environment" as a more fulfilling practice than the sometimes remote and often episodic relationships with clients that characterize modern large-firm specialists, particularly associates. Company lawyers are grateful to be free from that special large-firm impracticality, or "blindness," or obsessive focus on minutiae out of proportion to the worth of issues. But McGill argues there is a deeper level of fulfillment involved—identifying with, and caring about, what the lawyer is contributing to the client—that is often lacking in private practice, where lawyers may have deep personal reservations about the ends or policies of the client. The company's lawyers are proud of their client. It is satisfying to work for something you believe in.

Chapter 5

Tradition and Change
at the Maine Public
Utilities Commission

The Founder

Horace Libby, forty-nine year old general counsel of the Maine Public Utilities Commission, died of a massive heart attack at his desk in Augusta on 2 March 1982. Libby had worked eighteen years at the Public Utilities Commission after his graduation from Suffolk Law School in Boston. He was a shy, fretful, unassuming bachelor—a man acutely, indeed overly conscious of what he perceived was the modesty of his talents as a lawyer. Yet at his funeral, and in subsequent obituaries and letters to editors, he was characterized by those who knew him as a hero, an almost legendary figure.

Horace Libby began work at the Maine Public Utilities Commission in the early 1960s. At that time the two-man legal staff served a sleepy three-person commission that was entirely friendly to, if not completely dominated by, the utilities it regulated. It was not uncommon for lawyers working for the utilities to draft not only the decisions of the majority but also the dissents of the commissioners. After Horace was appointed general counsel in 1968, he began to emerge as a person of independence. He was the first senior employee of the commission to refuse the traditional gifts of liquor at Christmas and the trips and entertainment sponsored by the utilities. There was much groaning about Horace's "ruining it" for others. When presented a result reached by the chairman of the commission and a lawyer for a major utility and told to draft an order justifying it, Horace waited until the eleventh hour and then presented an elaborate rationale for a less cozy result that the commission had little choice but to accept. (The Public Utilities Commission still works under statutory deadlines, beyond which failure to act allows utilities' rate requests to take effect automatically.)

By dint of his longevity, conscientiousness, and unquestioned integrity, Horace, by 1970, had become indispensable to commissioners, whose experience and self-assurance in utility regulation fell short of his. Horace was lucky in another respect. The times were ripe for his views. The settled world of the power companies ("a big new plant every ten years named after the outgoing president by his successor, a fraternity brother at the engineering school of the University of Maine") began to unravel. The Arab oil embargo of 1973 stimulated cost increases that suddenly thrust utility rates into the public arena. One lawyer recounted the politicization of utility rates in this way: imagine how different the politics of the U.S. defense build-up of the early 1980s would have been if taxpayers had to write a monthly check to Secretary of Defense Caspar Weinberger.

By 1980, Horace had become a dominant figure at the Public Utilities Commission. He was fond of telling the story of how the chairman of the commission in the early 1970s instructed him not to "rock the boat" in hiring new attorneys for the Legal Division of the Public Utilities Commission. As a result, Horace took perverse pride in attracting to his staff young activists who were brighter and more capable than he was. Horace gradually increased his staff to a group of eight aggressive and talented lawyers. His leadership style was unusual. He did little direct supervision and established no formal training for his charges. He delegated most of the work. But he established personal relationships—one of his former protégés referred to these as "nurturing"—by serving as a resource of advice and knowledge and an example of institutional loyalty and commitment. A former PUC commissioner described Horace as "one of those soft-spoken individuals who had an unbelievable way of getting people to work as a team for him."

The Public Utilities Commission

In the words of the statute creating it, the mission of the Maine Public Utilities Commission is to assure that utilities "furnish safe, reasonable, and adequate facilities" at "just and reasonable" rates. The commission is charged to determine just and reasonable rates in terms of approving utility revenues "required to perform its [i.e., the utilities'] public service and to attract necessary capital on just and reasonable terms."[1]

The three-person commission presides over an agency of sixty people organized into five divisions:[2] the Administrative Division, which provides support services; the Consumer Assistance Division, which handles individual complaints from Maine utility customers; the Finance Division, which conducts financial analyses of utilities; the Technical Analysis Division, which conducts engineering analyses and inspections; and the Legal Division.

The commission sets regulatory policy through rule-making activities, but the primary activity of the commission and its staff is adjudication, or ruling on requests by utilities for rate increases. Personnel from the three substantive divisions (Legal, Finance, and Technical Analysis) form advocacy teams challenging the utilities, which have a statutory burden to prove that increases in rates are "just and reasonable," or that commission action is "unreasonable, unjust, or unlawful." Members of the three divisions also form separate advisory teams to advise the commission based on the evidence elicited in hearings. Other interveners (e.g., industrial customers, representatives of consumer and poverty groups) can present and challenge testimony at hearings. Most commission testimony is by experts, hired consultants, or in-house utility or commission employees.

Lawyers from the Legal Division traditionally assumed the leadership role in the advocacy teams if only because hearings before the commission are conducted pursuant to the Maine Rules of Civil Procedure and the Maine Rules of Evidence. Lawyers from the division also serve as hearing examiners (part of the "advisory team"), presiding over the proceeding on behalf of the commission. Other lawyers sometimes refer to lawyers from the Legal Division acting in this capacity as "Your Honor."

---

1. Maine Revised Statutes Annotated (MRSA), Title 35, sec. 51.

2. In addition to authority to approve all utility rates governing charges to consumers, the commission has jurisdiction over utilities' debt and equity financing, services to customers, contracts for power services outside of the state, and the siting and construction of new power plants. Some 148 water utilities, one gas utility, fifteen electric utilities, nineteen telephone companies, and four water carriers (ferry services on the Maine coast) fall under the jurisdiction of the PUC. In fact, three major electric utilities (of which Central Maine Power Company is by far the largest) and the largest telecommunications firm, New England Telephone Company, constitute one-third to one-half or more of all the regulatory activity of the commission.

This alternation of function in the Legal Division between advisor-examiner (quasi judge) and advocate (quasi civil plaintiff) is a matter of annoyance, amazement, amusement, or outrage in the private bar, depending to some extent on the experience of the lawyer with the specialty PUC practice. The Maine Administrative Procedure Act, first passed in 1978, prohibits ex parte communications[3] with commissioners or the lawyers who serve as hearing examiners or nonlawyer members of the advisory staff in the commission's adjudicatory proceedings.[4] The Legal Division long ago set up guidelines for its lawyers to preclude them from serving as both advocates and examiner-advisors in the same general field (e.g., electric, water, or telecommunications regulation). Nevertheless, one staff lawyer can be arguing in the morning as an advocate in an electric rate case before a colleague sitting as an examiner, who will, in the afternoon, reverse roles and be an advocate in a water case in front of the same staff lawyer serving as examiner. This "kangaroo court routine," as one practitioner puts it, has been challenged repeatedly and unsuccessfully in direct appeal from the PUC to the Maine Supreme Judicial Court. The most famous challenge arose from a notoriously acrimonious rate hearing in 1980–1981 in which lawyers for New England Telephone Company (NET) argued in an uncommonly heated brief to the high court:

> By the conclusion of hearings, it had become clear that the Examiner [Horace Libby] was not acting as an impartial, independent Examiner. Rather, he remained an adversary of NET.

---

3. An ex parte communication is one without a lawyer or representative from both sides to the controversy present.

4. MRSA, Title 5, sec. 9055. Ex parte communications; separation of functions:

1. Communication prohibited. In any adjudicatory proceeding, no agency members authorized to take final action or presiding officers designated by the agency to make findings of fact and conclusions of law shall communicate, directly or indirectly, in connection with any issue of fact, law or procedure, with any person, except upon notice and opportunity for all parties to participate.

2. Communication permitted. This section shall not prohibit any agency member or other presiding officer described in subsection 1 from:

   A. Communicating in any respect with other members of the agency or other presiding officers; or

   B. Having the aid or advice of those members of his own agency staff, counsel or consultants retained by the agency who have not participated and will not participate in the agency proceeding in an advocate capacity.

The numerous procedural due process violations and instances of unfair treatment that unfolded during the proceeding . . . demonstrate that the Examiner was not acting as an independent surrogate of the Commissioners. Rather, he repeatedly resolved questions—evidentiary, procedural, and substantive in favor of the Commission Staff position without regard to the evidence, the merits, or procedural fairness.

These last words were no doubt deeply troubling to Horace Libby for two reasons. If he had one conviction, it was that he was the guardian of fairness, a person who held a deep respect for the facts. (An experienced utility lawyer described Horace as someone upon whom you could depend to listen: "you always had a shot with Horace if it made sense to him.") Horace also knew how much he despised what he perceived to be the aggressive, high-handed tactics of NET and its counsel. Horace, in the days before staff specialization by category of utility, had, indeed, as the NET brief charged, "taken positions adverse to NET" in prior proceedings on issues similar or identical to the issues that arose in the 1981 rate hearing for which he served as examiner.

One of the mythologies that stand for more than facts at an organization like the Legal Division of the Public Utilities Commission is the conviction that NET's full-scale attack on Horace Libby and "due process" at the PUC in 1982 played a major role (along with overwork) in Horace's fatal heart attack in March of that year. The Supreme Judicial Court of Maine finally issued an opinion in July 1982 that was characterized by a NET lawyer as the "deification of Horace Libby." The court rejected most of NET's arguments, including the charges of bias, and stated that the Maine Administrative Procedure Act expressly permits a staff member to act as a presiding officer at a hearing; that a preconceived position in law, policy, or legislative facts is not grounds for disqualification; and that ex parte communications between the hearing examiner and the commission are permissible.[5] The advisor-advocate dual role at the Legal Division, whatever may be the objection of private lawyers, is entirely constitutional in Maine.

Horace Libby died at the height of his influence. The 1982 Legal

---

5. MRSA, Title 5, sec. 9055.

Division comprised eight young lawyers hired by Horace in 1978 and 1979. It was unquestionably the strongest and most aggressive component of the Public Utilities Commission staff. Indeed, the general respect with which Libby was held in state government meant that he and his staff dominated a sometimes reluctant commission, whom Libby technically served at will. One of the junior lawyers of the division, Joe Donahue, was made acting general counsel and eventually appointed permanent general counsel in May 1982. Joe revered Horace and consciously adopted Horace's low-key, hands-off administrative approach with his colleagues.

Changes at the Public Utilities Commission

Joe Donahue explains the mounds of stacked file folders, reports, and paper that cover his desk and side tables as the result of never fully moving in after the dislocation to temporary offices during the rehabilitation of PUC office space. His old office was similarly cluttered: Joe said he never really caught up since that day in 1982 when Horace died, leaving Joe, his coexaminer at the time, with a major Central Maine Power Company rate case to handle. Some mementos decorate the walls: Joe's law degree from Boston University, a photo of Horace, and Horace's law degree, which Joe picked up at an auction of some of Horace's personal effects.

Joe, a quiet person, as is most of his staff,[6] started work at the PUC in 1979. He was a particular protégé of Horace, who apparently had communicated with at least one commissioner before his death that he wanted Joe to succeed him. In only one respect does Joe seem incapable of emulating his mentor. Horace had an almost paranoid distrust of a few of his staff and generated strong feelings of dislike as well as affection in the division.

Joe takes pride in his lobbying skills. He has worked successfully with the state legislature's Joint Committee on Audits, responsible for the "sunset" review of the PUC. This generated a number of constructive proposals passed by the legislature to free both the Finance and Legal divisions from the confines of the state personnel classified system but that maintained the traditional protections of

---

6. An experienced lawyer before the commission described Joe and his group as "soft-spoken, but bulldogs underneath."

for-cause termination procedures. Although salaries remain low (most staff positions range close to $30,000 and Joe's close to $50,000 in the mid–1980s), Joe's work with the legislature and the state personnel department had helped to overcome some of the traditional structural problems of the division—low salaries and lack of a career ladder to higher salaries and greater responsibilities.

Joe continues to talk about "making himself" consider law practice in the private sector. Some of this derives from pressure he feels in his family life to achieve a higher income. He worries that he is stagnating, becoming a paper pusher and bureaucrat. He is concerned that he may have too high an opinion of the PUC, that he is too instinctively reluctant to move. He sees himself as a shy person, but genuinely enjoys "duking it out" with utility adversaries.

Shortly after Horace Libby's death, the commission began to change. In July 1982, two lawyers identified as proconsumer were appointed to the commission. One, Peter Bradford, a commissioner in the 1970s who had served on the Nuclear Regulatory Commission in the Carter Administration, was made chairman, and the other, Cheryl Harrington, had been chief of the Consumer Division of the Maine attorney general's office. The signs of a more self-assured and independent commission immediately became apparent. Hearings in 1981 reviewing the investment in the Seabrook Nuclear Power Plant in New Hampshire by the smallest of Maine's three large electric utilities led to a 1982 examiner's report, authored by Donahue, suggesting that the prudent course would be to adopt a wait-and-see attitude. The new commission rejected the report and issued an order requiring the utility to sell half of its investment in Seabrook.

The emergence of the commission as an independent force with strongly held views—or, as one outside lawyer put it, with an intuitive grasp of public policy unsullied by facts developed by the Legal Division—is welcomed by the lawyers of the Legal Division, who to a person express their respect for a more aggressive commission. In 1984 the commission was further strengthened by the appointment of one of the Legal Division staff lawyers, David Moskowitz. According to Donahue, the dominance of the Legal Division, and its conflicts with other divisions in the commission in the Libby days, was not a healthy system.

The commission has diminished the importance of the Legal Division in one other respect applauded by Donahue: major efforts have been undertaken to build up the quality of personnel in both the Finance and Technical Analysis divisions, which in the Libby days were weak and treated condescendingly by the lawyers. The vigorous and effective head of the Finance Division, Liz Paine, describes the intense campaign she waged with Libby to convince him to ignore the supine past history of her division and use her expertise. More assertiveness and higher levels of competence in the other divisions have had a tendency to relegate the lawyers to more of a "lawyer's role," that is, reduce their leadership role in policy making, lessen the extent to which they are able to use outside consultants to bolster their own views, and require them to negotiate their views within the PUC or represent the views of other staff. Under Donahue, relations between the divisions are not uniformly easy, but more consistently cooperative.

The biggest change in the Legal Division from the Libby era is the gradual departure from the staff of every lawyer who worked under Libby, except General Counsel Donahue. For one or two of the lawyers, being passed over for general counsel may have been a factor, but virtually all left for better opportunities. Moskowitz, mentioned earlier, became director of Technical Analysis and then a commissioner. The other "promotions" included general counsel to a new state hospital regulatory body, general counsel to an electric utility, homemaker, private practitioner, member of the legal staff of the largest electric utility, and commissioner of the Worker's Compensation Commission. The attrition occurred in 1983 and 1984 and significantly affected the experience of the staff. Libby died leaving a staff with an average of three years of experience. Donahue at the end of 1984 presided over a staff with one and a half years average experience. Most lawyers and nonlawyers at the commission argue that it takes about three years to become knowledgeable in the utilities field.

These changes to the landscape at the PUC were modest and incremental compared to the sensational case during Donahue's watch that was to transform permanently the Maine regulatory environment.

The Robert Scott Affair

The two major utilities in Maine are New England Telephone Company and the Central Maine Power Company (CMP). In the Libby days, both were represented by the same Portland law firm, and both were extraordinarily aggressive combatants in dealing with the PUC. CMP had a long tradition of stiff-arming the commission, playing "hard-ass" all the way with their regulators, in the words of one outside attorney. CMP witnesses before the commission were often difficult and evasive in responding to questions.

In September 1982, the commission was holding hearings on energy conservation, scrutinizing a request from CMP for additional funds for a consumer conservation loan program. At issue were extremely optimistic forecasts of consumer demand for conservation loans based on a survey of public attitudes conducted by CMP's subsidiary polling company. The surveys also included political popularity questions, which the management of the company shared occasionally on a confidential basis with leaders of both political parties.

On the morning of 23 September, Robert Scott, senior vice president and member of the board of CMP, testified, in response to probing questions about the public opinion surveys, that CMP had destroyed their surveys and no copies existed. Few, if any, in the hearing room believed his testimony. Scott was asked to return to the company over the lunchtime break and to search his files. At the company, the CMP lawyer, Gerald Amero, told Scott that he was not credible and urged him to find the surveys. Scott, instead, assured Amero all was well, asked Amero to leave his office, and called in a subordinate whom he instructed to go about the company to collect all the existing surveys. Scott returned as a witness in the afternoon and repeated his lie, thus, in the words of one private lawyer, delivering himself to the commission impaled on his own sword. Scott subsequently put together an edited version of survey data, ordered the company's computers purged of survey data, and convinced the president of CMP, whom Scott knew was protective of the activities of the polling subsidiary, to approve backdated memoranda calling for destruction of all surveys.

The PUC advocacy staff, which knew no details of Scott's activities, issued a brief following the hearing highly critical of Scott. The commission expressed its negative reaction. The resulting adverse publicity in the press stimulated Scott to give another high CMP official the freshly edited version of survey data, which was produced at a later PUC hearing. The commission promptly referred Scott to the Maine Attorney General's Office for prosecution for perjury and called a special hearing to probe the effort to withhold information from the commission.

The avalanche of negative publicity convinced the company of the seriousness of the situation. Outside CMP directors began to conduct their own internal investigation, with independent counsel. Scott made the mistake of lying to his own board and was immediately suspended. In December 1982, Scott pled guilty to charges brought by the attorney general of "false swearing" and was fined five thousand dollars.

The commission hired Peter Murray, one of Maine's most respected trial attorneys, to work with Moskowitz, at that time their staff member, in conducting an investigation.[7] Moskowitz and Murray in their report to the commission recommended that Scott and CMP be held in contempt and that CMP "give specific consideration . . . to . . . [the] discharge . . . of specific employees."[8] By the time the commission entered its final decision in September, accepting a settlement calling for a twenty thousand dollar fine of CMP, Scott had been fired, the president of the company had retired early, and the CMP board was looking for new outside management. In one of the most remarkable chapters in the history of U.S. utility regulation, the Maine Public Utilities Commission had brought down the management of its chief adversary. David had become Goliath.[9]

The relationship between the commission and Central Maine Power Company changed dramatically in the wake of the Scott debacle. The new CEO of the company, John Rowe, testifying before the commission, described CMP and his own role in these terms:

---

7. Sec. 296 of the PUC statute empowers a probe into "any matter relating to any public utility . . . for any reason." Such an investigation can result either in contempt citations or orders respecting any "practice . . . or acts" the commission finds unreasonable.

8. In a memorandum filed to dismiss a subsequent action for damages brought by Scott against the CMP leadership and Moskowitz and Bradford in 1985, an assistant attorney general intimated that the commission had statutory authority to order the termination of "employment of officers who no longer enjoy the confidence of the commission."

9. Bradford, then chairman of the commission, disagrees. It "really hasn't happened," he argues. "[I]f one must use that metaphor, David held a mirror up in front of Goliath for long enough to persuade him that he was pretty ugly and that curing the ugliness was a matter of changing character rather than plastic surgery."

During the 1970s and early '80s CMP was beleaguered by a number of events including changes in demand, generating costs, the intensity of regulation, two referenda seeking to shut down its most valuable asset, Maine Yankee, and a bombing in CMP's building. It seems clear that during the period CMP became more inward and defensive. These events were in the background to the misfortune of the Scott testimony and led the CMP Board to go outside to obtain a new Chief Executive Officer. Because CMP's management already had substantial operating and financial depth and experience, they were able to look for someone who would emphasize responsiveness to the public and elected or appointed officials.[10]

Rowe advocated a "collaborative" approach to working with the PUC, characterized by "dialogue and interchange" and early indications by the commission of the direction of its thinking. He expressed concern over the restrictiveness of ex parte rules and the costs (to the consumer) of lengthy adjudicatory proceedings.

After he arrived on the scene, Rowe met monthly with Bradford in the first half of 1984. Bradford felt it was "important that he [Rowe] have a thorough and candid understanding of my view of the causes of past problems, unfiltered by CMP employees or representatives who might view them differently."[11] Most of the meetings, however, concerned the mounting problems with the nuclear power plant at Seabrook, New Hampshire, in which CMP held a 6 percent stake. After CMP filed a request for a rate increase in June 1984, the meetings between Rowe and Bradford ceased in order to comply with ex parte prohibitions. Commissioner Bradford defended his contacts with Rowe in terms of the statutory language that the PUC "shall keep itself informed as to the manner and method in which each [public utility's business] is conducted" and explained he had never "hesitated during 13 years as a state and federal commissioner to meet informally with people interested in the commission's doings as long as pending cases and formal rule makings were not discussed."[12]

10. State of Maine, Public Utilities Commission, Docket No. 84–120, May 1985. Central Maine Power Company Re: Proposed Increase in Rates, Order Denying Motion to Investigate and Disqualify, at 2.
11. Ibid. 3, citing 35 MRSA sec. 4.
12. The test of the relevant statute is set forth in footnote 4 to this chapter.

The Changing Regulatory Environment

One rather important development from the point of view of the staff of the Legal Division is the emergence of more outspoken consumer-oriented voices. The loudest consumer gadfly, former state senator Bruce Reeves, heads a self-proclaimed Maine Citizen's Committee for Utility Rate Reform. Reeves's barbs are so indiscriminately aimed that he has alienated not only many of the staff and members of the commission, but also members of the legislature and other state agencies.

In 1980, Bruce Reeves initiated a referendum proposal to make the Public Utilities Commission an elected body. He gathered the number of signatures necessary to put it on the ballot in 1981, to which the legislature responded by creating the Office of Public Advocate as an official intervener in Public Utilities Commission matters on behalf of consumers. The public advocate legislation was explicitly conditioned on the defeat of Reeves's referendum and contributed to its defeat by the voters in the fall of 1981. Bradford was brought back from the Nuclear Regulatory Commission in Washington as the first full-time public advocate in 1982, but within five months he took the appointment as chairman of the PUC and his general counsel, Paul Fritzche, became public advocate.

The public advocate serves at the pleasure of the governor and has a staff of four lawyers and access to an energy-resources office that can provide technical assistance, particularly in the areas of conservation and alternative energy sources. Fritzche was a former legal-services lawyer who was an experienced intervenor in rate cases.

Utility lobbyists in the legislature enjoy raising the question of the distinction, if any, between the public advocate and the staff advocates of the Legal Division of the Public Utilities Commission. Fritzche, the commission, and Joe Donahue are careful to distinguish the two. They argue that it is useful in the complex arena of utility regulation to have a number of different public-interest positions represented. They also point out that the public advocate may not lawfully intervene in a hearing when the PUC staff have a substantively similar position. The advocate is responsive to the social goals and philosophy of the governor, while the PUC staff are civil servants meant to take a longer or broader view. In particular, the advocate must represent "the using and consuming public," while the PUC staff must also take into account the interests of the utility and deal with competing claims of industrial users.

The reasons for the close relationship between Fritzche and his staff and the commission's Legal Division stem partly from the fact that Fritzche went to law school with some of the PUC lawyers. Fritzche takes pride in his lawyerlike approach, that is, he feels he does not use the office to harvest publicity either for himself or the governor (a former attorney general who has adopted a strictly hands-off approach to the work of the PUC). He articulates an "adversarial but not abrasive" style. Staff in the Legal Division point to the usefulness of the public advocate: he permits them to play the "good guy," to adopt a "Mutt and Jeff" approach to "dealing with" the utilities. Fritzche points out another way in which his office is useful. He has more experience than most of the PUC legal staff, and a smaller, less cumbersome operation. The utilities in some cases can come to him and "cut a deal" in a short period of time, since he is a quick decision maker, and that arrangement, due to his credibility with the Legal Division staff, usually stands up as a basis for a settlement with the utility. (Settlements, in the parlance of the PUC, are termed stipulations.) The utilities, Fritzche argues—and outside lawyers confirm—find this process timesaving and useful.

The new world of stipulations in Maine utility regulation faced its most severe, indeed titanic, test with one of the largest bankruptcies in the history of New England, the Seabrook Nuclear Power Plant.

Seabrook

The three major Maine electric utilities purchased about 10 percent of the Seabrook Nuclear Power Plant, owned by a New Hampshire utility, Public Services of New Hampshire (PSNH). Costs of the project escalated along with repeated delays. In October 1982, PSNH announced a revised estimate of total costs of Seabrook from $3.16 billion to $5.2 billion, a 47 percent increase. The PUC itself estimated that the PSNH figures were unrealistic and that the project was likely to cost in excess of $8 billion. Prior to 1982, there had been no official recognition by the PUC of investments in Seabrook because, under commission rate-making policy, consumers do not underwrite the cost of a power plant until it comes on line.

By early 1984 it became clear that PSNH, which had been in tenuous financial condition for some years, was on the brink of collapse. There were serious questions whether the first phase of the project, Seabrook I, could be completed after work had been halted on the second phase, Seabrook II, with just over $800 million sunk in it. To prevent PSNH from going into bankruptcy, utilities with interests in Seabrook such as CMP agreed to borrow funds for up-front contributions, so that Seabrook I could be finished. The PUC would be asked to approve prefinancing the Maine utilities' contribution for Seabrook I, as well as to recover investments in the canceled Seabrook II, which amounted to $48 million for CMP and $13 million for a smaller utility, Maine Public Service. The financial viability of the Maine utilities was now linked to the Seabrook disaster.

In May 1984, there were meetings involving representatives of the three major electric utilities, the PUC staff, the public advocate, and a representative of a number of small, largely municipal, electric utilities. The PUC investigation focused on the reasonableness of continuation of Seabrook I as well as the investments sunk in Seabrook II, that is, the extent to which the utilities should recover prefinancing costs and lost investments through higher rates imposed on their customers. Three different sets of economic consultants were hired, and almost everyone in the Legal Division was mobilized either to deal with these Seabrook studies or the additional workload in other cases generated by shift of personnel to Seabrook. These were tense times, and relationships within the staff were strained as a result of a sense of being overwhelmed by the effort.

Chairman Bradford hired the Washington, D.C., firm of Covington and Burling as special counsel for some legal aspects of the Seabrook investigation, in particular the authority of the PUC to order Maine utilities to disengage from their investments in the nuclear power project and the contract implications and liability of the utilities in the event of disengagement. Bradford acknowledged that it was hard to say that the Legal Division needed help, and it certainly was not good for morale in the division to go outside for help, but it was essential to have sophisticated corporate law expertise and important to send a message to the utilities that the commission was prepared for any ultimate showdown. Joe Donahue concurred in the decision.

In the fall of 1984, the commission issued an interim order sug-

gesting that the continued investments in Seabrook I were not economically sound and that the three Maine utilities ought to seek
buyers for their shares under threat of the commission ordering disengagement plans. The interim order was appealed by the utilities,
and the Maine Supreme Judicial Court rejected the commission's position that interim orders were nonappealable. Before the case was
argued on its merits, Nancy Brockway, a Legal Division staff attorney,
the public advocate, and representatives of the Central Maine Power
Company engaged in intense negotiations and arrived at a series of
stipulations. The stipulations provided for some recovery of Seabrook
costs from ratepayers on the assumption that CMP would divest itself
of Seabrook interests. The commission approved the stipulations.
The effect of the Seabrook stipulations was to split the post-1985
costs for Seabrook I evenly between CMP stockholders and ratepayers, and to disallow for rate purposes 30 percent of all Seabrook
capital costs prior to 1985. This stipulation stimulated an immediate
and dramatic increase in the price of CMP stock, as well as charges
by Bruce Reeves in his newsletter that it was the "Big Bamboozle of
1985" and that the PUC was "had." Similar stipulations were negotiated and approved by the commission with the other utilities holding
Seabrook investments. By the end of 1985, all three utilities had
pending before the PUC requests to approve sale of their investments
in Seabrook I, and divestment was completed by 1988.

Seabrook is a significant chapter in the history of the PUC, quite
apart from the scale of the investments and the potential catastrophe
to Maine utilities. Seabrook was the most notable of a series of
stipulations with utilities beginning in 1985. The utilities and Legal
Division staff advocates feel that negotiated settlements through the
stipulation process work better than lengthy hearing processes. Obviously, a mutual understanding of the position of the commission, or
the predictability of the commission and Maine's Supreme Judicial
Court, plays a major role in facilitating stipulations. A number of
the division lawyers are somewhat uneasy about the growing prev-
alence of decision by stipulation, the full implications of which are
not clear.

The People at Home in the Legal Division

The Public Utilities Commission is housed on the second floor of a
nondescript two-story brick building on State Street in Augusta, not

far from the capitol. The entrance is at the back of the building, which the commission shares with the driver-testing and license-renewal station for the Maine Secretary of State. Recently rehabilitated, the offices present a rather aseptic appearance, with gray carpeting and off-white walls, decorated with contemporary art. It is a far cry from the years of working in a huge open area (the building once housed the computer facility for the state) cut up into a maze of partitions and dividers that gave the appearance of temporary quarters.

For the Legal Division, the greatest change in the newly rehabilitated space was the loss of a small, rather disheveled library room across from Joe Donahue's office. It was less than sumptuously furnished with a table and old glass-paneled wooden shelving that could pass for hand-me-downs or a poor buy at an auction, but it was home. The library was the center of the Legal Division, the site of the weekly staff meetings and other conferences, as well as the social center for talking about issues in the relaxed style of the division, a place to have lunch or coffee, a hangout. Schmoozing in the library was central to the functioning of the Legal Division. It was the exchange place, the forum for continuing education on the mores and dilemmas of public-interest law. In the library "the thinking of the staff" was gradually formulated, along with something of Horace Libby's legacy of caring about the facts, being both tough and fair to adversaries, and worrying about the integrity of the work. Joe fought unsuccessfully to keep the old library room, and now he is still plotting to create a room to serve the old function.

A large commission library now stands at the center of the building. The chronic disarray of the old Legal Division library has been replaced by a more efficient facility for all divisions staffed by a full-time librarian, who maintains an organized system of reports and commission decisions and computerized research capabilities. The new library represents a conscious effort by the commission to better organize their official files, reduce the "elitism" of the Legal Division (and the jealousy of the other divisions over the special space of the lawyers), and encourage all divisions to work together. The lawyers are contemptuous of a room without a conference table: "it is not a place where you can take coffee and doughnuts"; it is technically open but foreign territory "like the living room in your parents' house."

The friendly, talkative air of the Legal Division does not meet with universal acclaim. One wag elsewhere in the agency has described, only half in jest, the working habits of the Legal Division as work till midnight justified by wasting the morning shooting the breeze.

The lawyers of the division come from a variety of backgrounds and have a high opinion of the PUC compared with their prior experience in practice.

Peter Ballou graduated from the Maine Law School and after clerking for a justice of the Supreme Judicial Court of Maine, spent ten years in the Portland district attorney's office as a deputy district attorney specializing in appellate work. When the district attorney was not reelected, he moved to the PUC, where he enjoys representing the public interest, which he defines as "what is best for the customers in the long run."

Nancy Brockway, the most outspoken member of the staff, serves as senior attorney examiner, another position established by Donahue to create more possibilities for a long-term career in the division. Utilities regulation work is extraordinarily interesting to Nancy because it involves public exposure, and association with important people in public and private life in the state. One can be responsible and visible, a self-confessed "statehouse groupie" who plays a role in policy making on a state level. The job is also an excellent stepping-stone to other work in the private or public sectors—and still one has the pleasure of serving the public. (Nancy has since moved on to become general counsel of the Massachusetts Public Utilities Commission.) She says that, compared with her earlier career as a legal-services lawyer following graduation from Yale Law School, a Legal Division lawyer has influence and the power to do good. It is a joy to protect—with fewer resources—the consumer and the underdog from being "ripped off." More than any other job she has had in law, it is intellectually stimulating work that requires long and hard thinking. Energy policy has become her first love, and it will be a long time before she gets bored.

Tim Buckley graduated from the University of Maine Law School in 1979, clerked for a judge of the Maine Supreme Judicial Court, and spent two years in the attorney general's office, chiefly on tax matters. He switched to the PUC for a number of reasons: it was less political, it was more interesting to an undergraduate economics major, the legal staff had a good reputation, there are better lawyers on the other side, and one is more clearly wearing the "white hat" at the PUC. Besides, the pay was better.

Deborah Ross took her undergraduate degree from St. John's College, moved to Portland, and eventually enrolled in the University of Maine Law School. Before joining the staff of the PUC in April of 1985, she worked two and one-half years for a Portland insurance defense firm. She points with some pride to the fact that she is the only member of the legal staff who has been in private practice. This background carries some advantages, in particular a more problem-solving and negotiating perspective, which she finds is not the universal attitude in the Legal Division. She also has real familiarity with the rules of civil procedure and bankruptcy from private practice, which is useful in the Legal Division. She took a pay cut to come to the PUC, chiefly because of her disillusionment with private practice. She found it difficult to maintain her ideals. She came to the PUC because she "wanted to do good for the soul." She had become cynical about litigants: "People who use lawyers are not people you would really want to hang around with."

The lawyers associated with the division like to talk about the unusual quality of the place.

To Nancy Brockway, the Legal Division is a hardworking, zany kind of place with lots of kidding and camaraderie. The people are splendid. Everyone is doing a high-quality job. Compared to almost any other place she has ever known or heard of, this is a place without "ugly pissing matches." It is flexible, but not anarchic, relying heavily on the good faith of individual lawyers. It feels good to be trusted and respected. The commission has a very loose chain of command. While important new undertakings must go through the general counsel (Donahue), commissioners can work directly with staff and staff are free to trade cases. This is not a rigid structure. It is pressured and people do sometimes bump into other people, but the job is simply to pick up and go on. Her overall evaluation: "I'm happy as a pig in shit."

One advantage Ballou sees of working at the PUC is that the people who practice before the commission are far superior to the criminal-defense bar of Portland. The lawyers are friendly, cooperative, tough, but don't play games. He suspected the private bar probably had a fairly high opinion of the Legal Division.

Morale among the lawyers on the staff of the Legal Division, according to Tim Buckley, was better than his previous workplace, the attorney general's office. There are no slouches here. The legal staff are all civil service positions. One has the sense that prior commissions followed the recommendation of the Legal Division examiners most of the time. Now three experienced lawyers are commissioners, and you cannot buffalo these people.

Buckley assumes the reason morale is high in the Legal Division is that it is interesting and challenging work of real importance to society. The lawyer can really have an effect on things. Joe Donahue has continued Horace's practice of hiring young, energetic, and talented lawyers. Joe generates within the staff a current of togetherness, an "us against them" attitude. The utilities have the high-paid economists and lawyers. There is in the staff a sense of personal commitment to work for the public sector. People care here. They take their work seriously. There are no grudges. Joe uses no specific techniques for keeping up morale. The interaction among the staff outside of the office is spontaneous. When one is working until two or three in the morning and finds other people doing the same, as happens a few times a year, there develops a kind of team spirit. The tension of the workload is balanced with relatively high morale.

Pointing to a little coffee cup with the insignia of the Maine Public Broadcasting Network on her desk, Deborah Ross says the people at the PUC are the kind who donate to public radio. There seemed to be more of a commitment at the PUC to excellence and a willingness to take time to put in a good product. It is such an extraordinary feeling of freedom to take as much time as she likes to do a first-rate job, rather than to have the relentless pressure of moving cases and figuring out her billable hours. One of the frustrations of private practice was that the primary goal of the senior partners was to win a case in an efficient manner, which created tension because her interest as a beginning associate was doing a first-rate job that would impress the legal community. She was pretty much left alone by supervisors both in private practice and at the PUC. The one difference is that a PUC lawyer serving as an examiner-advisor has commissioners who edit the work. She enjoys the role of examiner and the respect one gets as "the judge." She likes the dedicated competent staff of the Legal Division and thinks perhaps one of the reasons she feels more at home is the presence of more women on the staff.

Although she is well aware of the fact that there is a "high burnout factor" at the Legal Division, Ross finds that there is a much more leisurely pace at the PUC than in private practice. She is aware of the fact that it will probably take a couple of years before she develops a full sense of the pressures at the PUC. She enjoys the fact that she has a few cases that she can do well. She is particularly excited about her assignment as an advocate supervised by Nancy Brockway. They are attempting to put together the various conservation and cogeneration and interruptible-service cases into a study amounting to a profile of power companies over the next twenty years. She has a lot of learning ahead of her. One of her small cases, a stipulation regarding a conservation program, has given her enormous satisfaction: it is the most significant thing she has ever done because it has a real effect on people.

Charles Dingman, a Columbia Law School graduate, started at the PUC in the summer of 1978 and left in 1984 for the newly created position of general counsel to the Maine Health Care Finance Commission, a hospital regulatory body. He speaks glowingly of Horace Libby as the force who shaped the whole approach to regulation of the PUC. Dingman looks to his experience at the PUC as a model for the health care agency. So much at the PUC depended on the philosophy of the people Horace hired and what Horace communicated to his staff as he shaped their practices.

The lawyers of the division are not reluctant to voice their concerns and criticisms of work at the PUC.

Joe Donahue has some regrets about the division. There has not been time or emphasis placed on encouraging staff to attend the many utility seminars and training programs around the country. He attributes this to the sense of overwork in the division, the strong peer pressure to work hard, and the high expectations the commission has for the Legal Division. Joe feels the best way to react to this pressure is a certain flexibility: he is pleased he does not need to run a tight ship and a hierarchical structure. There isn't time to go around getting one's nose out of joint about lines of authority. Since so much depends on the individual responsibility of the lawyer, it is extremely important to hire carefully. Joe's greatest fear is of a bad hire. Under the old classified system and the new rules, it is hard, next to impossible, to get rid of someone if the person wants to stay on. Although he perceives the division as overworked, even with the two or three law-student clerks in the division, he still has vacancies in the staff.

Joe also regrets that there is not as much deep legal and policy discussion as there was in the old days, not enough deep thinking. The appellate record of the division is also worrying. There are only two or three appeals a year, compared with the mid–1970's sustained attack by the utilities, when as many as twenty appeals were filed in a year. In those days the commission (through the division) won from 75 to 90 percent of its appeals, but its winning rate has dramatically declined of late, reflecting perhaps changes in the court, changes in the perceptions of the commission, and the utilities' acceptance of the commission and greater selectivity in what they appeal.

Peter Ballou confesses some nostalgia for purely legal work. He feels he is practicing in a specialty that is perhaps not quite as rigorous or as intense as traditional corporate practice. The questions in the office tend to be more policy or technical issues of economics and engineering than legal questions. Even the law of evidence formally applicable to PUC hearings is more "free and easy." There is an unwritten code of manners in adjudicatory hearings to the effect that "if you don't object, I won't object to the garbage that you want to put into the record." There are now intelligent lawyer-commissioners who can ignore irrelevancies in the record.

Nancy Brockway does not like the commissioners disagreeing with her. There are not enough resources, particularly clerical backup. The files in the office are disorganized and it is impossible to be on top of everything. She is overworked and feels that her work is occasionally slapdash and superficial: she would like to do better-quality work at times.

Tim Buckley's frustrations with the job are essentially the bureaucratic hassle, although in his experience it is far less of a problem at the PUC than at other agencies. (The PUC engineers and economists were much better than their counterparts in other agencies, most of whom put their pencils down in midsentence at 5:00 P.M.) Supplies are an annoyance. Buckley went for two years without a Rolodex and finally bought one himself. He buys his own punched paper in order to avoid having to punch state paper. He has to do much of his filing.

Meg Green, a Bowdoin and University of Maine Law School graduate, started at the PUC after clerking on the Augusta Superior Court in September 1984 and left the PUC in April 1985. She found her work boring and frustrating. She thought the staff people in

Finance and Technical Analysis with whom she worked were lack-
luster, and that there was too much "shifting about" if the commission
overruled the staff or the commission changed its mind. She did not
have interesting cases to work on, and she missed the law: most of
the work was fact-finding and policy. Joe Donahue was too apprehensive about treading on toes and therefore would not direct staff
firmly. The lack of office walls and doors at that time and inadequate
secretarial staff made it seem most unprofessional. It was disorganized, particularly the library and files. People were left on their own,
and there was too much sitting around and talking. She liked to be
productive: "tell me what to do and I'll do it." She particularly found
frustrating a confusion about her mission. There was a general liberal,
proconsumer, antiutility ethos about the place, but she was not experienced enough in utility law to have the big picture. There was little
direction, other than "if that's what the utility wants, we probably
don't want it." She was uncertain who her clients were. The public?
Who is the public? Ultimately she guessed it was a mixture of her
own conscience and the view of the commission.

Meg Green's concerns about the indeterminacy of the client, along
with the troublesome dual role of lawyers serving as both adversary
of utilities (the advocate), as well as impartial judge of the utilities
case (the examiner) are often discussed by Legal Division lawyers.

Tim Buckley's initial work had been largely as an examiner, but
he began doing work as an advocate, which requires better preparation. One feature of the work he finds peculiar is that there is no
client. The advocate cannot be told by colleagues or commissioners
what to do as a result of the ex parte rule. It really is an apolitical
process. The advocate must use his or her own judgment and draw
on the judgment of colleagues. Many decisions of the PUC involve
no clear right or wrong: for example, any treatment of an allowance
for a canceled plant is probably legally defensible. Of course, there
are a few guidelines of the Supreme Judicial Court and prior commission decisions. You can always talk with someone, because there
is always someone around not disqualified. The advocate's position
fundamentally derives from his or her best judgment of what is in
the public interest, a balancing of achieving the lowest rates consistent
with sufficient revenues to raise capital. You are not trying to beat
down the utility, although in practice it is usually the consumer that
needs more. You try to do what is fair.[13]

13. Bradford, the former chairman of the commission, expresses the public-

Buckley is uneasy with the advocate/examiner distinction, not because of the switching of roles, which makes the job far more interesting, but because "the lawyer in me says this doesn't look good." The utilities probably do not feel that it generates undue influence, or that there is unfairness, or they would complain more severely.

Charles Dingman does not believe there is a problem of unfairness in the dual examiner/advocate roles because both roles have the same end—to seek out a correct result, not "to win." He has never seen an instance of unfairness resulting from this system, although psychological and temperamental sources of bias can creep in. The industry sees all the cards stacked in favor of the regulatory agency. But the agency's resources are so limited and it is so busy responding to what the industry seeks that it is critical to have people who are experienced and knowledgeable as a result of their training in both the advocate and the examiner roles. Turnover and lack of expertise are the greatest threats to an agency. The current Public Utilities Commission is certainly more activist than in past years, but not necessarily more expert.

Dingman obviously enjoys his career as a public-service lawyer. He admits to momentary discouragement only when he asks himself how he will finance the replacement for his car, which has 150,000 miles on it, or when he is puzzling over his relationship with "the client." Am I the client, so my job is to persuade the commission of the right result? Or should I help the commission most easily defend the result I expect they want? Or do I just help them focus their thoughts so they can come to some decision?

Peter Ballou feels that there used to be much more fanaticism about ex parte communication when he first started at the PUC because the Legal Division viewed itself as something of a watchdog. Things are looser now because the commissioners are all lawyers, and no one believes there has been any effect on the outcome of cases as a result of inadvertent communications. One can, of course, get advice from commissioners, except on issues where one is an advocate in a matter under adjudication. But it makes sense to ask commis-

interest goals of the agency in these terms: "The mission of the commission in a nutshell (the long form is in the statute) is to make utilities behave as if they had competitors. Thus the commission evaluates rates and services as if customers could choose to go somewhere else and seeks to convince utilities to behave and set rates at levels as if they would lose customers if they did otherwise."

sioners questions that test which way the wind is blowing so that an advocate in a subsequent adjudication can tailor a position, or strengthen a position if it is counter to the wind. Ex parte communications were more relaxed in the Portland Superior Court than at the PUC.

Beth Nagusky, who graduated from Case Western Reserve Law School, expresses real reservations about ex parte problems. The appearances are not good. Staff has distinct advantages over outsiders because advocates are colleagues of examiners and obviously have more influence. It is impossible not to overhear things in PUC offices. All the outside consultants, such as economists, hired for the advocate's case must be approved by the commission. Advocates have more influence with the commission as a result of their close relationship with the commission formed in their examiner function. There is, however, an office rule that an examiner may not make a recommendation to the commission on an issue in which he or she is taking a position as an advocate in another case. It is not at all clear to Beth that the commission has defined its goals for the state's energy policy, so that it could adjudicate and make rules consistent with those goals.

Bill Furber graduated from the University of Maine Law School, clerked in the superior court, joined the PUC in 1978, and left in early 1985. Furber feels the examiner/advocate distinction is not a good system because it relies on everyone's personal integrity, not an appropriate base for a system. It was one big office and there were too many temptations. The only reason people accept the system is that it seems to work. The temptations involve having an interesting problem and wanting to talk about it with other people. Although care was taken not to talk about something over lunch because the commissioner or examiner was present, there is tolerance for "non-significant ex parte contacts." There is, of course, an advantage for a lawyer to play both advocate and examiner roles. It makes the advocate more objective, less rigid, better balanced than some wild-eyed utility foe. Furber never experienced an examiner who was biased as a result of a colleague's serving as advocate; if anything, the bias went the other way, the examiner leaning over backward to avoid the appearance of institutional favoritism. To some extent, the advocate/examiner system encouraged a homogenized institutional view, in which people began to think alike. This view was proconsumer, a notch more proconsumer than Furber judged himself to be. Perhaps it would make more sense to move the whole advocacy function to the public advocate and provide that office with accounting and finance backup. The current system is really designed to share access to limited technical resources. The cost of differentiating the advocate and examiner role with appropriate technical support would be excessive.

The View of Outside Lawyers

The lawyers who practice before the commission were understandably cautious in their comments about the people against and before whom they make their living. They are conscious of the fact that changeover in staff of the Legal Division lowers the level of experience. Inexperienced people are costly to private litigants: when junior people ask a question that indicates they do not understand the company or the issue, it takes time and effort to unpack the question and educate them. It is always unclear just how good staff will be when they acquire sufficient experience to make them thoroughly knowledgeable utility lawyers.

Lawyers practicing before the PUC in 1985 and 1986 expressed less concern about ex parte practices than the Legal Division staff did. The outside lawyers tended to favor the separation of the adjudicative and advocacy functions through the creation of some form of administrative law judge system, as in the federal government and many larger states. There were no complaints—indeed there were compliments—about the integrity of the staff, but the lawyers also believed that the system "must" affect the staff's decision making.

One of the concerns of utility lawyers is that the commission and Legal Division have such an acute sense of being overworked and understaffed that they do not perceive that the utilities may suffer from the same problem. The commission and staff have high expectations of time and effort, data, experts, and computerized studies from a utility filing with the PUC, even when the dollar amounts requested do not justify these expenditures.

Both the emergence of the commission as independent of the Legal Division and the creation of the public advocate have complicated the formal hearing process. The public advocate, in the words of one lawyer, "lowballs everyone." The PUC has become a three-step process, where the utility faces the conclusions of the Legal Division staff advocate (often not completely thought through for their full implications), the recommendations of the examiner, who may be competing with the advocate to come up with a better result for the ratepayer, and finally the commission itself, with its own conception of the public good.

Epilogue

In January 1988, the Public Utilities Commission dedicated the new hearing room of their refurbished offices, naming the room after Horace S. Libby. Present were Horace's mother, Peter Bradford, former chairman of the commission (who had become chairman of the New York Public Service Commission), commissioners, staff, lawyers, and utilities officials and dignitaries such as Chief Justice Vincent McKusick of the Maine Supreme Court, an old adversary of Horace when he was a practicing lawyer in Portland. Commissioner Cheryl Harrington opened the proceedings by stating that "we are where we are today due in large part to the vision and good work of the Libby years." A letter from the governor described Horace as a "public servant of unusual ability, fairness and dedication . . . who never lost sight of the public interest." Bradford then launched into some stories with the justification that "[w]e tell stories, after all, to younger people . . . when we're not trying to put them to sleep, because they seem to be interested in how the places and people that they have to deal with came to be the way they are." He recounted Horace rejecting Christmas presents from those he helped regulate, Horace hiring a group of young activist lawyers after being told not to rock the boat, Horace, disgusted with Detroit's treatment of consumers, putting his car up permanently on cinder blocks in the 1970s. He ended by describing how fitting it was that a hearing room, which stands as a place where fairness to all parties should take place, should be dedicated to a man of scrupulous fairness such as Horace.

The chief justice, in a gracious tribute, observed that what set Horace apart was his extraordinary "civility," a combination of politeness and courtesy and a sense of decorum that approached the "fine art of government." Joe Donahue, too, paid homage:

> I sit at this desk every day that I'm here in the office, and a lot of evenings, I have cause to think of him often as I sit here

among the piles of paper, many of which are mine, some of which are still his. I also have the opportunity to see the fruits of his work every day at the commission . . . and its people in what they do. I also find that Horace still helps me every day in my work and oftentimes I'll have a hard question that I have to address, particularly when there's a judgment call involved. I'll think to myself, what would Horace do in this situation, and it's amazing, but the answer is easy to me. . . . Horace had this innate sense of what's right and what's wrong and it was clear. What was right involved a combination of what the law requires, what justice requires and what humanity requires.

The ceremonies were memorialized by a plaque on the wall of the hearing room:

Horace Libby
1933–1982

Attorney and General Counsel for the Public Utilities Commission from 1962 to 1982—A man of Dignity, Courage, Fairness and Compassion. His efforts inspired Those with Whom he Worked and Left the Commission and the State a Better Place to Work and Live. May this Modest Memorial Commemorate his Work and the High Standards it Exemplified.

Afterward Joe described the ceremony as a kind of catharsis. He had finally put Horace to rest, less deified in his memory. It was time to move on. In April 1989, Horace's last two protégés at the PUC finally left. Joe Donahue resigned from the commission and joined a private law firm in Portland, and David Moskowitz concluded his term as commissioner and became a utilities regulation consultant.

Chapter 6

Marks and Feinberg's Struggle to Survive

The partners of Marks and Feinberg, a four-person firm specializing in criminal defense and civil rights plaintiff's litigation, are worried. They look over the prospects of fees due during the next few months and agree that things will be "tight." For the first time, they might have to use the twenty-five thousand dollar line of credit they took out with a local bank a few months ago. Morale at Marks and Feinberg "tends to vary with the size of the current bank balance." Although the Marks and Feinberg lawyers are deeply concerned about the economic future of the firm, money has played a backstage role in the development of their practice. The tradition at the firm has been to take on work oblivious, indeed "in defiance" (as Alan Marks puts it with a combination of ruefulness and pride), of the economic impact on the firm.

Background on the Firm

Alan Marks graduated from University of Michigan Law School in the late 1960s and clerked for a judge on the United States Court of Appeals for the Sixth Circuit. He then went to work for the NAACP Legal Defense Fund in New York City, doing prisoner-rights litigation. After moving to Detroit, he continued the prisoner-rights work in association with the Legal Defense Fund, financed by the Michigan Law Reform Institute and the Ford Foundation.

Joel Feinberg graduated from the University of Chicago Law School in 1964 and began work with a small, eight-lawyer Cleveland firm that represented a number of labor unions and specialized in low- and middle-income housing. Although he enjoyed his colleagues, he disliked his day-to-day diet of commercial litigation, tax law, and estates and trusts, and he asked for leave from the firm to spend the summer of 1966 in Jackson, Mississippi, as a volunteer for the Lawyers Committee for Civil Rights under the Law. He found the work in Mississippi so challenging and satisfying that he resigned from the firm and practiced civil rights legal work full-time in Mississippi. Two years later, he moved to New York City to become a staff attorney at the Legal Defense Fund, where he met Alice McKenzie. After Alan and Alice were married in Detroit, he and Alan decided to form their own firm, which they opened in Detroit in 1973 as Marks and Feinberg.

Alan and Joel started their firm on a shoestring, with a half-time secretary from the Michigan Law Reform Institute and a small office adjacent to the institute in a building occupied by other small firms that were part of the liberal public-interest law community— including the Michigan Advocacy Center and the Lawyers Committee for Civil Rights. Much of their caseload was a continuation of their Legal Defense Fund work, for which they were paid as cooperating attorneys. Alice, who had been working as a public defender, joined the firm a year later, and left in 1977 when she became a judge on the Recorder's Court (principal state trial court) in Detroit. In 1976, Alan and Joel took on their first associate. Their caseload consisted of matters related to school busing and desegregation, employment discrimination, a voting rights case, some criminal-defense work, and other civil rights cases generated either from the Legal Defense Fund or from referrals from other public-interest lawyers.

Marks and Feinberg's practice has expanded since the early days. They now have a third partner, Ruth Fried, an associate, Ann Burch, and their secretary and office manager, Carol McHugh, who has moved to full-time status. But the nature of their practice has changed relatively little since its founding. Thirty-five to 40 percent of their work is criminal defense, mostly referrals from other community-based lawyers. Little of this is lucrative white-collar criminal-defense work. Perhaps as much as a third of the practice is devoted to employment discrimination, particularly in the area of academic employment problems, including revocation of professional licenses. In addition to miscellaneous civil rights cases, including prisoner rights, they have recently begun to handle some personal injury, medical malpractice, and products-liability work, but it is a comparatively small part of the practice compared to the employment and criminal matters.

Both Joel and Alan enjoy their representation of criminal defendants. They cannot recall any irreconcilable differences, or head-to-head conflict, with their clients, whom they describe as people who trust the lawyer and rely on the lawyer's opinion. They also take considerable pride in the professional and scholarly aspects of their careers in law. Joel has regularly taught a course or clinic in prisoner's rights at Wayne State University and is working on a treatise on attorney's fees, an important subject for civil rights lawyers who are subject to a variety of court and statutory rules for fees and costs reimbursement. He continues to take a few court-appointed first-degree murder cases in the Michigan system because he enjoys the diversity this work offers and believes he has an obligation to deal with such important issues. Alan teaches a course on the Legal Profession at the University of Michigan in which he focuses on ethical problems in clinical practice. He is a leader of the National Network for the Right to Counsel. Both have strong ACLU ties and allegiances: Alan was the recipient of an ACLU award in 1987 for his work organizing against the death penalty in Michigan and for other public-interest work in which (the plaque reads), "He never shrank from taking the unpopular case on behalf of those most vulnerable to the inequities of our criminal justice system."

The other lawyers in the office are also cause oriented. Ruth Fried had been a schoolteacher for a number of years before entering law school. She worked for Marks and Feinberg as part of a full-time placement in the Urban Legal Laboratory program while she was a student at Detroit College Law School in the fall of 1978. She considered it her best semester in law school, and she found it hard to go back to the classroom. But she managed to arrange her schedule to work part-time with the firm after her return. Following graduation, she worked at the Michigan Civil Rights Commission (the State Fair Employment Practices Agency) because the firm had no openings. But she kept in touch and was hired on a three-day-a-week basis in 1980. Eventually her position was increased to five days a week, and she became a partner at the beginning of 1987. In order to finance herself in those early days, she found part-time work at the University of Michigan Law School in a clinical public-interest program for law students representing tenants in the Ann Arbor area. She still is an employee of the Law School, working roughly fifteen hours a week as a supervisor.

About two-thirds of Ruth's practice is employment-discrimination work at the agency and trial level. She greatly enjoys representing people who have lost their jobs, for whom winning is enormously important. Ruth finds that a "let's work it out" attitude with those company lawyers willing to look carefully at a case will almost invariably lead to good results through settlement. An occupational hazard is obsessive clients who spend years so wrapped up in their case that they are unable to move on with their lives. The remainder of her practice includes cases that are generated from her known expertise in landlord-tenant work and in tenant organizing in and around Ann Arbor, some immigration work, occasional tort work as second chair to Joel, and some civil rights work like police misconduct cases and a long-standing lawsuit initiated by Alan to remedy conditions at the Detroit House of Corrections (city jail).

Ann Burch had first become interested and active in prison issues while an undergraduate at SUNY Buffalo in the wake of the great Attica uprising. In 1977 she moved to Detroit and took a position at a state school for the mentally retarded, where she advanced from a caseworker to assistant division director in charge of 120 staff and six hundred to seven hundred clients in ten living units at the school. After constant struggles with the administration of the school, she entered the Law School at Wayne State in 1981, continuing to work as a consultant to establish community residential centers and innovative programs for the retarded. She clerked, while a student at Wayne State, at Marks and Feinberg, and she became an associate at the firm in the fall of 1984, specializing primarily in criminal work and prison litigation. Her prisoner clients are a great source of satisfaction to her because their situation is so dismal that she feels that virtually anything she achieves for them amounts to immense relief. Like Ruth's clients, Ann's jailhouse lawyers use their considerable free time to become deeply absorbed in their cases. Another source of encouragement has been the renewed interest of the Michigan Supreme Court, which has recently rendered more positive decisions in prison cases.

Ann expresses an appreciation for the experience of working with first-chair senior partners like Alan and Joel in major trials. One of their prisoner cases reached the United States Supreme Court. She works long hours, about fifty-five hours a week, but enjoys it. She believes both Alan and Joel are superb attorneys, always well prepared, with whom it is easy to work and feel comfortable. They show her respect. Everyone in the office "gets a voice in things." She is not told what to do but asked if she wishes to work on a case and asked her opinion on cases and office issues. The attorneys in the office do first-rate work and feel right about the position they are taking for clients. (Or as Carol McHugh puts it, people at the firm "care about what they are doing." There is a real "honesty" in the enterprise.) The firm will take on unpopular, "political-message" cases regardless of the fee.

The atmosphere around the firm is highly informal: casual dress except for court or clients, discussions around the lunchroom table about current cases and issues in the law. But this family-style atmosphere is, by all accounts, not as warm as it was some years ago, when the firm had its own set of offices. In the early 1980s, a fire in their building forced the firm into a nomadic existence while it negotiated with a landlord determined to increase the rents in the building, thus dispersing the old crowd of public-interest lawyers and agencies. Marks and Feinberg joined in a space-sharing arrangement with a three-person firm, and three solo practitioners (two of whom are of counsel to Marks and Feinberg) in a modest suite of modern offices with a conference room, kitchen, and small library. The dispersal of Marks and Feinberg lawyers throughout the space, and the complications and occasional frictions involved in dealing with other support staff, have sharply reduced the intimacy and quiet of the old office. The lawyers, however, get along well and the sharing arrangements work out more or less to the satisfaction of everyone.

Office sharing precipitated the creation of a special role for Ruth Fried, who shares the duties of the Office Management Team with Joseph Baum, the head of the other firm in the office. The two members of the team work out problems involving the building and space, the lease with the landlord, and common receptionist and secretarial services. Ruth also is responsible for interviewing and hiring the three or four law students who work for Marks and Feinberg throughout the year. The students provide valuable investigative and backup support for the attorneys, some at no cost to the firm because they earn law school credit during their placements. Ruth is having

more difficulty attracting paid clerks to Marks and Feinberg because
the wages at large firms continue to increase. Jack Osman, a student
intern in the office from Wayne State, describes how much he likes
the work of the office and the caring, informal style, but he doubts
he could afford to work at Marks and Feinberg: he couldn't earn
enough to pay back his student loans. "Besides," he adds, "there will
always be just four lawyers here."

Outsiders Look at Marks and Feinberg

Al Fox, a successful plaintiffs' personal injury lawyer, views both Joel
and Alan as highly skilled attorneys, "amongst the best" trial and
appellate advocates he has seen. They have had a very successful
track record in a varied criminal and civil practice. Joel, for example,
tried his first medical malpractice case a few years ago. It was a
difficult lawsuit against the manufacturer of an IUD and a health
plan and normally would require an expert in the field. Yet Joel got
a very good result. Fox is involved now in a case with Joel and
admires his intellect, his penchant to get to the heart of issues and
to think practically. Fox and Marks and Feinberg do not refer many
cases to each other, except that Fox sends criminal cases their way
because he does not do that work. Criminal law is a significant part
of the Marks and Feinberg practice. "They believe in it," remarks
Fox. If he were ever in trouble, he says, he would call Joel.

Fox describes Joel and Alan as dedicated to issues of social and
political importance over an extended period of time. This has hurt
them economically at times. Their longevity in these causes is remarkable. Fox recognizes that civil rights attorneys are caught in an economic squeeze, but he argues that much of this is a "change in the
times":

> When I was young, we lived in a two hundred dollar a month
> apartment and my wife worked. Ten to fifteen thousand dollars
> a year income was OK. But now I am close to forty and I have
> a house and three kids. The expectations of progressive lawyers
> have changed when everyone you know is living in a style which
> is expected and accepted. Your willingness to live in a certain
> fashion changes when the norms change. And so you take on

more personal injury cases, do less pro bono and develop a taste for a higher income.

Thomas Staughton is a Detroit lawyer with much the same practice as Marks and Feinberg. He once shared space with them and sees them socially. On occasion they have worked on cases together. Staughton ranks both Alan and Joel as absolutely first-rate talents. If he, God forbid, were ever indicted for a major felony, the first person he would turn to defend him would be Alan Marks. Alan is more charismatic in the courtroom. He makes people want to like and do things for him. Joel is more scholarly, and effective in a different way. Marks is not only extraordinarily skillful in the courtroom but has a special ability to mobilize public opinion in appropriate cases. For example, a few years ago Marks represented a man accused of being a serial rapist. The community was understandably frantic, and Alan not only succeeded in obtaining not guilty verdicts for his client, but he also was able to move the public to a general feeling that the man was innocent, an extraordinary service for his client.

Staughton is clear minded about the business problems facing firms such as his and Marks and Feinberg. A criminal-defense and civil rights practice is affected by inflation, as well as the increasing complications of the law. Very few private individuals can afford a private lawyer for criminal defense, except those accused of white-collar or drug offenses, or affiliated with organized crime. White-collar defendants do not usually choose civil rights lawyers: the large corporate firms now have criminal-defense departments and vie for that business. Work on drug crimes fluctuates dramatically, and many lawyers have concerns about organized crime work. The criminal appointment work through the federal court has kept such poor pace with inflation that the forty dollars out-of-court hourly rate and sixty dollars in-court rate make it difficult to sustain a practice without more lucrative specialties. Section 1983 work (lawsuits for infringement of constitutional rights under federal statute), which has been a contingency-fee staple of firms like his and Marks and Feinberg, got a shot in the arm with 1988 amendments permitting court-awarded fees. But generally, the handful of firms around the country that have practices like Marks and Feinberg are having difficulty staying economically viable.

A lawyer who can try Section 1983 or Title VII (employment discrimination) cases can, according to Staughton, easily try personal
injury, products liability, and malpractice cases. A client who has an
accident somehow never thinks that the person who handled his civil
rights action could do a superb job in the personal-injury case. The
civil rights lawyer is typecast, even by other lawyers who might refer
business. It is like the movie star who has made her name in TV sit-
coms who tries to get dramatic roles. It is a struggle telling people you
are available. Nowadays when Staughton is asked what he is doing,
he tends to respond by saying what he would *like* to be doing: "I've
started trying malpractice cases." Other lawyers think of firms like
Marks and Feinberg when they have cases they are afraid of, avoid
because of the unpopularity of the client or case, or feel won't generate
enough money. They think, "Alan will make something out of this."
But they would never send something Alan could really *make* something out of.

In Staughton's view, one of the tragedies of the profession is to
see featured in newspapers lawyers with lucrative criminal-defense
business who sometimes do terrible work and who haven't seen the
inside of a law library for years. He thinks they couldn't carry Alan
and Joel's briefcase. An honest lawyer is hard to find. A competent
lawyer even harder. But the great lawyers, thoughtful, highly analytical, and effective, like Alan and Joel, are truly rare.

Some Clients' Views

Alan's and Joel's characteristics are appreciated as much by clients as
by colleagues. Thomas McIver, a client of Alan, headed an interior
furnishings company for commercial customers. His wife of sixteen
years was on the town council of a suburban community, and they
had two children. McIver was a man of impeccable habits, with a
stable family life and successful business career. All this was shattered
by a hideous accident he suffered driving home on the freeway one
evening. The passenger in the other car was killed, and McIver was
briefly hospitalized and then charged with driving under the influence
of alcohol and recklessly endangering the lives of others. McIver was
terrified, barely able to function, but finally began to search for a
defense attorney. He interviewed eight attorneys and chose Alan
Marks. He remembers asking Alan why he should go with him.

Marks paused and said, "I'm thorough," the world's greatest under-statement, adds McIver admiringly. "He seemed genuine . . . someone who really *was* what he projected himself to be." For McIver, who has had "less than the best" relations with lawyers and accountants, it was crucial that he have confidence, and he never lost it. "It was the best decision I ever made." Marks's fees were extraordinarily modest—another illustration of something McIver had learned in business: what you pay doesn't necessarily have much to do with what you receive.

McIver began with what he describes as an extremely intense one-hour session with Marks where he discussed all his fears, after which the case was in Marks's charge. McIver had found his expe-rience after the accident so traumatic that he became something of an emotional wreck. He eventually sold his business, and Marks helped him find a therapist. McIver describes Marks as extremely sensitive to a client's vulnerabilities, someone who would never even consider manipulating the client. Marks never "yo-yoed" him emo-tionally, never gave himself points to make himself look good by playing on the client's fears (something that McIver obviously feels many lawyers do much of the time). Marks would not allow McIver to get emotionally ahead of himself by either building up his hopes or by letting him get despondent.

McIver's case was complicated by the fact the head nurse at the hospital where he was taken after the accident told a trooper friend of hers that McIver was "stinking drunk," which led to the charges against him. Contradictory testimony came from a physician, and the evidence also showed the driver of the other car had a history of alcohol and drug abuse. At his first trial, McIver was acquitted of all charges except driving while intoxicated, which was overturned on appeal. His second trial ended in a hung jury, and the prosecutor decided to drop the charges against him. McIver is now pursuing (with Marks as his attorney) a civil suit against the nurse in order to recover the $125,000 in costs he incurred in his defense over six years.

McIver has had a lot of experience with lawyers. Most are a lot of "pomp and circumstance," he says. Alan Marks has a "supreme sense of ethics," which is not to say that other lawyers aren't ethical, but that Alan has a much sharper vision of what is in the client's best interest. "*His* [Marks's] best interest is not at issue." McIver is convinced other lawyers would not have been so committed. They would have taken shortcuts and been unwilling to do the homework and take the extra steps Marks did. Not once did McIver have to remind Marks of a commitment. McIver had never felt such confidence in anyone before. He can only assume that Marks is motivated by his personal idealism. Marks and the people around him at the office give so much of themselves to so many causes. He does not seem motivated by profit.

"Lawyers are thieves," states another Marks and Feinberg client, Frederick Land, who went through four lawyers, lost all his savings and his car during a two and a half year ordeal of being charged with molesting two small children. Land was dating a woman he later married whose two children by another man were placed in the home of foster parents. He paid $1,000 to a lawyer to help him get custody of the children. The foster parents accused him of child abuse. When Land was arrested, his lawyer told him to get a criminal lawyer. Lawyer number two, a top criminal-defense lawyer by reputation, demanded a $5,000 retainer, and then another $5,000 on the eve of his pretrial hearing. When Land could not come up with the second $5,000, the lawyer instructed him to request a continuance and referred him to another lawyer. (Land was able to obtain a $4,000 refund.) His third lawyer, to whom he gave a $5,000 retainer, did his homework, but failed to prevent the grand jury from indicting him. This lawyer also demanded an additional $5,000 before trial. Land, having lost his job, was unable to produce the money. He finally went to a public defender, a nice young man who was so busy and overburdened that he was unable to respond. Land calls him "Mr. Depression."

Finally a woman who befriended Land's wife and was interested in helping her get her children back from the foster homes in which they were placed put Land in touch with Joel Feinberg and offered to pay Joel's $25,000 retainer. Land went to see Feinberg.

> He never built me up or brought me down. He was never judgmental. When I gave him information, he'd get the facts and say let's look at it from this angle and that angle: he *really* was listening to me! He was very exact in everything he did. Unlike the public defender, he sent me a copy of everything he did. He always returned my phone calls. He was very specific about what

he was going to do. He is a very quiet subdued man, not like other lawyers who "parade around" a lot. Can you imagine, with the kind of money he must be making, that he drives around in a plain station wagon!

Feinberg assembled all the evidence that had been gathered in Land's case, including two lie detector tests, psychiatric evaluations of both Land and the child making the accusations (one child withdrew her accusations), the lack of any physical evidence, and the testimony of Land's wife and former wife. Within a month of first meeting with Feinberg, all charges against Land were dropped. Feinberg followed up with a successful expungement proceeding and returned $15,000 of the retainer. A former police officer, Land said he would have committed suicide before going to prison. "If I had not had Joel, I don't know what I would have done. It is as if he was my heart surgeon. I will forever be grateful."

Jacqueline Frome describes her first visit to Joel Feinberg's office. She had heard from several different people how good a lawyer he was, and she was facing an academic tenure battle. She was impressed by the offices of the firm: they were unlawyerly. The offices felt homey, as if these discrimination lawyers had deliberately set up their offices not to intimidate people.

What was so striking about Joel was how bright he was. Hers was a complicated case. She gave him twenty names that first day. She never had to repeat anything. She always had his complete attention. Together they worked out an intermediate solution through internal procedures in her college. Five years later the issue of her promotion came up again, and the second round went well because Joel prepared the case so well the first time by constructing a good paper trail. Although he may be an excellent litigator, he was conservative in his advice, explaining to her that a court battle would cost a lot of time and money and that the odds were at best fifty-fifty before a judge. He encouraged her to develop an extralegal solution. Her confidence was strengthened by having him there to discuss the issues intelligently and to assist her in framing her strategy. Ms. Frome has dealt with many lawyers and felt most were interested in racking up time and indulging in last-minute, expensive maneuvers. She never felt Joel was greedy. He acted ethically. He was a steady, intelligent presence who had her case all in hand.

A Business in Difficulty

Alan's interest in computers in the office has led to the purchase of
personal computers for each lawyer, on which they do most of their
work—there is no dictation in the office—with Carol doing the printing and billing using a billing software package. But neither Joel nor
Alan is enthusiastic about law-office management or the business side
of the practice. Ruth has, by default and without much eagerness,
become the businessperson who has taken the lead in reviewing projected cash flow, collections, and expenses of the partnership. There
is no expense or income budget. The discussion at the sporadic meetings of the partners on these matters is informal, consisting of a
review and discussion of cases being handled by the firm, the prospects for billing, and the current status of the firm's bank account.

The firm has learned from bitter experience that it is wise to undertake few, if any, employment-discrimination cases on a contingent-
fee basis. Much of its work in this area involves court-awarded fees, if
the plaintiff is successful. The firm has been trying to take on more
financially remunerative work in civil litigation, but it is still known
primarily for its civil rights and criminal-defense practice. Rachel
Majev, who is of counsel to the firm, was active in recent years in
attracting some malpractice work for the firm but lately has been
focusing more on raising her young family than law practice. During
one summer, there was a consensus among the partners that they
should do something about client development. Both Alan and Ruth
called some friends in large firms to indicate their interest in referrals,
but the lawyers felt awkward about it, and there was no effort to continue the calls or follow through in other ways. Although a few cases
were generated from the calls, not much came of what all acknowledge
was a rather halfhearted effort.

Members of the firm have strong feelings about trying to be true
to their principles, and they have come to appreciate the costs associated with their sense of integrity. Two recent discussions in the firm
illustrate their thinking. A landlord rather notorious in the tenants'
rights community as an exploiter of poor people was known to be
looking for counsel to defend himself against a series of public charges
of misconduct, in particular for lying to a grand jury about payoffs
to housing inspectors. The firm ultimately was not approached by
the landlord, but they did engage in a discussion about what to do

if they were asked. Ruth Fried was deeply opposed to being identified with the landlord in any way, but she knows she would probably have been outvoted by her two senior partners. The lawyers of the firm have always felt it important to be on "the right side" of issues: advancing societal interests beyond the interests of individual clients is part of the special pleasure and satisfaction they take in their practice. While the firm never would have represented the landlord against a tenants' union or in an eviction, Alan and Joel would have defended the landlord in a criminal prosecution because they define criminal-defense work as the "right side," even though they are aware that few of these cases involve factually innocent defendants. Criminal defense, as Joel puts it, is a vehicle to advance rights that eventually protect us all. Joel and Alan regularly agree to accept court appointments to represent defendants charged with first-degree murder. They would only refuse to provide criminal-defense services if a case involved serious racial or ethnic prejudice.

Some time ago, Alan raised the issue of bringing into the partnership a fine lawyer he knew in the Wayne County district attorney's office who was exploring entering private practice. The attorney offered the possibility of engaging in products-liability defense work for major corporate clients. After a discussion, the strong consensus of the office was that adding this type of practice to the firm was a mistake. Joel's skepticism that the lawyer could actually bring in the business was far less important than the uneasiness everyone felt about getting on the wrong side of products-liability litigation. It did not fit with the firm's sense of its own personality.

The decision seemed in retrospect to be excellent when Joel became involved with products-liability litigation in which the same former United States attorney, now in private practice, turned up on the other (or wrong) side. But the precarious state of the firm's finances caused other problems in the litigation. A small group of civil rights and tenants' plaintiffs' attorneys began meeting to develop a novel strategy in lead-paint-poisoning cases. They devised a suit against paint manufacturers as well as landlords for damages resulting from the ingestion of lead-paint particles. Two of the other attorneys were from firms similar to Marks and Feinberg, that is, people who had established reputations for integrity and "cause" lawyering, with whom Joel felt totally at ease. The dilemma they faced, however, was the colossal cost of the litigation. The manufacturers, whose solvency would be threatened by a successful suit, would be bound to present the most comprehensive and dilatory defense imaginable, in short, a scorched-earth campaign. Virtually every major corporate law firm in Detroit—along with major national law firms—would be thrown into the battle, and the carrying costs of litigation with important ramifications for a whole industry would be enormous, far beyond the resources of the three firms. A fourth law firm, a plaintiff firm specializing in asbestos litigation that views lead-paint litigation as a new line of business, was therefore invited into the suit, chiefly because it had the resources to finance the litigation. The marriage of convenience led immediately to tensions within the group, as the asbestos firm refused to pool referrals generated by the publicity of the lawsuit and brought in a media specialist to publicize its role in the litigation.

The aggressive marketing of the asbestos-litigation firm is offensive to Marks and Feinberg, who see the asbestos firm as a group of unprofessional businesspeople. On the other hand, it underscores the absence of *any* planning for the economic viability and future of Marks and Feinberg. Alan Marks mentions in passing the multimillion dollar judgment in a contingency-fee case won by a friend with similar public-interest values. The wishful thinking for the big one, the mother lode, is the small law firm's counterpart to the Cinderella syndrome ("some day my prince [case] will come"). Gross income at Marks and Feinberg over the past few years has been erratic, moving from $298,000 in one calendar year to $389,000 and $313,000 in subsequent years. Gross income for forthcoming years is likely to grow substantially, but expenses are up even more sharply, particularly wages to employees and the commitment under the partnership agreement to Ruth Fried, who is paid a minimum of $33,000 plus a percentage of profits over $200,000. The annual net income of each of the two senior partners has fluctuated from $46,000 to $73,000 to $31,000, and more recently, a good year, $83,000. The two partners have doubts whether they can substantially improve their prospects for future net income.

After a period of inaction, and not a little despair (at least on the part of Alan Marks) over the hopelessness of their situation, the firm was persuaded that they had to engage in the process of marketing. They developed a three-page firm résumé describing the lawyers, their areas of practice, and their significant cases. Each lawyer resolved to contact people to get the word out that the firm was interested in most forms of trial work. Alan Marks was generally acknowledged to be the main "laboring oar," both because he felt more urgently the need to change the situation and because he had more contacts and friends in large firms. The marketing strategy was to talk to large firms and suggest Marks and Feinberg as an excellent small litigation firm to which the large firm could refer clients when prevented from undertaking litigation due to a conflict of interest.

The firm résumé serves as a written reminder and factual review of the quality of Marks and Feinberg's work. Sensing the inadequacies of their homemade résumé, the firm recently spent $4,000 for a public relations professional to clean it up, add pictures, make it look better, and reduce the verbiage and the civil rights stereotyping so that the brochure communicates more effectively the type of fee-paying work the firm seeks to do. Joel remarks sarcastically, "Next for us is radio and TV."

Alan has begun a series of contacts that is referred to jokingly around the office as "power lunches." Alan despises what he is forced to do, namely talk to his friends and acquaintances in the profession about his need for work and the quality work he is capable of doing, but he realizes that unless he makes a strong effort to market the firm and bring in more business, the firm simply cannot sustain itself. The painfulness and humiliation of it all recedes somewhat, the more he does it. The pace has slowed to one lunch a month.

Power lunches have not generated much business, although Alan suggests that they may be beginning to bear some fruit. All four lawyers are aware that results do not emerge from a low-key marketing process overnight, and Alan realizes he must continue the lunches and relentlessly remind people of the availability and quality of the firm.

One by-product of the firm's new determination to market itself did lead to some significant work. Alan talked about the needs of the firm to a faculty member at the University of Michigan who was of counsel to a large firm. The faculty member urged the firm to refer to Marks and Feinberg litigation for a major bank that the firm was barred from representing by a conflict. Although Alan had rarely handled commercial litigation, the matter was concluded successfully, the bank was pleased, and Alan has continued to do some work for the bank and to be referred work from other lawyers involved in the banking matter.

One other event has brought hope to the office. Alan and Joel remain on the list for capital cases because they believe they have an obligation to handle these matters. The assignment of a case occurs strictly by happenstance. The clerk calls the next person on the list for the next case that appears on the docket. Alan's luck of the draw was extraordinary: he was asked to handle a homicide of a policeman in the course of a drug bust, an extraordinarily high-visibility case in the local media that soon became sensational. The police raid on the drug operation that precipitated the shoot-out was based on a warrant that described the anonymous informant as West Indian. Since Alan's defendant was Puerto Rican, he requested early in the case that the informant be produced on the grounds that the informant might have exculpatory evidence that the defendant was not, in fact, involved in the drug operation. The state prosecutors delayed responding to the request for so long that the judge threatened to dismiss the indictment unless they produced the informant. The state finally admitted that the informant did not exist, and that the same mythical informant had been used in warrants involving fifty or sixty prior drug convictions. The judge dismissed the indictment, and the state appealed to the Michigan Supreme Court. The proceedings have been highly publicized and have generated a "fair amount of business," according to Joel, from people who have called because they read the names of Alan and Ann in the newspaper.

Some additional criminal business also arose as a result of another lucky coincidence. A fugitive from a bank-fraud indictment in federal court in St. Louis contacted a friend of Joel, who turned to Joel for assistance. When the fugitive was apprehended and returned to St. Louis, he asked Joel to continue to represent him in the trial and appellate proceedings there. The client then recommended Joel to others with whom he was incarcerated. Now Joel and Ann have developed a small specialty of representing federal drug defendants in St. Louis.

The lead-paint class action drags on as the defense firms create a mountain of paper out of the proceedings. The plaintiffs uncovered virtually nothing in discovery. There are now seven or eight individual lead-paint cases in the office, a modest but not insignificant result of this major litigation initiative. Ruth Fried has also taken on some additional employment-discrimination work. A friend of hers on maternity leave from another firm asked Ruth to take over her caseload.

Joel continues to teach the prisoner-rights course and clinic at Wayne State, in part because he feels he needs the money (about $12,000 total for two quarters of the school year). Alan has been teaching a course on advanced criminal-defense advocacy during both semesters at Michigan, for which he receives about $20,000, but he plans to cut back to one semester during the next academic year.

Joel reports that the current calendar year looks like a "good year." A couple of medical malpractice claims have settled, which helps greatly, and things look promising enough that the firm has decided to renew its option on its current space for one additional year. This next year will be an important test of whether the firm can make it together. Joel describes his hopes for the next year:

> It is hard to say if things will work out: I have a notion that we've managed for sixteen years, so we ought to be able to continue. Things are also changing in the profession. Competition is affecting us, creating more of a problem than before. We see many of the lawyers doing our kind of work facing difficulty, breaking up, restructuring into loose affiliations and the like.

Alan adds:

> Most of the lawyers who once had our kind of practice and are now doing well have specialized, usually as a result of one big successful case that gets them into a "pipeline" (steady referrals and reputation) for this work. They do almost nothing but lead-paint cases, criminal work, employment work, or stockholder-derivative work. Specialization and high volume reduces one's overhead and increases profitability. But I don't think I would be able to stand that kind of practice.

Joel agrees: "We probably don't want to be specialized." Ruth points out that the firm could learn from lawyers who specialize how to move their cases more effectively. Everyone agrees that employing paralegals would help, but that represents a significant cost they are unwilling to face. The firm, Ruth emphasizes, is busy; "We have no end of low-paying work: the question is how to get work (or as Alan puts it, get 'wired' to receive steady referrals of work) that pays better."

The volatility or fragility of the small specialty firm struck close to home when Baum and Caskey, the two-lawyer firm with whom Marks and Feinburg shares office space, recently broke up. Joe Baum took a job with the Michigan Grievance Commission and Fred Caskey joined a larger firm. This adds significant overhead costs and puts an enormous strain on the decision whether to renew the lease or seek new space. Luckily, one of the refugees from the breakup of another civil rights partnership will be sharing offices with Marks and Feinberg when Baum and Caskey depart. The big decision will occur later in the year, when Marks and Feinberg will be forced to decide whether to renew their option and to rent their space for an additional four years or negotiate for yet another one-year extension. The marketing campaign has several months left to bear fruit.

The economic uncertainty facing two highly trained, experienced, and respected litigators, and their partner and associate, goes beyond the immediate problems of their variable cash flow. It is the emotional impact of "managing to squeak by" that is most troubling. They both sense that it has become harder and harder to practice in the manner they have done for the past fifteen years: "Something has got to give." They talk of a need to find a method of bringing in regular, well-paying clients. For Alan, the economic problems are a symbol—a "club"—that hits a more troubling issue. He muses why money is not the major problem:

> I love to litigate, to win, and to contribute to the work as well as my clients' and our pocketbooks. Why, after close to twenty years of practice am I having to go through this? I have this strong feeling that I am a *very* good trial lawyer, comparable to some of the best people at the bar in terms of credentials and significant litigation experience. And yet I do not handle major cases. The day-to-day practice is not as challenging as it could be.

For the others in the office, the issues are more purely economic. Ruth would like to give up her demanding part-time work at the

University of Michigan Law School. Everyone would prefer the firm to be able to afford its own office, and to more easily make choices like the addition of the kitchen and conference room and the subscription to Lexis, a computerized legal-research service. Marks and Feinberg are a group who enjoy what they do, but they ask themselves with increasing regularity: How can we continue without increasing our income?

Part 2.
Reflections on the Profession

Chapter 7

Thinking about the Stories

Marks and Feinberg

Marks and Feinberg are cause lawyers, comfortable representing criminal defendants because of the important political and philosophical statement criminal defense represents under our constitutional system. This is unusual in itself, because a significant proportion of the criminal-defense bar in the United States finds it difficult to sustain faith that criminal defense is an important element in the American system of government and the American justice system. Marks and Feinberg bear no trace of the cynicism and blatant manipulation of clients that the literature describes as characteristic of some of the criminal-defense bar (Blumberg 1967; Mann 1985; Heymann 1988).

If a certain selflessness on behalf of society's downtrodden is a theme of the Marks and Feinberg story, Alan Marks sets the tone of this practice. He is distinctly an upper-middle-class lawyer, superbly educated, sophisticated, and committed to cause lawyering. But Alan worries about why he is not more successful, given his talent, education, and successes in the trial and appellate courts of Michigan. Joel and Alan have the stature of large-firm lawyers with respect to their education, litigation experience, and talent.

Other worlds of law practice dominate the story of Marks and Feinberg. Alan and Joel sense that the lawyers to whom they compare themselves are doing better and performing more interesting work. They understand the profession has changed. Yet, except for their small gestures towards marketing, they are unwilling to alter their practice to respond to the new realities they see. Alan Marks has a young family whom he wishes to educate, and a young partner and associate whom he is obligated to support. He has both a personal and a professional overhead to meet. His dissatisfaction is eating at him and worrying his colleagues. Alan and Joel, by virtue of having been educated with lawyers now in large firms, and by having a relatively sophisticated federal court practice where they repeatedly run up against the elite of the profession, cannot avoid the stark realities of their relative penury compared to the affluence of the top echelons of the bar. Or, more galling still, the affluence of even the lower echelons of the bar.

High in the Marks and Feinberg pantheon of virtues is the conception of professional craftsmanship and excellence. The Marks and Feinberg ideal of practice includes the special pride of the elite bar in the quality of writing, preparation, and the theoretical sophistication of their cases—the exactitude and finesse that judges admire in lawyers.

There is a rigidity in Marks and Feinberg, a lack of some of the skills needed to survive in the changed profession of the 1990s—skills of marketing, of business management, of understanding in a more sophisticated way the nature of their business and the way it underwrites the kind of practice they want to maintain. They have no budgeting system, no way of systematically measuring whether their current caseload can generate enough overhead and profit to sustain the business. Marks and Feinberg believe that being astute businesspeople involves relentless marketing, ruthless weeding out of "dogs" (i.e., cases that are insufficiently profitable), and the rush to specialization in order to increase the volume and profitability of their work. All of this is "unprofessional," something they eschew and find distasteful and unpleasant. Yet merging with another firm that would handle the unpleasant business realities would almost surely mean dealing with a clientele they feel would compromise their basic values as cause lawyers. So slowly, reluctantly, almost shamefacedly, they are attempting to expand the economic base of their practice and bring in fee-paying clients.

Stories are legion of former civil rights lawyers who have, in effect, abandoned cause lawyering when faced with the same pressures that loom large in the future of Marks and Feinberg. It is clear that Marks and Feinberg want to hold onto their tradition and not let the economic challenges to their practice undermine their kind of lawyering. Their single-minded commitment to the lawyering they have always done is the main asset of the firm, the concept of professionalism that keeps them together and that establishes their character. This strength is, at the same time, a source of their greatest weakness.

Marks and Feinberg is not an inventive firm. They are change resisters, even when that change is essential to serve their fundamental ideals. Lawyers from thousands of small firms throughout the country have attended seminars sponsored by the Economics of Law Practice sections of the American Bar Association and state and local bar associations,[1] as well as programs sponsored by continuing legal-education agencies and legal newspapers. These firms are trying to adapt to the economic changes in the profession, to learn, for example, how to bill more efficiently, how to market themselves to clients. Scores of firms have made the ultimate adaption and change by merging with larger practices, presumably on the premise that they are no longer economically viable or able to service their existing clients without a larger range of specialties and expertise at their disposal. Adapting to the new economies of lawyering in the United States is an excruciatingly difficult process for Marks and Feinberg. The possibilities of a successful transition are not remote: there are numerous examples of financially successful small litigation firms or boutiques in metropolitan areas around the nation.

Marks and Feinberg seems to be struggling with a transitional concept of professionalism. A professional is someone who manages the business structure of practice so that the practice can sustain itself. A professional is someone who attracts clients as well as serves them well. The idea that professionalism includes self-promotion and business acumen is not an entirely radical or new transformation in the legal profession in the United States. There are numerous examples in the nineteenth century, before the advent of prohibitions against advertising, of lawyers actively soliciting business and managing their affairs with the skill of businesspeople.[2]

Two major elements of change in the legal profession affect Marks and Feinberg: a substantial expansion in the size of the profession in

---

1. These sections, that is, committees, now carry more sophisticated, less reveal-ing names, like Law Practice Management.

2. King 1974 includes examples of Daniel Webster's acumen as a businessman in law practice (199–264, 243–59), and his solicitation of business (199–203). Webster was also an extraordinary financial success (266–69; Friedman 1973, 306). For adver-tising by lawyers in the nineteenth century, see Calhoun 1965, 82–83. I am indebted to Andrew King for these references.

the past decade, and a dramatic increase in income driven by more sophisticated business practices. Both have exponentially increased the intensity of the competitive environment in law practice. During the decade Alan and Joel became lawyers, there were about 250,000 to 300,000 lawyers in the United States. As of 1990, the best estimate is that there are 805,000 practicing lawyers in the United States (Curran 1991, 4; Sander 1989, 433). Had there not been such a dramatic expansion in the size of the profession in Detroit, Alan and Joel could have had an extraordinarily busy and lucrative practice in criminal-defense work that would naturally have sustained their other interests.

Marks and Feinberg are acutely aware of the economic success of certain segments of the corporate and plaintiff's bar. The *American Lawyer* reported in the summer of 1990 that more than twenty-one hundred partners in twenty of the largest law firms had average incomes just short of $1 million a year, a figure comparable to the 1989 average salary and bonus compensation of the eight hundred chief executives of the largest corporations in the United States. In 1987, only thirteen hundred partners in fifteen of the largest law firms had incomes comparable to the average of the eight hundred top CEOs, then about $760,000 ("The AM Law 100" 1990, 8, 10).

It is not clear whether the comparative affluence of certain elements of the corporate and plaintiff's bar at the close of this century is a genuinely new phenomenon in the legal profession. Lawyers historically have commanded high fees and made money in the practice of law. What is new in the last decade, however, is published data about lawyers' income; analyses of economic successes and failures; the creation of conferences and educational programs devoted to increasing profitability and the economic success of law practice; and the emergence of a new industry of law-practice consultants and nonlawyer managers who attend to the profitability of the practice, the attraction of talent, and marketing and public relations. The legal profession, in the decade of the 1980s and 1990s, has become extraordinarily self-conscious about making money. The tools of the new legal journalism hone this self-consciousness to a sharp comparative and competitive edge.

Marks and Feinberg are struggling. They are victims of an excess in the supply of lawyers and caught in a transformation of professional economic aspirations. They now are aware that success in the

legal profession requires managerial skills in addition to those attributes traditionally associated with competent practice, such as knowledge and professional skills, good health and work habits, and
willingness to follow through (American Law Institute–American Bar
Association 1980).

Lawyers have always had to manage practices in the sense of
organizing the way they deliver services to clients, relate to clients,
and arrange the structures of their offices to support these activities.
Management entails controlling the quality of the work in terms of
judgments about the law, understanding the situation affecting the
client, and what kind of lawyer the lawyer aspires to be. In the last
decade, pressures on traditional forms of management have changed
in virtually every setting of private and public law practice. New
management skills include the ability to understand and direct a
practice as an economically viable unit in an environment made
difficult by competition for clients, heightened pressures for income
as an element of professional success, and resistance by clients or
other funding sources to the high cost of using lawyers.

Management skills put a premium on efficient use (i.e., a much
more sophisticated management) of the capital resources of the practice, which are

1. staff (secretarial, paralegal, legal) with varying degrees of
   abilities and training;
2. space and new technologies for research, data management,
   and document production; and
3. clients, and the practice's understanding of clients' needs and
   clients' expectations with respect to time frameworks, costs,
   and desired results.

Efficiency is a function of both profitability and more qualitative
goals of the practice; and it includes attracting business, namely new
clients or existing clients sufficient to keep busy and fully productive
the other capital resources of the practice.

The major question facing the Marks and Feinberg practice is
whether they can develop enough of the new management skills to
survive as a practice. Marks and Feinberg have one extraordinary
asset: a clear sense of the kind of lawyers they want to be, an
established identity as a civil and human-rights practice. Taking on

other, more profitable lines of activity, such as commercial litigation or personal injury and malpractice work, is unlikely to affect this core sense of who they are. Their character as a practice may be an asset to marketing themselves, particularly to lawyers in large law firms who refer clients because of conflicts of interest. Large-firm lawyers may refer clients for both the business reason that Marks and Feinberg represents no threat to steal a business client, as well as the ideological reason that civil rights lawyers need support in an era when many firms are cutting back on their pro bono, or non-remunerative, public benefits and civil rights work.

The future for Marks and Feinberg can take several different turns: survival from year to year with a sense of uncertainty about their ability to stay together as a practice; a busier and more profitable practice that flourishes; or dissolution in whole or in part as a lawyer leaves the practice for a more secure economic future in a public agency or private practice, almost certainly (for departing lawyers) abandoning some control over the type and style of their practice.[3]

The dilemma facing Marks and Feinberg is that, in order to avoid dissolution that would signal loss of control over their vision of being professionals, they must assert more control over the direction of their practice and become, to some extent, different lawyers. They must be more effective at marketing their practice and attending to the bottom line of a business entity. Their choices are continuing as is, a relatively demoralizing prospect; catastrophic change (dissolving); or planned change, a difficult, demanding, and sometimes discouraging effort to improve their business. These are not happy or easy choices. They must decide whether to become victims or collaborators in the transformed legal profession of the late twentieth century.

The Legal Division of the Maine Public Utilities Commission

The practice of Marks and Feinberg presents relatively clearly honed concepts of professionalism, either serving a class of people who need

---

3. Lawyers who do not possess self-promotional or marketing skills appear to be relegated to being functionaries in organizations, the "grinders" (i.e., workhorses), while other lawyers serve as "finders" of new clients or "minders" of existing clients that give them a distinctly higher status (as well as income) in the profession.

the special protection of the law and the legal profession, or serving an important ideological foundation of American justice, namely the due process protections accorded criminal defendants under the Constitution. Clients tend to fit within the general categories of people deserving protection; Marks and Feinberg seem clear about their roles and functions in the legal system.

The role of the Public Utility Commission lawyers is less unambiguous. Every member of the Legal Division would say without the slightest hesitation that their function is to serve the public interest. But it is hard to fathom from this narrative what that interest is. A number of different definitions of the role of the lawyer in serving the public interest can be found in this story:

> A utility shall have safe, reasonable, and adequate facilities and just and reasonable rates with revenues required to perform its service and attract necessary capital on just and reasonable terms.
>
> The staff of PUC do *not* reflect the social goals and philosophy of the governor (as does the public advocate) or the using and consuming public but must take into account the interests of the utility and competing claims of industrial users.
>
> The job is "to protect . . . the consumer and the underdog from being 'ripped off.'"
>
> What is best for the customers in the long run.
>
> The individual must develop "his or her best judgment of what is in the public interest, a balancing of achieving the lowest rates consistent with sufficient revenues to raise capital."
>
> The goal is not "to beat down the utility, although in practice it is usually the consumer that needs more."
>
> Try to do what is fair.
>
> Utilities must be made to behave as if they had competitors, as if customers could choose to go elsewhere.
>
> The lawyer is the client and therefore must persuade the commission of the right result.
>
> The lawyer anticipates the decision the commission (the client) will make and helps them defend this decision.
>
> The lawyer helps the commission (the client) better focus their thoughts so they can make a decision.
>
> "If it's what the utility wants, we probably don't want it."

Public interest is an extraordinarily amorphous concept. The fact that there are so many differing concepts of this interest and the abstract and ineffable client who lies behind this interest called the public, is a fundamental feature of law practice at the Public Utilities Commission. Since neither the public nor the public interest is clearly defined, the goals of this practice are up for grabs and under constant threat of subversion. Stipulations, the negotiated settlements with the utilities that avoid the full hearing process envisaged in the statutory structure for rate setting, suggest that yet another definition of public interest is the desirability of deals that eliminate the high costs of legal process for both the utility and the PUC. The uneasiness in the PUC about stipulations further sharpens the dilemma of lawyers unsure who their client is and what best serves their client's unarticulated interests.

The public-utility lawyer is beset by what has been called the "problem of imputed ends." In private practice, lawyers tend to assume that their clients have certain typical goals like freedom, a larger share of the pie, and the like (Luban 1981, 454). Lawyers project these imputed ends or goals on clients, often pressure clients into accepting such goals, and often don't listen carefully to clients to determine the clients' *real* interests. But the public lawyer is unclear how to go about listening. Public interest is an imaginary projection by the lawyer of what the lawyer feels the public ought to have from the utility with a service monopoly in a region of the state.

The indeterminacy of the client and the client's interests is so fundamental to the PUC practice that it helps to account for some of the peculiar features of the Legal Division under Horace Libby and his protégé, Joe Donahue. The schmoozing in the library and after-hours camaraderie during busy times and the remarkable hands-off attitude of both leaders of the division are functional responses to the lack of definition of either client or public interest. Both leaders had an acute sense of process, of listening: "If he [Horace] thought it was fair, you always had a shot," as one of the private attorneys for the utilities put it. When no client gives direction, and when there is no process to ascertain the real goals of the nonexistent client, a conscientious lawyer, unwilling to come to snap judgments and skeptical of the cruder formulas for resolving this indeterminacy, will naturally be inclined to talk, to test hypotheses, to compare judgments, to articulate the dilemma in a way that helps the lawyer create the client or impute ends in the context of a particular hearing or settlement discussion. One goal of Horace Libby and Joe Donahue was to teach their lawyers how to come to some focus or to sketch in the probable outlines of client and client's interest. But equally important was the goal of respecting the indeterminacy, of not laying down "the law," of leaving the decision about the public interest in the hands of each staff member, whose judgment was honed and whose sensibilities were developed in the process of conversations around the office.

The concept of *public* and *public interest* changed during the history of the organization spelled out in this narrative. As the commission filled with people whose judgment and "generally proconsumer" biases filtered down to the staff, and the technical expertise and professionalism of the other units in the commission improved, the Legal Division found itself defining public interest in terms of the specific client, namely the commission, and the commission's own interests and goals. It is no accident that stipulations began to replace full hearings once it was clear that the lawyers respected the instincts of the commissioners, and the commissioners began to be clear about their policies. Both PUC staff and utility lawyers could draw a relatively clear picture of who was the client and what the client wanted. Some of the challenge went out of law practice at the Public Utilities Commission once the client had been found and the client's views were known.

The upgraded quality or professionalism of the other divisions of the Public Utilities Commission over this period of time is a widespread phenomenon affecting the contemporary legal profession. This narrowing of focus, this confining of lawyers to the technicalities of law, has recently been associated with the emergence of in-house corporate counsel, and the changing dynamic of practice in the large corporate law firm. As in-house corporate law departments become more professional, that is, more capable and highly respected by management, they do something much more significant than take routine business away from the large corporate law firm. They capture much of the judgment business, the general advising, the work of helping the client to determine the client's real interests, and they limit the role of outside counsel to highly specialized arenas (like litigation, pension and profit sharing, environmental law, etc.) in which the in-house group has limited technical expertise.

The Public Utilities Commission story suggests that the phenomenon of narrowing the definition of lawyering is much broader than
the in-house counsel movement (Chayes and Chayes 1985, 277; Rosen
1989, 64). The professionalization of organizations that lawyers traditionally serve has had a major impact on contemporary practice.
It is probably fair to say that lawyers under Horace Libby had too
much power in the agency and were in fact usurping some of the
authority of the commissioners to serve an imputed end of the interest
of the public. And the commission is no doubt a much stronger and
healthier institution today than it was under Horace Libby. But conversation about goals and the public and their governing statute and
the role of fairness to the utilities—those tough judgment calls that
made life in the Legal Division of the PUC so exciting under Horace—
are gone. The Legal Division is undoubtedly working in a less interesting, more technically defined environment.

The "professionalization of everyone" (Wilensky 1964) has
important implications for the legal profession in the 1990s. Corporate
managers, even those with limited in-house counsel, are often more
sophisticated, better educated, certainly more confident about their
ability to find their way in a complex world.[4] The lawyer is less of
a general-purpose advisor than in the past. The professionalization
of management is one force behind this changing role of the lawyer.
Another force is the escalating fees of lawyers, in particular the
billable-hour structure of fees. High-cost billable hours have two
effects: they make clients resistant to using lawyers for general advice
because clients are resistant to high hourly costs, and lawyers so
sensitive to the high cost of their time that they tend to resort to
forms of defensiveness such as relating time to more easily billable
document production. Both lawyer and client overreact to the phenomenon of the "clock running."

The sense of being a wise head, or counselor, of being respected
for one's judgment as well as for one's technical expertise, is a recurring
theme in conversations with lawyers about why they enjoy the practice of law. It is a recurring theme in large law firms because many
older lawyers, client-responsible lawyers whose judgment is valued

---

4. Obviously, there are major exceptions, such as "bet-your-company" merger
and acquisition issues, litigation that has similar life-or-death implications for companies, complicated tax-shelter deals for which investors needed meticulous and doc-
umented analytical advice, and the like.

by the client, bemoan the fact that the economic necessities of the firm force the younger generation to be so specialized that they lose some judgment training—the kind of training that Horace Libby provided his charges at the Public Utilities Commission. And it is part of the reason that in-house counsel jobs have become so much more attractive: because they offer the pleasures of collaboration with a client, rather than episodic fire fighting or technical servicing.

The Public Utilities Commission story illustrates another similarity between public and private lawyering, which are usually thought of as separate worlds. We ordinarily think of institutional leadership in law as almost exclusively expressed by the founders or formative leaders of private law firms. Horace Libby created a legal department strong enough to transform the state's major utility and alter fundamental relationships between the state and the utilities it regulates. Horace had none of the attributes we normally associate with great leaders. He was shy, self-effacing, unassertive, never a spokesman or cheerleader. But he had a sense of what he wanted in an organization. He commanded respect for his integrity, his consistency, and his caring. He built a fine institution.

The Legal Division of Standish Development Company

Standish is not untypical of the newly emerging, more modern, in-house corporate law department ("The AM Law 100" 1990b, 58–60; Kaufman and Henning 1990, 42; Wilber 1990, 40). It was organized to cut down on the high costs of using one large corporate law firm and to create a substitute legal capacity inside the company. The in-house department also manages outside law firms, choosing specialists in various firms in particular geographic regions that best suit the needs of the company. A singular and close relationship with one firm is by and large a thing of the past, as a company's sizeable investment in client-specific information about its goals, procedures, and complexities is relocated inside the company. The department engages in preventive lawyering with the managers of its existing properties. And the quality of the work is extraordinarily high, at least according to the evidence of the client, those people in the company who feel they are receiving more sophisticated, timely, and responsive (and lower cost) services than they could obtain from the best real estate departments in private law firms.

The story begins with an incident in which Standish was arrayed against its natural adversary, the large corporate law firm. Many Standish lawyers have had a firsthand experience working for law firms and found these experiences distinctly unpleasant, dull, or alienating. Standish employs similar firms and monitors them with a healthy distrust of their billing practices. McGill's ability to develop a support network for his lawyers and to reduce the costs of relatively routine work are a result of skilled and attentive personnel management, automation, and training of nonprofessional staff rarely matched in the private-practice environment. McGill is not just close to management and its thinking, but part of it (remember the letter with just the right "soft" tone). He now has the ability to recruit people many people in the company feel are better than the best outside transactional lawyers. Deep antagonism to lawyers—distrust of the "games" that lawyers play—seems to run high not only in Standish but in many other corporations. McGill is able to take advantage of this profound distrust to build an institution that has the confidence of the management of the firm while building a compensation structure that, at least for senior people who have the advantage of stock options, is comparable to senior-level compensation in large law firms. Virtually every element of the Standish practice is a challenge to corporate private practice—a challenge in terms of institutional design, a challenge in terms of lower costs, a challenge in terms of effectiveness and quality of services.

The Butler law firm is the villain of this piece. The billing struggle with Butler takes place in the context of a traditional mythology that the large law firm is the entity that provides independent, thoughtful, and sage advice to clients on complex transactions, while in-house corporate departments exercise little independence and do only the most uninteresting routine work. This story transforms this mythology and reverses it. Standish's lawyers had a more sophisticated understanding of the transaction and of the client's interests. The problem with the Butler firm in this case was not that it failed to exercise independent judgment, but that it failed to serve its client. Butler showed itself to be a self-interested and self-serving enterprise that accepted no accountability for the costs and quality of its work because it was protected by its status in the client bank, not by its effective functioning on behalf of the bank.[5]

The fact that Standish fought back and succeeded in convincing the bank's management to use a different, lower-cost, and more knowledgeable law firm in the future constitutes a powerful form of education to the bank client that legal costs need to be managed, that professionals must be accountable.

If legal services are a cost center that require sophisticated management, how is it different from marketing and cash management and a host of other corporate functions and activities? The threat of loss of professional independence is a daunting one to most commentators on the phenomena of the rapid growth, scale, and stature of in-house counsel (Chayes and Chayes 1985, 298; Rosen 1989). If the Butler story is a significant indicator, however, Standish seems to offer a company culture that offers *more* professional independence than do many private law firms (Lochna 1985, 312).

The fact that the company's CEO is a lawyer may be an important factor in the success of the law department, but it seems likely that many modern corporate managers *expect* law departments to be independent and active forces in decision making and management of the business. Every in-house law department is owned by a company. The issue is whether its regulatory and advisory role is respected by a company. No doubt there are numerous examples of lawyers working for corporations where unfavorable attitudes of management or fragile economic circumstances make impossible the kind of authority and respect and the independence of the Standish legal department. Most of the outside lawyers commenting on the Standish legal department point out how remarkable it is, how different from that of other companies.

A central feature of this story is the extraordinary tension in the law division over salaries apparently typical of corporate law departments ("The AM Law 100" 1990b, 58–60; Kaufman and Henning 1990, 42; Wilber 1990, 40). Salaries always produce anxiety over performance and an individual's role in an organization. At Standish, there are added comparisons with private law practices, to which the

---

5. Thus, Butler inverts the classic distinction of Talcott Parsons that a profession derives its authority from its function, rather than by virtue of its office, as do bureaucracies (Parsons 1954, 38–39).

division feels it is superior. Salary setting in the corporate environment also signals the status of law within the company, a matter of extraordinary concern to an in-house lawyer because it turns on the opinion of the client. This anxiety can be compared to the trauma of a private firm worried about a significant diminution in the use of the firm by a major client. At Standish, salary setting is an annual gauge of client satisfaction as well as a measure of the tensions between the lawyer's self-image as an important element of the deal-making team and the pressures "to keep lawyers in their place" as staff, not line employees, whose value is comparable to other forms of expertise in engineering, design, and marketing. In those corporations where lawyers "know their place" and realize they are not a significant factor in the value added by the corporate enterprise, no such tensions are likely to arise. The very success of the law department at Standish, its ability to guide and counsel the client and participate in the client's strategic decisions, puts heavy pressure on salary decisions. Indeed, a simple maxim may apply here: the better the corporate law department, the more difficulty and unhappiness there will be in creating a satisfactory compensation structure for the department.

Another distinguishing feature of the Standish Legal Division is its ability to manage the potentially exponential or runaway costs of leasing through its cadre of trained paralegal personnel with automated systems support. The sustained management work and attention to the needs of lower-level personnel suggests that there is more flexibility in the corporate structure than in most law firms under a partnership structure. Governance in law firms is much more horizontal and democratic, at least in formal terms, than in corporations, but law firms seem to generate a more hierarchical social structure—a kind of stratification that makes it extraordinarily difficult for law firms to engage in the structural innovation and management of nonprofessionals that Standish is able to achieve. Professionals seem prone to be slavishly bureaucratic in considering the roles of nonprofessionals, or in conceiving of a support structure that enhances *their* professional role.

The practice of law inside a well-managed corporation offers many potential advantages to the company: sharply reduced legal costs for both routine and sophisticated transactions; better quality and cost control over legal work performed outside the company; more efficacious systems of preventive law within the company; and more informed and influential advice, because it originates within a unit of management attuned to the goals and mores of the company.

Perhaps the primary lesson of the Standish story is not the satisfactions of the client, or the transformations required of large private firms to respond to in-house departments,[6] but the fundamental attractiveness of this kind of practice to the lawyers engaged in it. The lawyers at Standish sense that their practice is *superior* to private practice for a number of reasons. Stress is lower because of the alignment between the lawyers' and the client's goals and values. It is less obtrusively bureaucratic and less subject to dishonesty because lawyers are not subject to the relentless pressure of the time sheet and the bottom line of the firm. It is more interesting because lawyers may enjoy a more varied and generalist practice than do the perfectionists in minutiae who inhabit many large-firm specialty departments. It is more professional because the work is to function for the client, not to engage in the forms of marketing, hucksterism, or internal and external self-promotion required of large-firm partners. It is more satisfying because lawyers deeply understand the client. The lawyer can be highly valued and influential as she or he helps the client develop goals and strategies. Law is not narrowly or purely technical. For these lawyers, it is a better, indeed a far better, professional life than that led by their colleagues, friends, and adversaries in private practice.

Mahoney, Bourne, and Thiemes and McKinnon, Moreland, and Fox

Mahoney and McKinnon are profoundly different firms. They operate in different communities. McKinnon is about ten times the size of Mahoney and bent on rapid growth, while Mahoney agonizes over the challenges of growth. McKinnon operates with a large bureaucracy compared to the intimate, informal structure of the Mahoney firm. Their clientele are different. Mahoney has a small, stable group of clients with enormous loyalty to the firm, clients who respect what the firm stands for as well as the quality of service they receive from the firm. Although I did not speak with McKinnon clients, the impression given by McKinnon lawyers is that its clients are hard-driving,

---

6. For a short summary, see Freund 1985, 301, 305.

aggressive businesspeople who want hard-driving, aggressive lawyering to put together complicated deals, financings, security offer-
ings, and the like at a breakneck pace.

The fundamental differences between these two firms are great
but are less a function of size and clientele than of the social construction of the organizations. Here we may find some useful contrasts
in the art of building a law firm.

Mahoney and McKinnon engage in not altogether dissimilar,
largely transactional work serving profit-making or nonprofit organizations of considerable size and complexity. Both practices clearly
put a high premium on being financially viable and profitable, and
both can be said to be successful, particularly as a result of their
strong client orientation. They have grown and thrived largely as a
result of the effective service they provide their clients. Both are strong
organizations. The people who work in them are pleased with the
dynamic character of their firms. Both can point to what might be
called cultures that sustain the firm, give the firm a distinctive quality
that is a resource in coping with the challenges facing it.

One striking characteristic of both firms is the pride expressed
by their lawyers, their sense of the firm's special character, the feeling
that they are a community that expresses certain values. This sense
of cohesiveness is a function of what Philip Selznick calls *institutionalization*, a process that occurs over time and reflects the distinctive history of the organization, its people and their vested
interests, and the way the organization adapts to its environment
(Selznick 1957, 16). The organization's responses to internal and external pressures gradually "crystallize into patterns" that emerge as a
"social structure," according to Selznick, and "[t]he more fully developed its social structure, the more the organization will become valued for itself, not as a tool but as an institutional fulfillment of group
integrity and aspirations" (1957, 16). Thus in the case of both Mahoney and McKinnon, the organization becomes institutionalized, or
"infused with value" that has a special double effect. On the one
hand, the sense of common values creates "resources of energy" that
increase day-to-day effort, and may be summoned in times of crisis
or threat. On the other hand, the sense of identity or character that
these values foster limits the organization, binds it to certain aims,
procedures, and irreversible commitments, and makes it resistant to
certain forms of change (Selznick 1957, 17–19, 39–40).

The successful institutionalization or infusion of value that transforms a law-practice organization into a cohesive force with a character of its own occurs by building purpose into the social structure
of the organization. In this way the policies of the leadership of the
firm attain depth and support throughout the organization (Selznick
1957, 90). Mahoney and McKinnon have successfully assembled the
elements of local organizational structure that support the firms' policies and values.

McKinnon, for example, recognizes that interest groups[7] are not
entirely controllable and represent sources of energy for the firm.
The Michaels and Todd group, which socially did not fit the firm,
was integrated into the firm's "collection-of-boutiques" structure.
McKinnon provided support for the growth of their practice, and
Michaels and Todd generated business for the larger firm, primarily
as a result of its needs for tax and corporate expertise. McKinnon
encourages the creation of internal interest groups, even though some
of the Michaels and Todd environmental work duplicates the activities
and expertise of people in the corporate department. The conditions
the firm sets for this grant of departmental freedom is profitability.
As long as Michaels and Todd makes an appropriate contribution to
the profitability of the firm as a whole, it is free to operate as its
own boutique in the department store of the firm.

Mahoney, roughly the size of the Michaels and Todd boutique,
does not have, nor would it tolerate, separate internal interest groups.
The division of labor into the health care or real estate teams are
the only exceptions to the conscious attempt to break down divisions
so that everyone in the firm has some knowledge of the various
clients of the firm.

Mahoney makes major efforts to undermine any sense of rank
or social stratification. Lawyers and staff are accountable for their
treatment of each other; lawyers have offices of identical size; perks
are distributed in egalitarian fashion; lawyers and support staff social-
ize with each other.

McKinnon pursues the opposite policy: it plays up rank as an
important element in the value system of the firm. At McKinnon
rank is a function of compensation. Relations between support staff
and lawyers, particularly with the most powerful twenty or thirty

---

7. For more on interest groups see Selznick 1957, 93–96.

lawyers who are the oligarchy of the firm and wield the most power, are hierarchical and, at times, tension filled. Office size and location and positions on important committees are important emblems of status, so much so that negotiations on these matters threatened at one time to undermine the merger with O'Connor, Markham, and Flynn, which, in all other respects, was an extraordinarily attractive social and business combination.

The hierarchical structure of McKinnon is useful in other important respects: it limits the group of people with whom the leadership must communicate, that is, the people they must engage to participate in major decisions such as distribution of profits, major mergers, and the like. While committees at McKinnon have relatively broad participation by partners, this effort to attract the allegiance of partners by giving them decision-making roles in a variety of policy areas such as retirement plans, business development, training of associates, and recruitment does not obscure the clear understanding in the firm that the people chiefly responsible for the clients by and large run the business. Interviews with partners about the subject of compensation each year no doubt vary greatly, depending on whether the leadership is trying to negotiate consensus among owner-partners or communicating with employee-partners. Without a clear sense by the partnership, based on economic data to which all partners have access, of who are the owner-partners and whose decisions carry the most weight, annual compensation and other major decisions at McKinnon would be virtually unmanageable.

Another important function of hierarchy at McKinnon is that its dominant role is carefully limited to business values, the core values of the enterprise. Pluralism of viewpoint on other issues, such as departmental training of associates, professional and pro bono commitments, political commitments, and office organization are tolerated and welcomed.[8] Hierarchical controls are deliberately confined to a number of crucial issues in order to foster freedom of expression. This is a self-conscious decision by the leaders about the most effective way to manage a law firm. As Abe Fox puts it, a balance is achieved between a business that motivates and satisfies most people and a professional atmosphere of open interaction among people who are, by and large, resistant to change.

8. Of course, once authoritative decisions are made by the firm on a number of these issues, dissent is less welcome.

The reward systems of the two firms dramatically underscore the different uses of social stratification. McKinnon rewards lawyers for their contribution to the firm in terms of the billings and profitability of their individual work and those of partners and associates who work for them, as well as the business they attract to the practice. A substantial percentage of the annual compensation of individuals in the firm comes from lawyers' direct contribution to profits during the year. Information necessary to evaluate the fairness of compensation is available to every partner. Status is an open and fast-changing book at McKinnon. Mahoney, on the other hand, does not reveal individual lawyer billing or profitability information to its partners and distributes bonuses at the end of the year in an equal amount to every partner. Mahoney structures its compensation in a lockstep manner: compensation depends on seniority.

The intense loyalty that Mahoney generates from its lawyers is, in part, a function of the way it spreads the profits of the firm. The annual compensation of its most senior people are less than twice the amount of its most junior partners, and less than five times what the incoming associate earns. At McKinnon, comparable ratios are close to five to one for partners and thirteen to one for new associates. Ownership at McKinnon means taking substantial profits from the enterprise, commensurate with the partner's economic contribution to the enterprise. Ownership at Mahoney is something akin to holding a trust for the group of people who practice in the firm. In effect, the leadership at Mahoney chooses to contribute to the financial well-being of their colleagues and the stability of the enterprise by investing profits in the firm they might otherwise take out of it.

For Mahoney, moderating the income of the senior people is an important example of loyalty to the organization and commitment to an egalitarian ethos, while at McKinnon increasing the partnership income of the senior people is an incentive for the other partners, a goal, an aspirational level of compensation, an important attraction to lateral hires impressed with the compensation scale of McKinnon.

Community commitments of the two firms are markedly different. Mahoney is deeply engaged in a wide range of public-service activities, and McKinnon is by and large oblivious to such activities, unless they are part of the expectations of being a major firm in their community. McKinnon will contribute to pro bono activities when not to do so would be an embarrassment to their major-firm stature.

McKinnon is in no way hypocritical about its public-service orientation or philanthropic spirit: it does not pretend that this is an important part of its firm culture or a function of the enterprise. It is a business serving other businesses. It does not partake of the pretensions of a number of large firms of doing public service.[9]

Mahoney spends an extravagant amount of time promoting fellowship, camaraderie, understanding of the firm's clients, the ambitions of the firm, and the special character of the institution. McKinnon's internal dialogue is quite different: it considers itself successful because people feel free to talk, to express their complaints and concerns. There is no false idealism at McKinnon. Everyone at McKinnon has a clear understanding that the nature of the firm is to make money by serving clients well and to pursue such rapid growth as is economically prudent in order to remain competitive with other large firms.

Leadership at McKinnon charts the growth of the institution, maintains its financial viability, and structures the institution so that people feel a sense of loyalty, while providing a substantial return for the owners of the firm. The leadership at Mahoney appears to be less interested in immediate financial return than in building an institution that, although profitable for its participants, makes a difference with the clients they serve, enriches the lives of the people who work in the firm, and makes a substantial contribution to the betterment of the community.

Totally different conceptions of the nature of the profession obtain at the two firms. Service is the watchword at each firm, but the kind of client-advising services that lead to control of the client at McKinnon—that gives the senior lawyers their stake in the partnership profits and their power and authority within the firm—are invested by the Mahoney senior people in the organization and in inculcating in the younger people in the organization the same kind of client-fathoming, client-advising orientation.

McKinnon is, of course, a much larger and more profitable operation than Mahoney. It is located in a more dynamic corporate community. Its 1992 gross revenues were over twenty times the gross revenues of Mahoney. McKinnon generated about $85,000 more gross

---

9. In the 1991 ranking of America's largest law firms, McKinnon did not receive a good rating in the relatively crude designations of firm pro bono activity devised by the *American Lawyer* ("The AM Law 100" 1991).

revenue per lawyer than Mahoney did. Profits per partner, however, were a much different story: McKinnon generated over twice the profit per partner. Partnership profits are a high priority at McKinnon, which maintains a much higher leverage or ratio of total lawyers to partners in the firm.[10] The average number of billable hours worked by partners and associates is higher at McKinnon. In all likelihood, the rates per hour of lawyers at McKinnon are also somewhat higher, if only because McKinnon does more premium or high-compensation work in securities law and financial deal making.

The assumption about human nature of McKinnon's leaders is that money is the fundamental motivator, and that the major engine of growth for an organization committed to growth is the basic incentive of individual compensation pegged to the ability of the lawyer to attract and service clients. All these assumptions and incentive systems are reversed at Mahoney. Clients are the clients of the firm, not of individuals within the firm. Junior people are taught to service and bill, that is, develop a responsible relationship with a client as soon as possible. At McKinnon a much more hierarchical structure obtains in which senior people remain the responsible billing partners. The effective owners of McKinnon are not the partners, but the leadership group of twenty or so major billing partners. At Mahoney, there is a deliberate effort by the leader of the firm to inculcate a sense of ownership throughout the partnership and the ranks of associates, paralegals, and secretarial staff. The Mahoney leadership deliberately undermines a sense of hierarchy to convince everyone in the firm that everyone is an owner.

If ownership of the firm and the clients belongs to the entire Mahoney community, that community expresses certain values and requires a certain loyalty. Loyalty entails respect and decent treatment for its members as well as enjoyment of and caring and support for colleagues. Loyalty includes a strong commitment to public and community service. The community comes first at Mahoney. Unlike McKinnon, it is not a group of individuals who find the inconvenience of practicing together improves an individual's financial return. Mahoney is, rather, a group of individuals transformed in some way by

---

10. The larger the number of salaried lawyers billing in excess of their compensation and overhead costs, the higher the profits for the owners (partners) of the enterprise. New York City traditionally is the home of the most highly leveraged and profitable law firms in the United States.

their membership into a community that strongly expresses values about practice, the profession, and civic life. Being a Mahoney lawyer is to be a lawyer with a certain set of values, a far more formidable array of commitments and constraints than at McKinnon.

Recruitment is symbolic of the differences between the two firms. Mahoney invests hundreds of hours in each decision to hire a new associate or a lateral lawyer. McKinnon takes on scores of new associates each year and has generated most of its growth by laterally hired lawyers in specialty practices with existing clientele who create some synergy with McKinnon's clients and range of specialty practices. Mahoney's recruiting is values driven, McKinnon's driven by the numbers.

Because Mahoney recruits with such extreme care, it is relatively rare that an associate does not emerge as a partner. Hiring is almost an institutional commitment to make things work out. McKinnon, on the other hand, hires large numbers of associates who do not work out—indeed, there is some sense in McKinnon that the odds are increasingly against associate success, because the firm is unable to attract associates of a quality comparable to the owners of the firm. The preferred route to growth at McKinnon has been through lateral hiring of partners who bring clients, experienced associates, and expertise to the firm. Partnership criteria at the two places are markedly different: at McKinnon, it is a determination of whether the firm is adding a substantial profit center and a potential for growth. At Mahoney, the assessment includes quality of work and the servicing of clients, as well as loyalty to the values of the organization.

The differing perspectives on growth capture important differences between the firms. For Mahoney, growth is a necessity that amounts to a significant challenge to the values of the organization— a phenomenon that lurks like an adversary to their way of life. For McKinnon, growth is the savior, the engine of success, the ticket to the big leagues, the creative means of outdoing the firm's competitors.

McKinnon is a calculated risk taker, Mahoney extraordinarily conservative. No aspect of either firm underscores this difference more than their debt. Receivables—the amount of money owed by clients to the firm—are a major problem at McKinnon, and virtually negligible at Mahoney. Although I was not privy to the outstanding debt at McKinnon, the high growth trajectory of the firm has certainly led to the creation of a substantial debt structure. Financing new office space and state-of-the-art automation, carrying newly acquired firms until their billings and synergy pays off, and the substantial scale of their receivables require the borrowing of short-term capital. Mahoney, on the other hand, has self-funded most of its expansion through accumulated partnership capital and is rapidly reducing debt for its new offices. Mahoney's total debt payments scheduled for 1993 were $100,000 (against gross income in 1992 of about $5.5 million).

Mahoney and McKinnon can be seen as characteristic of two types of organizational styles in contemporary law practice: the tight, homogeneous organization (Mahoney) and the loose, heterogeneous organization (McKinnon). The Mahoney, tight style is found in a variety of personal service industry firms as well as in corporation organizations. David Maister calls these organizations *one-firm* firms and describes their characteristics: strong emphasis on loyalty, a cooperative approach that encourages teamwork and conformity and de-emphasizes stardom; a strong work ethic; a sense of special mission of serving clients; open communication that is used for "bonding"; the absence of status differences; consensus-style governance; controlled growth; a relatively homogeneous client base; and huge investments in recruiting talent carefully and "growing their own" professionals (Maister 1985; Swaine 1946, 1–12).

The loose organizational style of McKinnon is, in many respects, the opposite of one-firm values. Priority is given to acquiring proven talent over growing it in the firm's own culture. A social Darwinist approach prevails in attracting substantial numbers of lateral and entry-level talent, with the clear understanding that recruits will be jettisoned if they do not prove themselves capable of enhancing the profitability of the firm. The firm promotes rather than controls growth. Consensus governance occurs only among the real owners of the firm, namely the lawyers responsible for major clients who have highest status in the firm. And the encouragement and reward of stardom is a means of attracting clients to the firm. The loose organization promotes teamwork more as a means to achieve profitability than as a value in itself.

Loyalty, the work ethic, and a client-serving ethos are indeed values at McKinnon but are more functions of economic self-interest than inherent goods for which the enterprise stands. These values seem more enforced than reinforced by the compensation and retirement systems of the firm. Even the extraordinary communication style within McKinnon, which plays a crucial role in sustaining the firm's sense of community, has a strongly instrumental aroma about it. Without it, the newly acquired lawyers with practices important to the firm would not feel they have access to governance and decision making. Openness is crucial to the successful record of the firm in managing disparate practice groups, coping with inevitable conflict, and identifying quickly sources of discontent that need the attention of management.

If the process of helping an organization develop a character or identity is that of "infusing it with value" (Selznick 1957, 17–19), the Mahoney and McKinnon leaderships are talented and thoughtful organization builders. McKinnon's leadership wrestles with a difficult balance between assuring the commitment of independent professionals and running a business bent on high growth in a competitive market for clients. The primary values articulated by the firm are an open environment for decision making and business success, defined in terms of compensation for its professionals in the short run and the long-term prosperity of the enterprise. An environment that fosters intense client loyalty and a strong work ethic is the corollary to these fundamental commitments.

Mahoney values do not exclude an interest in strong financial performance and long-term plans for the economic well-being of the firm, but these appear to have equal status with the positive, if not redemptive, value of colleagueship and a supportive work environment, and the crucial professional importance of an ethos of service— not only to clients but to the larger community. Mahoney's is a larger basket of values and commitments than McKinnon's. Many, if not most, law firms at least articulate and in some ways support these other values. But Mahoney is unusual in the relentlessness with which the practice goes about reinforcing noneconomic values. These values are as dominant in the social structure of Mahoney as the compensation structure is at McKinnon. They are built into the character of the firm, which is infused with, or embodies, these values.

Which type of organization—the tight Mahoney style or the loose McKinnon style—is better able to withstand the centrifugal forces of an intensely competitive marketplace for talented lawyers in the 1990s? This is a central question for people thinking about the organization of large firms. What does a firm offer that prevents a lawyer, who could earn more elsewhere, from leaving or disrupting the firm by demanding more compensation? What motivates lawyers in organizations to work hard for the firm, to avoid coasting and not contributing to the firm?

The case for the superiority of the tight firm would focus on the wider range of values characteristic of a firm like Mahoney. At McKinnon, all the eggs are in one basket, the economic success of the firm and the ability to achieve consensus on a fair distribution of the fruits of success to individual lawyers. Mahoney's portfolio of values suggests it is likely to be more resilient than McKinnon to threats to its integrity and well-being.[11] In other words, if one may ask of any professional organization, "What is the glue that holds the organization together and keeps it functioning well?" Mahoney has more glue, more lines of allegiance that bind the lawyers together, a wider range of connections that will sustain the group, should one of the elements weaken. In contrast, one series of business misjudgments by the leadership of McKinnon, or some financial bad luck of a few major clients, or a recession, might leave McKinnon vulnerable to disintegration. Mahoney may be more likely to weather bad years (in business terms) because business success is only one element of the loyalty and commitment of its personnel.

The case for the loose firm turns on the advantages of money as the medium of agreement among partners. Obtaining agreement on nonmonetary values is complicated as a firm grows larger and takes on more diverse groups of lawyers. Money may be crude, but it has a brutal honesty about it; it bears no subtle or hidden strings or intimations of partiality,[12] an advantage particularly valued by some women and minorities who point out that they did not fare well under the traditional mixed-values dispensation of American law firms of which Mahoney can stand as a modern exemplar. Not only

---

11. See Gilson and Mnookin 1985, 313, 321–29. Gilson and Mnookin use portfolio theory, an economic model relating to the pricing and management of securities investments to explain the disadvantages, in terms of an undiversified investment strategy, of lawyers practicing outside a diversified portfolio of human capital in a large corporate firm. My use of *portfolio* suggests more a set of consumption, not investment, values (Gilson and Mnookin 1985, 324, n. 22) that serve to bind the law firm together and address the agency theory problems that worry Gilson and Mnookin, such as grabbing, leaving, and shirking. Clients, of course, are the ultimate consumption value that binds lawyers together in law firms.

12. The argument in this paragraph is drawn from Galanter and Palay 1991, 128–29 n. 10.

are there different constituencies for different "goods" (such as leisure time, pro bono service, child-rearing time), but these goods are incommensurate:[13] there will be unresolvable arguments about how to value them against each other, how to measure their worth. Monetary compensation, on the other hand, is relatively high on every lawyer's list of desirable values because it is easy to measure and consensus among partners is likely for using it as the measure.

McKinnon's emphasis on the bottom line and openness about virtually all other issues illustrates the strengths of the loose firm. The McKinnon approach is particularly responsive to the threat of lateral hiring, now commonplace in the world of the large corporate law firm. In a mixed compensation firm, the people who rank money at the top of their list are particularly vulnerable to raiding (or tempted to leave) because their monetary compensation is reduced by the other goods partners are taking from the firm, and they can be attracted to organizations that focus all rewards on monetary compensation. Indeed, McKinnon has exploited this vulnerability in other firms in the course of building the firm through relentless raiding of talent from other practices. Even if the money-ranks-number-one people are in the minority, the money-ranks-lower people will want to protect them because they realize that a mixed rewards scheme invariably makes everyone less mobile. And there is always the odor of distrust, the nagging concern that a mixed-rewards firm, whose lawyers would have difficulty finding the same mix elsewhere, and therefore in some degree are stuck where they are, may be tempted to take advantage of its people.

Mahoney and larger one-firm firms have tried to develop ways to solve these problems. These are not leisure-time or alternative-lifestyle firms. The work ethic, indeed a rather relentless work ethic, predominates and helps make coherent and commensurate the "other goods" valued by the firm, all of which have strong community significance. The general understanding is that the time the firm finances for pro bono work, civic activities, politics, and family responsibilities are values everyone in the practice respects. They are a form of giving that fits the firm's service ethic. They have a kind of social equivalence in the Mahoney scheme of things. Substantial time playing squash and writing poetry do not.

13. For an extended discussion of the importance of incommensurability, see Pildes 1992.

The Mahoney style, or one-firm firm, has a special way of perceiving and handling clients that builds cohesion. Law firms are not simply assembled by lawyers. Firms grow and structure themselves as a response to clients, current or potential. But for the one-firm firm, the quality of the client, the interest and diversity and challenge of the work the client represents, is a fundamental building block or premise of organization. There is a kind of bonding that goes on between such firms and their clients, a cultivation of an intense loyalty of firm to client. Lawyers deem it a privilege to serve these clients; only through the mechanism of the firm could lawyers have access to clients of this size and quality. It is as if both the client and the law firm were carefully chosen by and for each other. Thus clients are treated systematically as clients *of the firm,* and responsibility for the client is dispersed throughout the firm regardless of seniority, not lodged in an individual lawyer or responsible or billing partner who gets billing credits for bringing in or maintaining the client. A Mahoney lawyer has no clients, or portables, he or she can take to another firm.

Finally, Mahoney and other tight-style firms make an enormous investment in management, by which I mean concerted and broad-based efforts to sponsor firm wide conversations about the directions of the institution, its special character, and actions appropriate to this character. Management is seen less as a burden in such firms as an opportunity to grow as a group. The pervasiveness of this management style puts pressure on the lawyers and staff to treat one another with courtesy and respect, and to work hard for clients and the community and the good of the firm, all of which are part of the firm's character. Schultz derisively refers to the "Holy Grail" firms, a shorthand reference to the arrogance of the large firm. But the secret to the Mahoney style is the conviction among its lawyers that the real Holy Grail resides in a firm (like theirs) that embodies the professional ideal. It is through the firm, with the challenges and opportunities and social interactions it offers, that a lawyer can find genuine fulfillment in service to others.

Tight and loose-style firms have different vulnerabilities. The McKinnon style is highly dependent on the fortunes of its major clients and its major business-generating lawyers, who are susceptible to leaving the way they arrived, laterally. The firm's long-term strategy is to diversify by region and substantive specialty in order to modulate volatility in their income. Negotiations over partnership distribution of income will remain the toughest management function that determines the cohesiveness of the enterprise. The economics of the Mahoney-style firm may be dependent on a kind of bonding with the client that appears to be on the decline in a world of clients seeking a variety of individual cutting-edge specialists and taking advantage of fierce competition within the legal profession. Another vulnerability turns on its capacity to sustain high-quality leadership. The multiple arenas of life in the firm that need vigilance and thoughtful planning put heavier demands on management. A few misjudgments by Mahoney with respect to lateral hires, or policies to cope with the demands of larger size, or support of a pro bono cause that turns out to be highly controversial inside the firm, could seriously upset the equilibrium of the institution.

McKinnon and Mahoney represent two profoundly different approaches to building a law firm, or defining professionalism. Their leaderships stand for deeply contrasting systems of value, but they are alike in two respects: they have a clear idea of their understanding of professionalism, and they have built organizations that effectively embody these meanings. Their commitment to their vision of the profession is not cosmetic. It is actualized in the structure of their organizations. They have created different legal professions.

Chapter 8

Thinking about the Story
of the Profession

What reflections do I draw from my experience as a traveler in several different law practices? Generalizing from this group of lawyers is a highly speculative venture. Lawyers who would let an itinerant academic write about them are not typical lawyers. They are confident that an observer will not find deep inconsistencies in their practice. And the evidence underscores how unusual, or nonrepresentative, some of these law practices are. The outside lawyers who dealt with the Legal Division of Standish Development stated it was exceptional in the universe of in-house corporate law departments. The Mahoney firm appears to be thriving as it defies the conventional wisdom of professional journalism that small general practice firms cannot survive in the competitive environment of the 1980s and 1990s. The practices described in this book are enormously varied in size, in clientele, and in their perspectives on the practice of law. Nevertheless, some themes emerge, refracted through the prism of these stories, that may contribute to a discussion of the contemporary practice of law.

Probably the least interesting generalizations from these stories concern the sociology of the profession. No doubt some details from the descriptions of these practices fit concepts about stratification and the relative prestige or status of lawyers, depending largely on the clients they keep (see, for example, Heinz and Laumann 1982). Marks and Feinberg generally represent individuals, while the other organizations deal by and large with corporate entities. The McKinnon firm fits the model developed in Robert Nelson's structural critique of the large corporate law firm as an organization in tension between its success as a business bureaucracy run by its client-controlling owners and its needs to engage the commitment of other members by appealing to their sense of professional pride and independence (Nelson 1988).

The stories capture something of the turbulence and extraordinary pace of change in the contemporary profession. Marks and Feinberg is struggling to keep afloat in the strong competitive tides that buffet small firms. The Mahoney firm and the Standish legal department see themselves almost as oases in a profession dominated by the dynamic but destructive and alienating values of large firms. McKinnon is engaged in systematic headhunting and mergers to enlarge and strengthen the organization in the challenging large-firm competitive environment. And the Maine legal department faces some of the same changes that the growth of in-house legal departments have generated for private practitioners, as the upgrading of the commissioners and the other divisions of the commission reduces them from generalists to more technical legal specialists.

Surely the stories in part 1 underscore the risks of any general theory of professionalism. Each organization described in these stories defines professionalism in its own terms. Any comprehensive definition of the meaning of being a professional generates immediate difficulties. Take, for example, Robert Nelson's choice of autonomy as a core idea of professionalism. The perception and, in important respects, the reality of autonomy may be strongest in the Standish organization, in which lawyers are literally the employees of the client they serve.[1] The larger Standish corporate environment fosters decision-making freedom in an organization that contrasts sharply with the extraordinary lack of autonomy of Angus Hawkins of the Butler corporate law firm.[2] Autonomy seems peculiarly ham-handed as a way to capture the contrasting ideals of professionalism in this story. A different concept of autonomy pervades the Mahoney firm, but it seems to have been transferred to, or subsumed in, an organizational ethos and set of constraints that some lawyers would find confining and view as limiting their autonomy. Mahoney chooses clients for the values that the law firm wants to express, clients who respect their independent judgment and their civic activism. Marks and Feinberg appear to conceive of rights vindication as the core

---

1. Perhaps this only reinforces Nelson's skepticism that the partnership is necessarily well suited to the delivery of professional services to large corporations.

2. I am assuming that Hawkins's actions can largely be accounted for by the fact that his value to the firm, his place and role in the practice, consisted more in racking up a substantial number of billable hours at a high hourly rate than serving the vital business interests of First Midwest National Bank.

meaning of professionalism. The lawyers in the Public Utilities Commission of Maine focus on the meaning of the public interest as the fundamental force that drives their professionalism.

The Standish and Mahoney stories are particularly subversive of a business-professional conflict thesis. Standish expresses many of the values touted as professional: the client's respect for the independent judgment of lawyers, the lawyers' deep immersion in the client's business so that thoughtful and broad-reaching counseling can occur, the encouragement of public service, and supportive and generally cordial relationships among the professionals. Yet Standish is not a law firm but a department in a business, a branch of a corporation, the goals of which are presumably to turn a handsome profit. Indeed, the Standish legal department itself is a rather sophisticated business operation that makes superb use of paralegals in creating a highly efficient lease-negotiation process.

Mahoney is even more damaging to any idea that professional values are necessarily opposed to business values. A case could be made that the real significance of the Mahoney story is the creation—from the financial chaos sown by its founder—of an extraordinarily successful business enterprise in a regional center. The firm generates revenues per lawyer that would not shame it on the latest list of the one hundred largest law firms. Its leaders, however, choose to invest in the people of the business and civic goodwill rather than to draw substantial profits from the business. This is a business that has all the earmarks of looking to the long term, carefully building its human resources, nurturing its client base, and creating a strong and sustainable firm-specific capital.[3] It has deliberately kept its debt structure low, and its negligible accounts receivables would be the envy of any law firm in the country. Mahoney lawyers could plausibly argue that a number of the big firms against which it competes are poorly managed businesses that do not cultivate sensitively their two greatest assets (clients and their own lawyers), take too much income for the owners out of the business, and carry too much debt instead of self-capitalizing.

Even if the concept of professionalism, or a simple business-profession dichotomy, is too murky to provide an accurate view of the contemporary practice of law, perhaps analyzing the nature of the

3. For an explanation of this concept and its importance, see Gilson and Mnookin 1985.

changes in the legal profession may prove fruitful. The last few decades unquestionably witnessed a substantial growth in the size and strength and specialization of the organizations in which professionals practice. A strong argument can be made that this corporatization, or increasing organizational rationality and bureaucratization, is transforming the nature of law practice.

Alasdair MacIntyre argues that this new rationality or strengthening of the institutions of practice is a "corrupting power" (1984, 81). MacIntyre comes to this conclusion after developing a provocative distinction to illustrate the contemporary viability of classical and medieval concepts of virtue. MacIntyre describes what he calls a "practice," a term of art meaning a coherent and complex cooperative human activity through which goods internal to the activity are realized in the course of trying to achieve excellence in the activity (1984, 175). To MacIntyre, piano playing, baseball, physics, sculpture, even raising a family, are practices. For the moment, let us assume law also is a practice.

The crucial distinction relating to a practice, in MacIntyre's view, is the difference between goods internal to the practice and goods external to the practice. Internal goods are the sense of satisfaction and excellence in performing the practice well that can only be identified and recognized in terms of the practice and through the experience of participating in the practice. To enter into a practice is to accept the authority of the standards of excellence and obedience to rules, to subject one's attitude, choices, preferences, and tastes to the standards of the practice, and to judge the inadequacy of one's performance by these standards. External goods are things like prestige, status, influence, and money, which may come from success in a practice but are also generated in other ways "by accidents of social circumstance" (81).

The achievement of internal goods is a good for the whole community that participates in the practice, while external goods are objects of competition in which there must be losers and winners. Certain virtues—MacIntyre names truthfulness, justice, and courage—are acquired qualities essential to achieving goods internal to a practice (1984, 178–79). Institutions, argues MacIntyre, are different from practices, and are "characteristically and necessarily concerned with external goods"—acquiring, structuring, and distributing goods like power and status and money. And practices cannot survive without being sustained by institutions:

> Indeed, so intimate is the relationship of practices to institutions—and consequently of the goods external to the goods internal to institutions—that institutions and practices characteristically form a single causal order in which the ideals and creativity of the practice are always vulnerable to the acquisitiveness of the institution, in which the cooperative care for common goods of the practice is always vulnerable to the competitiveness of the institution. In this context the essential function of the virtues is clear. Without them, without justice, courage and truthfulness, practices would not resist the corrupting power of institutions. . . . We should therefore expect that, if in a particular society the pursuit of external goods were to become dominant, the concept of the virtues might suffer first attrition and then perhaps something near total effacement. (1984, 181)

MacIntyre's view of institutions as representing the corrupting power of external goods leads him to adopt a grim view of contemporary culture, in which practices and the pursuit of internal goods have become only marginal activities.[4] Thus, MacIntyre can appropriately serve as official philosopher for the story of the decline of the profession, a man who details the corruption of the contemporary practice of law.

MacIntyre's Manichaean instincts tend to relegate external and internal goods into respective worlds of darkness and light, corruption and virtue. But why the contempt for external goods? These are, in MacIntyre's words, "characteristic objects of human desire, whose allocation is what gives point to the virtues of justice and generosity" (183). One problem with MacIntyre's distinction is that goods external to one practice are internal to others. Raising a family, a practice according to MacIntyre, includes providing for the family. Income or support or money, at least in moderate amounts, becomes

---

4. MacIntyre suggests much of modern life (presumably including law) "cannot be understood in terms of the nature of a practice with goods internal to itself" owing to the industrialization and bureaucratization of "institutionalized acquisitiveness" (1984, 211–12).

an internal good of this practice, along with other goods presumably internal to the institution of the family such as nurturing, guidance, and love. It is not clear why the practice of law and the leadership of organizations, which MacIntyre hints, correctly, are practices, should not, in similar fashion, have an internal good of "providing," or sustaining the economic base of the practice (181–82).

MacIntyre correctly identifies that the institutions pose significant threats to the practices they make possible if they neglect other goods of the practice for the pursuit of fame or the dollar—if they have an unbalanced portfolio of internal goods—just as we would judge harshly the parent who lavished financial support, but little affection and care, on the family (MacIntyre 1984, 274; Stocker 1990). Angus Hawkins's "churning" of the Standish Development account, for example, his practice of piling up unnecessary hours on a case in order to run up a bill, which both improves a lawyer's status in a practice and builds the overall profitability of the practice organization, is a contemporary, all too common case of business values undermining the internal good of the client-serving ethos of law practice. On the other hand, we cannot dismiss the business ethic of contemporary private practice as relentlessly corrupting without "a certain hypocrisy" (MacIntyre 1984, 183) or a fantasy-like "wistfulness . . . [for a] world in which external goods posed no temptations" (Stout 1990, 289). Money and prestige cannot be extricated from the history of the American legal profession.[5] How could it be otherwise in a culture where wealth is a factor in determining status, social position, and political power? The story of Marks and Feinberg illustrates the danger that neglect of the financial side poses to a practice focused almost exclusively on professional values and attention to excellence. Practices embedded in institutions (to use MacIntyre's phrase) are worlds of ambivalence, mixed motives, and inextricable connections between financial and other values, where income is often not easily sorted into the external or internal goods account.

---

5. See, for example, Gordon 1988, 2–6. Robert Gordon has assembled literally hundreds of statements by leading American lawyers who, for at least a century, argued that the profession was in decline due to its commercialism, its loss of independence from craven service to powerful clients. External goods have been with the profession of law since its inception. Gordon's current project is to argue the viability of one tradition in law in which the profession plays a conscious role in promoting the public good (Gordon 1990, 255), but he is too good a historian to fail to recognize countertraditions. For a critique of Gordon's project, see Osiel 1990, 2009, 2045–66.

The emergence in 1989–90 of nontotalitarian values in Eastern European societies after forty to seventy years of suppression is widely applauded in the West. But the fragility of democratic society in the East—expressed through open discussion, public responsibility through majority rule, and representative elective government—is in no small measure a function of the catastrophic decline in external goods and the weakness of independent traditions of institutions used to mediating the tensions between the allocation of external goods and the sustenance of goods internal to social practices. Social practices devoid of worldly goods are a chimera. Chess and violin playing, archetypes of MacIntyre's examples of "practices," do not capture the nuanced external-internal or mixed internal goods world of the client-responsive institutions of law or most other social practices.

Jeffrey Stout's thoughtful critique of MacIntyre calls for a more "stereoscopic" view that "brings social practices and institutions, and internal and external goods, into focus at the same time" (Stout 1990, 279) rather than limiting them to reductionist perspectives that tout only internal goods (the story of decline of the legal profession) or external goods (the story of gain and growth). Stout cites the example of "the kindly old physician who took himself to be pursuing only the health and comfort of his patients." We can approach the physician in a romanticizing mode that wishes away the realities of hospital politics and power struggles with colleagues, or we can reduce the story of this physician to that of a system moved by the levers of desire for status, money, or power (Stout 1990, 280–81). Making the physician's life intelligible requires "situating his actions within a network of social practices and institutions" that help account for the meaning the physician draws from the health and comfort of patients and the relationship with a spouse, as well as the physician's interest in fame and wealth and enough institutional power to influence the hospital. "To understand [the physician] well, we shall need a dramatic narrative," Stout argues, "replete with moral appraisals, a coherent interpretation of his . . . language, and a rendering of the mutual determination of character and circumstance." Stout continues:

Despite our concerns about their fallibility, the corruptions of prestige and wealth, and the facelessness of modern medical bureaucracies, we still pay tribute to the virtues and worth of medical practitioners. Few of them are saints, but most are more than technicians. Most of the cases they treat in our hospitals and clinics raise no serious moral problems for us. It would therefore be mean-spirited or grossly hyperbolic to deny that medical care survives in our day as a valued and valuable social practice with much of its authority intact.

Stout's more sympathetic stereoscopic view of the "kindly old physician" does not foreclose a critical perspective. It sustains a balanced view that accounts for the plurality of values that constitute a social practice like medicine or law (Stout 1990, 279–82).

Another approach to identifying the nature of the transformation of the legal profession is to turn from focusing on external goods, such as income and prestige, to an examination of organizational change. Sociologists, Nelson included, tend to correlate the efficiencies of bureaucratic organization with a business-oriented ethos of an organization. Many extraordinarily profitable law practices in the United States, particularly in personal-injury practice, are counter-examples; these are organizations that are both staunchly business oriented (i.e., highly oriented to making a profit) and highly disorganized. But let us assume that, for most practices and particularly the larger practice organizations serving larger corporate clients, bureaucratic forms of organization represent a rationalization of the institution that make it more efficient and effective in responding to the needs of its clients. W. Richard Scott has proposed two models to capture the essential characteristics of bureaucracies and professions and to highlight the tensions and differences between them within organizations (Scott 1966, 265–75). The professional approach is to instill in each worker all the basic work skills and norms that will govern performance in an effort to have the worker internalize controls; the bureaucratic approach is to divide the task into constituent activities and among different workers, establish a system of rules for the work, and create supervisors to coordinate the workers and the work (Scott 1966, 267).

All three organizations that service corporate clients—Standish, Mahoney, and McKinnon—can be described with some fairness as bureaucratized. Each has adopted budget and financial accountability disciplines serviced by computer and accounting professionals who report to the organization's leadership.[6] Each has a leadership-responsive

---

6. Standish no doubt uses resources generally available within the company.

bureaucracy that manages support staff, although McKinnon's size involves the firm in a more extensive range of activities (through staff or consultants) such as management of the library, duplicating, messenger services, catering, internal communications, automation and telecommunications, marketing, and headhunting. McKinnon's bureaucracy is highly valued by the Michaels and Todd lawyers who came from a firm with an undernourished support structure.

More revealing of the extent of bureaucratization are certain flash points, or what Scott identifies as classic areas of conflict that can arise between professionals and bureaucracies. Three of these areas of conflict are resistance to bureaucratic rules, resistance to bureaucratic supervision, and conditional loyalty to the organization. McKinnon, by far the largest and most departmentalized of the three organizations, experiences considerable professional tension with bureaucratic rules and displays more conditional loyalty, since loyalty is largely dependent on the compensation structure. But supervision, a realm in which power in the organization (the client relationship) is most clearly expressed and respected, generates virtually no systematic tension at McKinnon. Mahoney, the least departmentalized, experiences almost no tension with respect to rules and supervision but is able to attract an unconditional loyalty that might be viewed as more typical of bureaucracies. Standish stands midway between these two poles.

What conclusions can be drawn in terms of the relative bureaucratization of these organizations? Scott cautions that these tensions can be sharply reduced in cases where the organizations are controlled by professionals, so perhaps this factor leads to idiosyncratic results.[7] But it is no less plausible that use of the bureaucratic-professional distinction and equating bureaucratization with the business ethos is not a particularly useful mode of analysis.[8] Mahoney may be the least bureaucratic, but in important respects it is the most tightly managed, the most controlled and controlling, of all three organizations. But the mechanisms of control at Mahoney are not imposed from above so much as through collaborative self-imposition. The internalized controls that sociologists claim as characteristic of professionals

---

7. Scott was not analyzing professional organizations as such but bureaucratic organizations that employ professionals. His principles seem to apply to professional organizations (1966, 275).

8. See similar doubts by Celia Davies (cited in Sterett 1990, 381).

have been given organization status: lawyers identify the organization as the instantiation of the professional ideal. They have created—indeed, they are always in the process of working out the meaning of—the profession and submit willingly to the controls of the professional idea.

Robert Rosen has pointed out the similar orientation of professionalism and bureaucratization in terms of concern with rationality, affective neutrality, achievement, and focus on means displacing ends (Rosen 1984, 47). Perhaps this conceptual affinity leads to the remarkable degree of assimilation and variation of bureaucratic operating methods in law-practice organizations, often under the rubric of increased professionalism. Paul Cravath, who as much as any man can be said to have invented the modern law firm, developed a system of dividing associates' work into small manageable units that were strictly supervised. The system was designed for recent law graduates to develop a loyalty to the firm, rather than the broader professional community. The route to becoming partner at Cravath required a lengthy apprenticeship training of markedly bureaucratic cast (Swaine 1946, 4–6).[9] More recent organizational models idealized from the Japanese experience seem to professionalize (at least in Richard Scott's terms) traditional bureaucracies like manufacturing organizations. The variety of adaptions of both the bureaucratic and professional models in contemporary business suggest these are not helpful analytic categories for identifying business values or peculiarly business-oriented organizations in the practice of law.

Another way of analyzing the contemporary legal profession is to begin by assuming that the profession is a business, that the sharp rise in lawyers' incomes and organizations' orientations toward profits in the past decade has made the legal profession more businesslike. What is the significance or meaning of such changes?

If we draw an analogy between the law business and business in general, a striking feature of the current dialogue in the legal profession about the decline of profession and the rise of business is how reminiscent it is of the setting, the dialogue, and the unease of the Progressive Era, an important chapter in the history of American business.

The late nineteenth and early years of the twentieth century in

---

9. I am indebted to Robert Post for bringing this implication of the Cravath system to my attention.

America, were, like the 1980s, prosperous years in terms of the growth in the material fabric of the United States. These years were also characterized by unhappiness with the nature of the changes in American culture, chiefly expressed by a diverse group of people generally labeled "Progressives," who sought to restore something of the values lost through the industrial transformation of America. Progressives were disturbed by the implications of an emerging industrial society that exploited labor, aggrandized the few, created numerous dangers and harms, corrupted the regulatory and legislative process, and undermined traditional concepts of personal responsibility. Progressives called on government to control the trusts, larger businesses and monopolies, and major concentrations of industrial power.

Lawyers played important roles in the leadership of Progressive forces, as well as the opposition to Progressivism by certain corporate interests.[10] By and large, however, the organization or structure of the legal profession escaped the forces that generated the Progressive debate.[11] Whether the independence of the profession was being compromised by representation of large corporate interests was vigorously debated, but the forms in which lawyers conducted their practices remained largely unchanged during the early decades and between-war years of the twentieth century.

More recently, the legal profession has undergone structural change, most notably in connection with the exponential growth in the size of practices and incomes of corporate lawyers practicing in large firms. The vocabulary of contemporary professionals concerned about the way in which organizational values have overwhelmed traditional modes of practice carries, at times, a Progressive aroma: concerns about the transformation of traditional values of individualism, the breakup of personal relations, the impersonalization and corporatization of America. It is as if it has taken roughly eighty years for the conflicts fought out in American society at large to reach the precincts of the professions. Ethical confusions of conceiving

---

10. For an account of how complex the various themes of Progressivism were within the legal profession, see Gordon 1984, 51–74.

11. One could argue with some justice that the invention of the American corporate law firm originated in the Progressive Era at the turn of the century, but the scale and growth and impersonalization of these enterprises was limited until the years after World War II, and the dynamic of growth in these firms—the modernism of their structure—has not, until quite recently, been recognized. See Galanter and Palay 1991, 747 and note 10 of chapter 1.

law in terms other than the individual lawyer-client relationship, anger over the pervasive symbols of accountability (red tape and bureaucracy), and discomfort caused by the new muckrakers of professional practice are Progressive in tone. Only the unusually powerful idea of professionalism associated with our cultural idol of individualism—and the strong market controls professions until recently exercised—have preserved the privileged position of the professions and kept larger cultural developments from overtaking the professions before the late 1970s and early 1980s.

The Progressive Era was, of course, far different from the current watershed in professional life. Lawyers telling the story of the decline of the profession have no tolerance for the Progressive call for government intervention. The Progressive sensibility among lawyers is more of a small back current or eddy: it does not resonate in a society that is far from Progressive in time and spirit. The strength of Progressivism was, in part, a product of the have-nots disturbed over the accumulation of wealth generated by industrialization. Lawyer-critics of the 1980s may share something of the same status as they complain about the gigantic incomes and sweatshop atmospheres of some of the largest corporate firms. But the unhappiness of large-firm senior lawyers tends to be muted by the extraordinary increase in their incomes generated by the business success of their organizations.

The metaphor of Progressivism offers a perspective—through examination of a similar but much larger-scale social phenomenon some eighty years earlier—that undermines the salience of conceiving the current transformation of the legal profession in terms of a struggle between professionalism and business values. American business in the Progressive Era and in subsequent decades developed into an extraordinarily heterogeneous set of institutions, with sharply differentiated degrees of bureaucratization, vertical and horizontal management structures, size, profitability, growth, internal harmony, ability to harness the creative energies of employees and managers, and community responsiveness.[12] A similar future is likely to occur in the legal

---

12. I am not arguing that Progressive themes disappeared. A plausible case could be made that a Progressive agenda has reemerged in the last few years in contemporary debates, sharpened by the Japanese record, about the relative advantages of participatory management, long-term rather than short-term perspectives on corporate success, and the responsibilities of boards of directors (when deciding whether to sell a company) to consider community and employee constituencies as well as the immediate gains of stockholders.

profession, which will continue to grow and change and differentiate itself as it responds to the needs and concerns of both clients and lawyers.

The spectacular growth and visibility of the corporate law firm may obscure an understanding of the significant strengthening of virtually all organizations of law practice in the United States during the past three decades. A lively market exists for continuing education programs dedicated to the development of more business controls and efficiencies in smaller organizations, as well as procedures to protect against the growing specter of malpractice liability. In-house corporate law departments, organizations providing legal services for the poor, solicitor and attorney offices in state and local government, prosecutors, and public defenders have grown substantially in numbers and in management sophistication.

The stories told here of five law practices underscore the importance of the organization, the pervasive interdependence fundamental to the contemporary practice of law. The lawyer one-on-one with a client (or an officer or employee of a client) remains a powerful and important relationship in the practice of law, but a lawyer acting alone in a matter of any consequence is an unusual event. Marks and Feinberg are incapable of undertaking their class action suit without joining with two other firms. Lawyers in the Maine Legal Division are dependent on colleagues, even in an environment bound by fears of ex parte communications, to work out the practical implications of the public interest. Lawyers in the McKinnon and Mahoney firms and Standish office are not simply reliant on the support structures of a law office; their clients, reputations, and the character of their approaches to practice are in large measure a function of their organizations.

Law-practice organizations are the landscape or context of the practice of law in the United States. It is a landscape of small communities or villages, a metaphor that captures something of the closeness and interdependency, the character-defining role of the contemporary practice organization. Professional success or failure—whether gauged in economic terms, clients served, style of practice, pursuit of excellence—turns on standards or conditions set by the practice organization. The organization affects not only the practice of the individual lawyer but also, increasingly, nonclient connections to the world outside the village, from charitable giving to the style of relationships with business and civic and professional communities. Robert Jackall uses another metaphor to describe the strength of being part of a village, something he calls "institutional logic":

> I mean the complicated, experientially constructed, and therefore contingent, set of rules, premiums, and sanctions that men and women in a particular context create and re-create in such a way that their behavior and accompanying perspective are to some extent regularized and predictable. Put succinctly, institutional logic is the way a particular social world works; of course, although individuals are participants in shaping the logic of institutions, they often experience that logic as an objective set of norms. (Jackall 1988, 112)[13]

These stories suggest that the concepts of profession and professional in the years to come will be set less by the organized bar than by the practice organization. Balkanization of the legal profession is already underway. House norms of the practice organization— the local village or town standards or institutional logic create a rich and diverse landscape of thousands of legal professions.

If we conceive of the current instability of the professional ideal as the tension between concepts of professionalism that cut horizontally across the entire spectrum of the profession and organizational values that draw lawyers together vertically within an institution, the most robust horizontal learning affecting lawyers in organizational settings these days is reinforcing the vertical axis. One of the most powerful new modes of professional education in the legal profession is new economics-of-law-practice learning that includes automating practice activities and routines, creating information systems that facilitate the analysis of costs and profitability, and implementing practice controls ranging from budgeting, to marketing, docketing, conflicts of interest, and communication systems. It is an open question whether the high decibel levels with which segments of the organized bar and judiciary call for renewal of professional ideals of public service will develop an equivalent salience.

Understanding this more polyglot, sometimes rather confusing,

---

13. Steven Winter's use of "situatedness" and "sedimentation" from Merleau-Ponty seems closely related to Jackall's concept of "logic" (1990, 1485–92).

legal profession may require new skills of reading or analysis for lawyers. The stories in this book offer clues or directions of how to approach understanding a village system, its internal logic, its local professional code.[14] Deciphering an organization requires answers to rather basic questions. What are its origins? How did it arrive where it is now? What is happening to it? Where is it going? To make sense of these questions, to create a coherent picture of the organization, we need to make the ultimate move to what Hayden White calls "a primary . . . form of human comprehension, an article in the constitution of common sense" (White 1981, 252; see also Taylor 1989, 47–52; MacIntyre 1984; Wollheim 1988; Stocker 1990), namely a narrative or story of the organization that ties things together, that permits people to fathom the meaning or judge the significance of the village of which they are a part, or plan to become a part.

What accounts for lawyers choosing one practice setting over another? The explanations probably range from sheer accident (tied to a perception that this is the best one can expect) to meticulous investigation and analysis of the practice. It is likely that most lawyers are attracted to practices in which other people have told them interesting stories about the practice and served as advocates who influence and mediate the lawyer's attitudes toward the practice. A danger in any world where marketing skills are at a premium is the possibility of the phony story. What makes a story credible or revealing enough to form the basis of a sound choice to join the organization? One initial response might be that any practice comfortable enough to tell stories about failures as well as successes is likely to be giving a plausible account of itself. A more systematic response would attempt to develop criteria of a complete or insightful narrative of a law-practice organization, an inventory of fundamental elements or story components. A rudimentary list of these basic elements should include

---

14. Since writing this section, I have discovered a remarkably similar approach taken by Burton R. Clark 1970. Clark describes his historical narratives of three colleges as an exploration of distinctive organization character through sagas or legends. He alludes to crucial factors of these sagas: leadership and organizational elements such as the belief and power in a personnel core (senior faculty), the program core of curriculum and teaching, the external social base, and the student subculture. The saga or common narrative of the organization generates an ideology that binds people to the institution as a community, focuses the organization's identity, and creates a resource and activity mission for everyone in the enterprise (Clark 1970, 6, 8, 9, 233–62). A summary of the book can be found in Clark 1972, 178.

the history of the organization, its economics, clients, style, its handling of conflict, and leadership. Let me exemplify the meaning of
these elements by referring to the stories in this book.

In both the Maine and Mahoney stories, the heroic dimensions
and values of the founder are the heart of the tradition, the starting
point of the firm and division. The business acumen and ambitions
of the founders and current leaders of McKinnon are the reference
point or frame that continues to inform all the firm's decisions. Similarly, Marks and Feinberg are still rooted in Alan's and Joel's early
origins in civil rights work. And difficult times for Standish Development in the early 1970s reinforces the recurrent budget message
to its legal division: stay lean. What is striking about the historical
context in each of these stories is the way it is used or reinterpreted
or extended by the organization. Most of these groups have experienced some tensions or conflict over the meaning of their tradition,
and the conversation or debate associated with this conflict appears
to strengthen the organization and extend the sense of a special
tradition.

The Ashton-Miller merger debate at McKinnon can be seen as
the rejection of a crude interpretation of the tradition of the firm,
namely that it has prospered and grown by acquiring significant
clients through merger with other law firms. The tradition was reinterpreted to a more sophisticated gloss: McKinnon has prospered by
being canny enough to avoid some of the obvious problems that
mergers have generated in a number of law firms. Ashton-Miller was
not a smart move, among other reasons, because it could disruptively
move into the upper levels of the partnership some client-controlling
lawyers who were not workers at a time when the firm was still
adjusting to other major mergers and the lower levels of the firm
were overtaxed. The Mahoney firm's rejection of its leader's efforts
to bring to the firm a major client-generating lawyer reinforced its
traditional commitment to organic growth that only responds to
existing clients and does not threaten the unique culture of the firm.
Standish's conflict over stock grants for lawyers, the Public Utility
Commission's attack on the leadership of Central Maine Power Company, and the agonizing of Alan Marks over initiating his power
lunches also stand as examples of an organization's redefining its sense
of the significant elements of its history and tradition.

Money is a major part of every one of these stories. The future of Marks and Feinberg is jeopardized by questions about their economic ability to sustain the practice. Joe Donahue must resourcefully create middle-level management and senior-attorney positions at the Public Utilities Commission in order to provide salary incentives for his more experienced lawyers. The law department is an extraordinarily cost-efficient investment for Standish Development Company, and compensation issues within the department raise acutely the extent to which the company values its lawyers. The financial success of Mahoney underwrites the structure and style of practice of the firm. And money is the motivating and organizing principle of McKinnon. Ambitions of individuals for levels of income in these stories are transformed into expectations on which the organization must deliver. The ways organizations generate and allocate these goods are major issues in at least three of the stories: Marks and Feinberg, Standish, and McKinnon. And, as one observer of Marks and Feinberg puts it, levels of ambition and expectation about money have risen, probably dramatically, in the last decade in the profession as a whole.

Clients—and the extraordinary value and satisfaction in serving clients—are another crucial component in the story of any practice organization. The stories of these law practices capture a striking sense of commitment to clients, a fact that should cause no surprise. These are stories of successful and effective lawyers. Of course, no lawyer is likely to describe cases of client disloyalty to an outsider. But the extraordinary client orientation of these practices appears to be authentic. The clients of Marks and Feinberg are largely people in trouble who need a champion, and these clients, by all accounts to which I had access, receive an extraordinary level of commitment and devotion. The Public Utility Commission lawyers are dedicated to serve the commission that employs them, but they can also be seen as dedicated civil servants in a quest for an imputed client who embodies the concept of the public interest. Both Mahoney and Standish lawyers in some sense *choose* their clients, have exceptionally close relationships with them, and consistently work to promote an ethos of client service. McKinnon's reputation is derived from aggressive and effective work for its business clients. The scale and entrepreneurial bent of the McKinnon enterprise may on occasion create some problems of substandard service, but all the evidence from McKinnon is consistent with a client-driven, client-supportive, effective service organization.

Is client orientation synonymous with client transparency, that is, the invisibility of lawyers as a force affecting clients? Do lawyers exercise any influence on their clients? In the five practices described here, not one lawyer described to me an incident in which he or she used legal or prudential arguments to convince a client to alter plans. Yet I would be hesitant to draw conclusions from this. I was not specifically looking for such incidents, although on occasion I questioned lawyers along these lines, and client-oriented lawyers (namely successful lawyers) are not likely to recall incidents unless they amount to a rare crisis in client relations. My suspicions are that much more alteration of the purposes of clients goes on in law than surfaces in surveys, at least among self-confident and successful lawyers and organizations that enjoy the confidence of their clients. The way Standish lawyers and clients talk about their work suggests that advice that modifies deals—legal and otherwise—is not uncommon in the conversations between project director and lawyer. Horace Libby often overmatched and outmaneuvered his commissioners to arrive at what he thought would be a better decision for the public, and his successors constantly aim to influence the commission, even though their advice is sometimes rejected. Some Mahoney clients use Schultz as a general advisor and strategist, something of a co-venturer, with obvious influence on the direction of their businesses. An outside lawyer recounted to me the story of attending a breakfast where the Buffalo archbishop responded to an introduction by Schultz by acknowledging that his lawyers sometimes helped the church take a more enlightened (i.e., ethical) course than they otherwise would have done.[15]

Another crucial part of the story of any organization is what might be termed its personality, its style, the way it conducts con-

---

15. In fairness to Robert Nelson, who devoted an entire chapter of *Partners with Power* to this question, I have no evidence from McKinnon, the one large corporate firm I have described, to dispute his conclusions that large-firm lawyers do not much change the plans of their corporate clients. McKinnon was the only practice that refused to put me in touch with clients. One could argue whether Nelson's survey results are as negative, or as suggestive, as he paints them. But it seems entirely plausible that the intense competition for corporate business in the large-law-firm market tends to drive the level of client-influencing behavior down to a floor approximating the line marking potential malpractice liability for the lawyer.

versations, the conditions (of respect? caring? indifference?) under which colleagues relate to each other. Style comprises modes of communication and refers to matters like inclusiveness (who are the conversationalists?), range of subjects (what, if anything, is out of bounds as a topic owing to its sensitivity or its nonbusiness character?), frequency (how often and how easy is it to get together? is someone responsible for making it happen?), and structure (how organized is communication? is it agenda items, or stories, or both?). The laid-back atmosphere and conversations about a wide range of topics in the Legal Division of the Public Utilities Commission and Marks and Feinberg are important values to the lawyers. The Marks firm spent money it could not afford to add a small kitchen schmooze area to its office, and the loss of such an area in the remodeling of the Maine Public Utilities Commission offices is keenly felt by the lawyers. Schultz is the master of organized communication and institutional storytelling in Mahoney. McGill's success in developing a strong and effective cadre of legal assistants at Standish is, in part, due to their sense of being included in the major conversations concerning the division and the company. He is less successful in his communicating with the lawyers whose relationships and conversations are more closely shaped by colleagues elsewhere in the company. The leaders of McKinnon have been exceptionally skilled at promoting an ethos of open conversation by a policy of listening to, and tolerance of, discordant views. This atmosphere is highly valued by the firm's lawyers, who would give it prominence as a factor in the success of the firm in responding to the challenges of newly merged practices.

Individuals gifted in decision making, and understanding of the stakes involved and the path to follow, are crucial to success of virtually all organizations. These stories reveal how vital leadership is to the life of every law-practice organization.[16] Leaders are people whose judgment about integrating or arranging or working out the competing values of law practice is respected by fellow lawyers. Marks and Feinberg's future will turn on the ability of Alan Marks to overcome his scruples about selling himself and his firm so that

---

16. I take leadership to be something altogether different than governance, although the two might coincide (as they do, for example, in Mahoney). Governance is the legitimation of authority to make certain decisions for the practice. Leadership is the ability to persuade, to show the way to making critical and correct moves in the ongoing narrative of the life to the organization.

he can generate business compatible with the basic values of the firm. The Mahoney firm is so completely a function of the thinking of its current leader that its lawyers (following the lead of the managing partner) have become acutely sensitive to the vital importance of broadening the base of leadership thinking and preparing for succession to the leadership. McKinnon's leadership is fundamentally responsible for its business success.

There is virtually no literature on leadership, this most crucial of functions in modern law practice—no book, no continuing education, no manuals or consultants for law-practice leadership.[17] How is leadership learned? Chiefly by example, of one's own mistakes and successes, and attentively listening to, or watching unfold, stories of other leaders making important decisions. A leader makes intelligible the connections between the actual and the possible by having (on the one hand) a deep understanding of the traditions, character, and inclinations of the members of the practice and (on the other) a sense of, or imagination for, alternate futures or appropriate goals for the practice.

Conflict plays a remarkably large role in all these stories, perhaps because it captures best for the storytellers the true character of their practice. The professional character of Alan Marks and Joel Feinberg is defined in important respects by their great cases, their battles on behalf of individuals through the legal system. Two of the stories cast large law firms in the role of villains: Standish and Butler struggling over the control of fees to the company, and Mahoney engaged in ongoing efforts to keep their clients from migrating to large firms. McKinnon lawyers are proud of the way their leadership encourages the expression of internal conflict. It is hard to imagine any law practice organization that does not clash with other lawyers or experience internal conflict. But many law practices stifle or conceal these stories. Most of the organizations described here celebrate their conflicts and make parables of their successes and failures as a means of defining the character of the organization. The accuracy of the stories told in a practice, the extent to which important stories are not suppressed, is an important indicator of the character and health of the organization.

I have mentioned some basic elements—history, money, clients,

---

17. Dietel 1992 and Greene 1990 require no caveat to this generalization.

style, leadership, and conflict—that are likely to be present in any coherent narrative of a law practice, by which I mean any rudimentary understanding of the course, character, and predicted future of an organization. If I had to name a single theme of these stories— and any story by which we can assess the practice organization as a microprofession—it is the quest for organizational integrity.

Each of the narrative elements I have described involves the potential for tensions and trade-offs: the pleasures of informality in social relationships with colleagues and clients versus the need for more formal organization to service larger, more complicated, and more demanding clients. Or the income needs of lawyers versus their desires for a certain style or type of practice. Or leadership pressing a direction for the practice versus the commitment to respect dissenting views. These are normal pressures in the practice of law that inevitably require a series of accommodations for the practice to thrive. Choices invariably involve subordinating the goals or ambitions of some for the sake of the collectivity—a working out of differences to determine the course of the practice. It is not possible for a practice to let all do precisely what they want. Decisions must be made, directions must be set. This is what is meant by organizational integrity, and it resembles closely the core meaning of personal or individual integrity. Here, for example, is a recent exposition of the meaning of integrity:

> [I]t is . . . important to discover which way of life is most likely to preserve a relation of fellow-feeling or friendship, as Aristotle calls it, among the different parts of one's own self, some of which must necessarily be subordinated for the sake of others. A person whose soul has, in Aristotle's phrase, "friendly feelings" toward itself, a person whose parts are not openly at war or engaged in subtler contests of repression and revenge, possesses a quality of wholeness that is best described by the simple term "integrity." (Kronman 1987, 854–55)

Can there be a sense of wholeness or friendship or fellow feeling among the different parts and people of a law practice? For many lawyers, experience at a school or college or law school captures the idea of belonging to an institution, or having a commitment or institutional self-image that transcends using the school to obtain a degree.

There is an extra value, a source of personal satisfaction, associated with being part of the institution. When a law practice has established an identity, through a history of responding to the world, and an internal structure and a sense of itself, it develops character. And maintaining the character, of an individual or an institution, is an exercise, often difficult, of preserving integrity (Selznick 1957, 17, 38–41).[18]

All the practices described in part 1 share an important attribute: they have a relatively clear sense of who they are, what are their goals as an organization, and the set of values that inform how they act. We can call this their concept of professionalism. Even Marks and Feinberg, who are experiencing conflict about adapting to the necessities of marketing, have an idea of the practice they wish to preserve, and their main concerns appear to be how to avoid letting marketing undermine their goal of cause lawyering. Many contemporary law practices are disoriented, primarily as a result of buying into competitive business methods and techniques of managing the practice without serious examination of the goals of practice that are important to the members. They have adopted business techniques of practice rather than adapted these means to serve the objectives of their practice. As a result of the incorporation of state-of-the-art billing or accounting, or compensation structures, they have failed to anticipate, understand, or care about the impact of these measures on their character structure, integrity, and the aspirations of their organization.

Organizations can thus be said to have an identity, a character, and value that affects the distinctive outlook, habits, and other commitments of organizational life (Selznick 1957, 40). Each organization described in part 1 faces challenges to its character and commitments in which the values and directions of the organization are at stake: Marks and Feinberg grapple with the survival of their style of lawyering in a fiercely competitive world; the legal department of the Maine Public Utilities Commission faces rival champions of the public interest in their own agency and in the public advocate; the Standish Legal Division struggles to devise a compensation structure com-

---

18. Selznick comments that few aspects of the study of organizations are so important or so badly neglected as the problem of institutional integrity (1957, 130). I am indebted to Robert Post, who in reacting critically to an early draft of this passage on institutional integrity, referred me to Selznick's *Leadership in Administration*.

mensurate with its self-image as a group of outstanding transactional lawyers whose skills add value to the company's product; Mahoney faces the challenge of growth both to respond better to its clients' needs and its own conception of the unique character of its practice; and McKinnon's business goal of rapid growth is tested by its commitments as a professional service organization to collegial governance. Each of these challenges amounts to a form of self-definition, reconstruction, or reevaluation of the "friendship" among, or equilibrium between, the various pressures and competing values of their practice. The identity of the practice is at stake.

The interest of these stories involves efforts by lawyers to create or continue a framework for their lives in the practice of law through the integrity of an organization that they find coherent and satisfactory. The framework of a life lived in a law-practice organization comprises some way of arranging, giving order to, or integrating the incommensurate values of earning a living, attracting and serving clients, maintaining a sense of group character and loyalty (in relation to clients, colleagues, and the work itself), managing conflict, and expressing one's ideals through the identification of their mission, or what it means to lead a good life in the profession.

The key to reading a law-practice organization, or understanding the professionalism it represents, is to assess its integrity, its unique sympathy toward itself or self-respect in resolving and ordering the inevitable pressures and conflicts of contemporary practice. Do the stories told by a practice fit together, cohere as a narrative that bespeaks "inward friendship" (Kronman 1987, 855) in the choice of organizational policies and directions? As Philip Selznick expresses it:

> The study of institutions is in some ways comparable to the clinical study of personality. It requires a genetic and developmental approach, an emphasis on historical origins and growth stages. There is a need to see the enterprise as a whole and to see how it is transformed as new ways of dealing with a changing environment evolve. As in the case of personality, effective diagnosis depends upon locating the special problems that go along with a particular character-structure; and we can understand character better when we see it as the product of self-preserving efforts to deal with inner impulses and external demands. In both personality and institutions "self-preservation" means more than

bare organic or material survival. Self-preservation has to do with the maintenance of basic identity; with the integrity of a personal or institutional "self." (1957, 141–42)

A number of contemporary law-practice organizations would not bear scrutiny under this formulation. If the independence and autonomy of the lawyer and the legal profession can be described as the central challenge to the professional ideal from the mid-nineteenth century through the 1960s, solving the dilemmas of organizational integrity is the comparable challenge to the legal professions of the 1990s.

One conclusion I draw from reflecting on these stories is that the idea of a legal profession grows less and less coherent as the organizations of practice become stronger and develop their unique identities in the face of competing professional ideals and competitive market forces. There will be extraordinary demand and opportunity for leadership in this Balkanized profession. The preservation and construction of institutional integrity is the primary challenge to the leadership of these organizations.

A threat to organizational integrity is opportunism, "the pursuit of immediate, short-run advantages in a way inadequately controlled by considerations of principle and ultimate consequence" (Selznick 1957, 143). Certain forms of opportunism are almost instantly lethal, such as ill-considered mergers that unravel both merging firms, or attempts to co-opt partners threatening to leave with compensation arrangements that demoralize the other partners and undermine the firm's sense of itself and its character. Other opportunistic moves may simply be a form of drift that attenuates or confuses the character of the organization (Selznick 1957, 145), such as poorly conceived geographic diversification, churning or overbilling clients, exploitation of nonpartner lawyers, or emphasis on new specialties as product lines that have little or no coherence with the identity of the organization. The story of the growth and renovation of the profession carries with it the odor of opportunism, a failure to think through the full, character-transforming implications of business strategies and technologies available to law practices in the decade of the 1980s and 1990s.

Another challenge to leadership is utopianism,[19] a flight to

19. I am indebted to Selznick for the idea of opportunism and utopianism as

abstractions that are a substitute for the hard choices of building an organization responsive to the economic or competitive realities of contemporary practice. The story of the decline of the profession is a manifestation of a failure of stereoscopic vision, which by its vagueness and romanticization of the profession, lends itself to unrealistic or overgeneralized goals of a practice and therefore makes the practice vulnerable to the peculiar drift of uncontrolled opportunism. Thus, some of the most vocal advocates of the tragic model are senior partners of law firms that have slowly and inexorably changed character while its older leaders steadfastly champion nostrums about the traditional public-service mission of the legal profession.

One way of looking at what lawyers do is to characterize legal argument as the competition to tell the best stories. One story infuses a clause of a constitution, a statute or rule, or a set of court opinions, with meaning that organizes or puts into order its origin and place in our system of laws, which might be called legal narrative. A second story is an account of the facts of a situation, which could be called local narrative. The legal and local narratives must work together: the facts must exemplify the legal problem, and the law prefigures the factual situation. The two stories must dovetail, mirror or correspond to each other in order to legitimate the conclusion or the point of the two stories that the lawyer wants to make or achieve (Luban 1989, 2152–53). As my colleague David Luban puts it: "Holmes was . . . wrong: The life of the law is neither logic nor experience, but narrative and the only partially civilized struggle for the power it conveys" (1989, 2154).

Luban does not pursue the hazards of fitting narratives together. If we think of this process as a kind of mutual adaption, there are many dangers of misfit, or inappropriate attempts to connect the two stories. One danger, for example, of improperly conforming the factual story to the legal narrative is subornation of perjury and its more sophisticated variants like the "lecture" from *The Anatomy of a Murder*. And it is common to misread the law, or wrongly interpret the legal narrative in order to bend it to the use of local narrative.

The lives of lawyers are also a form of multilayered narrative, an effort by lawyers to merge satisfactorily their individual life stories

---

threats to institutional identity, but I use utopianism in a somewhat different way than Selznick (1957, 147–49).

with the story of the organization in which they practice.[20] The search for organizational integrity is closely connected to the search for personal integrity by the individual lawyer. Law-practice stories are a significant part of the personal histories of those who are part of the organization. As I hope the stories in this book illustrate, the intersection of personal and institutional stories can enrich each of the stories, as it does the life of the organization and the lives of individuals working within them.

But the intersection of individual and organizational stories can also become unintelligible. The evidence is strong of adaptive failure[21] or disequilibrium in the contemporary profession. Thus, our two metastories mentioned earlier, the story of loss told by individuals complaining about the adaptive demands of organizations, and the story of gain told from the perspective of organizations complaining about the adaptive demands of individuals. Law firms disintegrate as a result of the recalcitrance of lawyers who pursue agendas inimical to the organization. And the accounts of thousands of lawyers leaving the profession each year suggest (apart from an overabundance of lawyers) the inability of organizations to adapt creatively to the needs of lawyers.

I have described the search for organizational integrity as the major theme of the stories told here and an important concept in examining a professional organization. This sense of integrity or wholeness or internal self-respect may also be conceived in terms of the intersection of two stories, the reciprocal or friendly adaption of individual life stories to organizational needs, and organizational biography to individual needs—a kind of contract for the mutual good, or shared working out of the contradictions inherent in the practice of law.

While this adaptive process, or working things out, is relentless

---

20. See MacIntyre's idea of a life narrative in 1984 chap. 15.
21. Cf. the suggestive remarks of Steven J. Gould:
Adaption, in the vernacular sense of working or fitting, characterizes entities at various levels of an inclusive hierarchy—and the various levels are often in overt and ultimately tragic conflict. What's good ("adaptive") for the organization may destroy the group in the long run. Baseball may die because players pursue their own advantages so single-mindedly. What's good ("adaptive") for the group may require the suppression of personal benefit. America may die because Japan understands the balance of individual and corporate good far better than we do. Adaption is not a unitary concept. (1990, 26)

in its demands on the time and energy and imagination of law-practice leaders and followers, the task is by no means daunting. Organizations are routinely and often wrongly cast as villains in our culture. There is relatively little acknowledgment of the realization and fulfillment that many individuals achieve in the organizational setting. Most lawyers with whom I spoke in the course of writing these stories derived enormous satisfaction from work within their practice organizations. It is their way of defining what it means to be a professional.[22]

Stories within and about law practices are commonplace in the legal profession. The senior lawyer impossible to satisfy with anything less than perfect prose. The time people stayed up all night to meet a crucial deadline. Outlasting, or being outwitted by, an adversary known as a skilled negotiator. The insoluble conundrum or incoherent argument solved or put right by the wisest head in the practice. These stories, told in admiration, or cynicism, or criticism, capture something of what is valued in a law practice. We need to extend these stories about the practice of law to lawyers and the organizations in which they work and make them as true as we can so that we can learn from the joys, the disappointments, the battles, and the cares that inform the working lives of lawyers.

---

22. Only in the McKinnon firm did I find some sense of unhappiness over the trade-offs required by the organization. McKinnon lawyers were more prone to articulate a sense of tension between the intensity of work in the practice and the time they wanted for their families and private lives.

Afterword: Writing the Stories

One way to appreciate these stories may be to recount why I came to write them. Twenty-nine months after I had become a full-time law teacher and before I had developed an established specialty or field of scholarship, I became dean of the University of Maryland School of Law. The teaching dean is a tradition in legal education. I decided to offer the course on the legal profession, a subject historically termed "legal ethics" or "professional responsibility." This seemed to me to be a logical move for someone aspiring to lead an institution purporting to train professionals. But there was a more pragmatic reason: in 1975, professional responsibility was not something respectable law teachers were enthusiastic about teaching. The course was required of all students at most schools, including my own, as a result of historic pressures imposed by the organized bar and amplified in the wake of Watergate. Still, faculty members were skeptical that it was an intellectually coherent subject. I decided that it was easier for me to teach the course than to twist arms to get other professors to teach it. While there is still no consensus about the precise contours or definition of the subject of legal ethics, the last decade has seen a substantial reawakening of academic interest in professional responsibility, and the development of a more sophisticated scholarly literature in the field. We have emerged from the arm-twisting era.

During the late 1970s, teachers of the course on professional responsibility generally agreed that the most effective pedagogy was the problem method. Many of the topics covered in the course—confidentiality, for example—do not have a rich array of judicial cases suitable for classroom discussion. Typically, therefore, writers of casebooks create problems or short scenarios that raise significant issues, and students read background materials such as law review articles, reported cases, and opinions and reports of the organized bar. The purpose of these problems is to focus discussion on difficult or borderline areas that raise significant issues in lawyers' decision making.

Casebook problems never worked to my satisfaction. Successful textbooks in professional responsibility present students with quandaries of how to apply different systems of norms to individual decision making and the larger issues of the structure of the profession. Criteria range from the regulations of the Code of Professional Responsibility or the Model Rules of Professional Conduct to judicial decisions, ethics opinions, general moral or religious principles, obligations entailed by the special role of the lawyer, and individual relationships with clients. This way of thinking about ethics as discrete decision making based on concepts and rules has come under attack by such modern Aristotelians as Alasdair MacIntyre (1984),[1] but even if one accepts this framework of analysis, it leaves out a crucial component of all decisions: the constraint or guide of what could be called ambition, or a life plan or career concept. A person's sense of place and future in a practice organization is enormously influential in decision making by lawyers.

The problem method has additional problems, not unlike the criticisms leveled at business-school case studies by economists and professors of finance. It often amounts to a celebration of ad hoc decision making that abandons any pretense of a coherent approach to a subject. I cotaught the legal profession course for a few years with David Luban, a brilliant moral philosopher, in an effort to provide both general perspective and analytic tools with which to work through the subject. I ultimately abandoned overt use of philosophy in the course as a result of the incomprehension of both students and law teacher, and a growing realization that contemporary moral philosophers have little to offer in terms of systematic perspective to solve many of the dilemmas posed in the world of legal ethics.[2]

---

1. Other contributions to this revival of virtue or character ethics are Wollheim 1988, Stocker 1990, and Taylor 1989. Taylor makes a distinction between ethics seen as thinking about decisions or actions, and ethics as a form of inquiry about the meaning and direction of a life. The latter best describes the idea of ethics underlying this book.

2. I take some pride in having led Luban astray, however. The result is a superb book that offers both systematic and analytical insights on legal profession issues (Luban 1988). See also Rhode and Luban 1992.

Any classroom is an unreal place, and all classroom decisions are vicarious. But the structure of play decision making in the classroom can affect the depth and sophistication of discussion. Casebook problems fail, in particular, to *place* decisions, to put them in the social context in which they are invariably made, such as in a law firm or legal department or agency. Few of the classic dilemmas of lawyers—for example, weighing a sense of social responsibility against professional duties to individual clients—present themselves outside the particular pressures of a particular client in the setting of a firm or organization that has its own ways of approaching such issues. The legal profession course seems to generate even more pontificating and blather than the normal law school classroom, precisely because the presentation of the profession, particularly the dominant context of the practice organization, is so abstract. Casebooks do little more than offer background snippets about the sociology or realities of the profession.

My dissatisfaction with the course on legal profession went beyond the superficiality of the classroom dialogue. Lawyers, particularly those I considered the most thoughtful, seemed totally disinterested in the course I was teaching, except for the area of conflicts of interest, which has important practical or tactical significance in client relationships and litigation. These same lawyers, however, were deeply concerned about the problems of the profession, particularly tensions within their organizations between the need to create environments supportive and attractive to lawyers, and competitive pressures in ferociously difficult marketplaces for both clients and talented lawyers. These lawyers were wrestling with problems for which no real literature existed, other than the new legal journalism touting the size, the troubles, the average partner's income, and the biggest deal makers of the nation's largest law firms.

By the late 1970s, it had become clear that there were major transformations occurring within the legal profession, changes that have accelerated in the 1980s and 1990s. The more self-consciously business and bureaucratic focus of the organized profession has led to considerable discontent and unhappiness among lawyers. Yet the casebooks and teaching of the legal profession course in law schools seemed oblivious of a profession in major transformation.

I set myself the task of writing about the legal profession in order to capture for the classroom something of the complex forces of change and adaptation at work in the institutions of practice. I began with a largely instinctive decision to write case studies of law practices. I was trained as a medieval historian and as a lawyer, not as a sociologist. Narrative accounts of people and institutions come naturally to me. But my preference was grounded, I believe, in a form of reasoned instinct. At the time I began writing, there was almost no theoretical work available to enable one to understand the transformations occurring in the profession.[3] One advantage of descriptions is their power to generate (rather than test) hypotheses, which in itself is a useful contribution to a theory-lean field. But there was also the problem of too much theory. Law professors are particularly quick on the draw when it comes to pointing out the decline in professional values generated by some phenomenon, such as the rise of in-house corporate counsel.[4] Like their students, they tend to focus generalizing attention on the large corporate law firm, which is home to probably no more than 15 percent of American lawyers. A deliberate effort to put aside theorizing and do some basic fieldwork seemed to me to be a positive contribution to understanding the profession.[5] Watching the profession attentively might be a helpful leaven to some of the half-baked pronouncements of academics about a world some of them had once visited early in their careers.

Case studies also respond to problems I saw in law school pedagogy about the profession: they have what I felt at the time to be the advantage of being real, not fictional scenarios or constructed problems, and they provide much richer contexts in which to examine decision making by lawyers. They may be particularly useful because a student lawyer, through cases, has access to a particular leader in a firm as the leader approaches an issue and solves a problem. Reviewing how a thoughtful lawyer works through a decision in context,

---

3. But, more recently, we have both Nelson 1988, a sociological study of four large Chicago firms, and Galanter and Palay 1991. Nelson reviews the impoverished state of theory about the changing nature of the corporate law firm (1988).

4. See the related complaint of Galanter about "macro assertions . . . as if the motions of social life could be grasped without any attention to the institutional sinews and joints that connect and shape individuals and great social structures" (1989, 507).

5. Since we all carry about with us a huge, relatively unexamined bag of understandings of the world, I recognize that it is preposterous to suggest that doing field work is a renunciation of theory. My method, if that is not too dignified a term for the way I went about my work, could be described as spare of theory, not unencumbered by theory.

given the peculiar pressures of his or her firm, may be as informative to a budding decision maker as studying the structure and economics of practice in general. Cases reveal what counts, that is, how a decision maker evaluates the incommensurate worlds of personal loyalties, the ideals of the firm or agency, the structure and economics of the organization, relationships with relevant clients, general professional ideals, and a variety of other principles.

My preference for cases was not based on the conclusion that they are superior, that one necessarily learns more from them than from a more structured exposition of concepts and ideas. American law schools offer many examples of cases doing poorly what a good lecture or serious text can do better. But case learning has peculiar virtues. Cases are stories, and thus obviously more open textured, less conclusory, more susceptible to varied interpretations than analytic material. They may stimulate questions and answers the reader is looking for, rather than the questions and answers of the writer. Like any parable, they can prompt nuanced learning, layers of meaning, reinterpretation, and retelling over time. Cases are often vivid. They stay with us because they are stories, each with its own setting or framework, its characters and movement, and sometimes even an illusive point or moral.

Stories or cases have another notable distinction. They work well in conveying character. If the world of law is beset by many different pressures and lawyers adapt their practices to a rapidly changing environment, the likelihood is that talented lawyer-leaders are making decisions about their practices without any clear set of guidelines of the right thing to do. The coherence of decision making is discovered over time, or after the fact, as the character of leadership and a leader's innate sense of professional mission is revealed. Character is taught largely by example, even the vicarious example of a story. In a world where the direction of a profession and its standards are controversial and up for grabs, the character of leadership may be the surest guide to professional integrity.

Having determined to write cases, and having chosen the business-school case study as my model for creating accessible teaching materials, I arranged a sabbatical visit to the Harvard Law School, where for a number of years the Program on the Legal Profession sponsored the writing of case studies.[6] During the sabbatical I enrolled

---

6. Some of these studies have been published in Heymann and Liebman 1988.

in a business-school course on teaching by the case method and became aware of the peculiar constraints of writing cases that work well in the classroom.

Many business-school teachers view cases as vehicles to put vicarious managers in vicarious decision-making environments. A case must be relatively short, contextually rich enough to generate competing analyses and discussion, but not so rich as to create a cacophony of conclusions. A case is structured to require students to solve a business problem. It must seem real and be relatively open-ended. Sequels to the initial story reveal decisions made and attendant results, and these, in turn, can stimulate further classroom discussion. A business-school case is fundamentally a story of a decision to be made. And it is part of a course representing particular lessons the instructor wishes to build into the syllabus of the course. The art of writing case studies is to help students find the moral of the case but not make the process too facile. Case-study pedagogy is an exercise in disingenuity: the power of the learning comes from students discovering or finding for themselves the lesson of the case within a series of lessons that comprise a course. The craft of teaching by cases is to make an interesting experience out of helping students discover what the instructor has planned for them.

I began by writing stories of both individual lawyers and organizations. The individual stories came relatively easily and, when used in the classroom, worked well. In contrast, the organizational accounts were much more demanding and seemed less suitable for classroom use. They required scores of interviews. The stakes to the organization were high and created much more tension in relationships with people. Both capturing the feel or character of the enterprise and organizing the materials in a coherent fashion proved to be challenging. But I found myself drawn to the organizational stories, and I turned away from the individual accounts. The stories of individuals were, in fact, largely about people reacting, in some fashion, to organizations, and I was fascinated by the puzzle of these organizations. Thomas Hardy in *Tess of the D'Urbervilles* wrote, "Every village has its idiosyncrasy, its constitution, often its own code of morality." I felt it was more interesting to capture the spirit or essence of the professional villages I was describing. The stories of individuals only reinforced my belief that organizations, or lawyers acting in their organizational capacities, are the main force, the effective actors generating change in the contemporary profession. I became intrigued with how lawyers in an organization structure the terms, the conditions, and the norms of contemporary practice—how they respond to, remake, manipulate, sometimes transcend their organizations—how the pieces or dynamics of the organization work to create an organization's personality, or special character of the house or village.

I began to chafe under the pedagogical distortions required by the business-school case method. I did not want to write to a lesson plan, or to design a series of important decisions in law practice around which I would write stories meant to stand for the contemporary legal profession. My initial instinct, driven by my classroom teaching, was to look for ethical issues. I soon had to abandon this approach when, in my first story of the Legal Division of the Maine Public Utilities Commission, I found myself drawn to write about a law-practice organization that seemed to have its own logic or story rather than the ethical problems for which I was looking.[7] The logic of the classroom seemed to interfere, or be incommensurate, with the logic of what I was seeing and attempting to describe in the practice environment. My instincts as an historian got in the way of being a teacher with an agenda. I decided to go with my instincts, abandon the pedagogical focus of the writing, and describe honestly what I saw and heard.

If I was drawn by a certain logic or order that imposed itself on what I saw and heard in these practices, I also found myself developing, quite by instinct, and with just as strong a sense of logic, a method of dealing with the practices. I was able to write only about organizations with people or friends of people willing to vouch for me.[8] Law firms and lawyers are notoriously jittery about outside analysts scrutinizing their work. Nothing remotely resembling the business-school case study tradition prevails in law. And lawyers are particularly squeamish about revealing confidential client-related information and articulating internal procedures in their firms, because these could be relevant and damaging in potential legal claims against them. Since the only way I could gain access to a firm was

---

7. Several years after drafting this account of discovering a logic in these organizations, I stumbled across Robert Jackall's more sophisticated description of "institutional logic." See Jackall 1988, 249.

8. My difficulties in finding practices willing to take on an observer parallel that of Jackall 1988, 14–15.

by saying, "Trust me," I moved to methods to reinforce this trust. I cannot say these procedures were well thought out, but they seemed the decent thing to do.

The protocol with which I approached the organizations consisted of several commitments. I gave assurances of anonymity to the organization, and in some cases individuals within the organization, in short, creating a veneer of fiction in order to strengthen the quality of the nonfiction.[9] I also felt the need to assure those whom I interviewed that I would give them the text of whatever could be attributed to them in my account of the organization. I was interested in describing the practice honestly and deeply, not in scoring points on the practice or individuals within it. I wanted them to see how I was using their words and insights before their colleagues saw them. Although I did not explicitly make a commitment to edit or censor quotations of individuals, I found myself accepting almost every correction a lawyer wanted to make in the attributed material. An extremely high percentage of people—perhaps nine out of ten—made no changes whatsoever or made utterly inconsequential changes. The changes by the one in ten consisted of toning down or lessening the acuity or cynicism of a remark or expanding a remark to make it more intelligible.

A second review occurred when I circulated to everyone I interviewed the complete text of my description of the organization for comments and corrections. The only commitment I made to change the text at this stage concerned sensitive financial information and the cosmetics needed to assure the anonymity of the organization. But I often changed the text to respond to comments, either to clear up what I became convinced was an inaccuracy in my description, or to remove material so sensitive that it would be gratuitously offensive to members of the organization to include it.[10]

After my first experience with the Maine case, I decided it was important to question people in an open-ended and nondirective style. I had a few basic questions with which I usually started most conversations (after laying out my method, which I hoped set a tone of my trustworthiness): Where did you come from? How did you land in your current situation? What do you like about the practice? What do you dislike or what annoys you about the practice? What is likely

---

9. The Public Utilities Commission of Maine is the only exception to this rule.

10. Some, if not most, of the removal of sensitive subject matter occurred in the writing on my own initiative, not in response to comments.

to be next for you? Where might you go, when or if you take a new position somewhere? What's happening around here? After these opening questions I simply pursued questions that interested me from the answers I received from people in the practice. Only in the McKinnon firm, where the task of interviewing some two hundred lawyers was daunting, did my sponsors in the firm organize, with my agreement, an initial framework of assessing two recent mergers that limited my interviewing to fifty or sixty people.

I started from these individual histories to obtain some sense of how people's lives intersected with the practice. The lawyers were of particular interest, but I made it a point in virtually every practice to interview secretaries and support staff and clients so that I would have a variety of perspectives with which to assess the practice. In one practice, my initial draft described how women with family-rearing responsibilities were less active in the social functions of the practice, something I believe is an accurate description of the reality of that practice. The women in the practice were deeply distressed to read this description and urged me to remove it on the grounds it unfairly singled them out. They argued that some men were also limited participants. I removed the offending material, which I thought was peripheral to the description of the practice.

Gradually I realized I had created a kind of method.[11] I wrote from what people in the organization told me. If I did my job well, I created out of these materials an accurate description of the organization, at least as they saw themselves, a mirror that people in the organization could use to look at themselves. I am not certain I understand all the implications of this method, but some are obvious. Inherent in it is some self-censorship, or a decision that certain subjects are too awkward to raise without the organization feeling betrayed. Narratives of this kind run the hazard of face-saving and self-justificatory accounts by individuals of their relationships and roles in the practice. I worked hard to make sure that my generalizations seemed honest reflections of consensus in the organization, not necessarily idiosyncratic perspectives of individuals. If I had one methodology it was as an historian—checking, verifying, making sure I had it right. As a result, I suspect I did not give full justice to dissenters, people who had cynical or disparate views. And, of

---

11. See Geertz 1988.

course, the self-selection through which I had access to these organizations meant that I was dealing with self-confident groups, willing to open themselves up to scrutiny, and therefore not likely to be experiencing substantial conflict or sense that they were operating with false assumptions about themselves. In virtually every case I was dealing with mature, stable organizations willing to tell their stories to an historian.

Fictionalizing was a pledge I made to the organizations I visited. All the pieces involved replacing real names and places with fictional ones, except for the people in the Public Utilities Commission of Maine. Particular markers or identifiers of the organization, for example, an employee benefit unique or notorious in the local community, were omitted to avoid identification. I also changed specialty areas or altered elements of a story within the story. For example, the high-profile case described in Marks and Feinberg is fictionalized to prevent people in their community from identifying the lawyers. I feel confident this fictionalizing is superficial and does not affect fundamental elements of the practice I was describing, with one major exception: ethnicity. The ethnic identity of members of the organizations—an extremely important element of practice culture—was often lost in an effort to protect the identity of the practice. Some practices were too clearly identifiable if I did not change or neutralize their ethnic character.

Some information I uncovered would fit in the we-can't-talk-about-this-openly category, such as arrangements made to cope with various forms of incompetence. Sometimes I did not have time to pursue an issue. For example, in one practice there was a hint of a problem of sexual liaisons in the office. I did not consider this matter a major theme critical to delineating or characterizing the organization. Focusing on these problems, in my judgment, was inaccurate, in view of my own sense of purpose as well as the relationship I had with each group.

Some incidents in the histories of the organizations are written with much less detail or richness than the information I had at my disposal. A few examples that come to mind are the assumption by Schultz and Isaacs of the leadership of the Mahoney firm, and the controversy over compensation of senior lawyers at Standish Development. My accounts of these events are not inaccurate, but they are not as detailed as they could be. The cost of making the stories more vivid and richly textured (as, for example, the one-sided story of the Butler and Standish fight over fees) would have been to open wounds needlessly or require a long period of investigation, sifting of evidence, and weighing the accuracy of different participants' perhaps sharply differing recollections of events. I had insufficient time to undertake such investigations.

Some stories contain thumbnail sketches of lawyers in the organization. I asked every lawyer to review these, and the changes I received were minimal. Only one lawyer asked to have the brief biography deleted completely, and I complied with that wish. Quotations or comments by individuals were rarely changed, and the request to change usually involved tidying up the quotation.

Sometimes people convinced me I was inaccurate, had drawn the wrong inference, or was too loose in my characterization of opinions. The reaction of a number of people at Mahoney to my initial draft, which indicated (as does the current text) the dominance of Schultz in the firm and the crucial importance of succession to leadership at Mahoney, led me to add some material that I believe accurately reflects the efforts of Schultz and others in the firm to broaden leadership and policy-making functions within the firm.

The Marks and Feinberg lawyers corrected only obvious mistakes—matters I had wrong. This was the only story in which I became a player, an unpaid consultant or stimulus to the firm to consider various ways to bring in fee-generating cases. I assisted in framing the initial draft of the firm résumé mentioned in the story.

The most difficult set of negotiations over the text occurred with McGill, the head of the Standish Legal Division. McGill worked over my text as if it were an indenture agreement for which he was responsible. Seventy-five to 80 percent of his suggested changes were corrections of factual mistakes, or improvements in the text which I found helpful. But he was also the relentless advocate for his division, determined to negotiate for the best face on everything. McGill wanted profanity removed from the text. I refused. McGill wanted a rewrite of a footnote listing of the schools—many of which are fictional—of Standish lawyers. He wanted fictional schools of higher status than some of the schools I listed. I refused. McGill objected strongly to an inference or interpretation that he felt reflected poorly on the department, or parts of the department, and I sometimes modified the text slightly, but in my view not significantly, to respond to his criticisms.

One could argue with some accuracy my method pulls a lot of punches. On the other hand, if I was at all successful in building a relationship of trust with the people I interviewed—including those not entirely happy with the organization—the second review (during which I sought criticism of the description of the practice) was an opportunity to determine whether people in the organization felt my writing was an unrealistic perspective, or some form of glossy journalism, or a public relations piece. My overriding concern was to capture what it was like to be in that organization, so that the people in it would say I was being fair, that it was an honest portrait—not brutally honest to the point of indiscretion, or a needless reopening of old wounds—but an honesty that reflected the realities of the place, a portrait by an honest friend, not an enemy or an academic showing off.

The fact that I was writing for the people I observed as much as the audience of readers observing the practice solely through the writing unquestionably shapes the structure of this work. These stories are both less revealing, in terms of unveiling some of the embarrassments of the organization, and more revealing because they are written with a form of assent, or participation in the story writing, by the characters of the story.

In my estimation, these are relatively superficial portraits of law practices compared to what an extensive amount of time and more sophisticated methodology might generate. They are the descriptions of a visitor or traveler who spent some time talking with the inhabitants about village life. I had virtually no access to those most private and vital lawyer-client interactions that could reveal dimensions of professional quality more poignantly and persuasively than any amount of self-explanation by lawyers.[12] I engaged in some participant observation of meetings within offices, barely enough to convince me what I was being told about the organization was not clearly inaccurate. More time and effort devoted to watching interactions might have greatly enriched my accounts of the practices.

I am convinced that the people I interviewed were more forth-

12. For one of the rare examinations of such interactions, see Felstiner and Sarat 1986.

coming because they felt that a dean, unlike most academics, is more understanding and tolerant of how the world works. There were advantages brought to the intellectual table from the perspective of the dean as manager: a generalist's unfocused curiosity, a tolerance for personal and institutional foibles, an instinct for reading organizations. But there were also disadvantages, in particular, the constraints of a busy administrator with negligible time for in-depth research. Some decades ago, the world of legal education was closely identified with the profession. Today, the worlds of legal academic and practitioner have drifted so far apart that it is necessary for one to write the anthropology of the other. Indeed, the profession itself is so divided that stories that talk across cultures are necessary if one part of the profession is to understand another. Perhaps deans, peculiarly cross-cultural figures who work with academics, law-practice managers, lawyers, and various professional associations, have special translation skills to bring to writing about the profession.

I have mentioned the logic of the organizations I was describing and the logic of the procedures to which I was drawn in relation to these practices. A third logic emerged as I began to organize my material, the peculiar demands of writing narrative. Some of the stories of practices, in first draft, came out shapeless or flat, and I felt the need to round out or finish the story or give it some framework. If I was to respect the logic of the organization, the story frame could not be imposed artificially like some injection of drama designed to pique interest. Rather, it had to be discovered in the material itself, and it had to be true to the material, representing a perspective that caught the practice in the right light, so that the account had resonance, depth, or clarity. I can only use metaphors to describe this pressure or logic. Perhaps, if I were trained as a social scientist or literary theorist, I could better evoke this sense of obligation I felt to the demands of narrative—and to the demands of portraying honestly the law practice. The account of the Legal Division of the Public Utilities Commission of Maine, for example, languished for almost four years before the course of events helped me tie it up with the ceremony honoring the founder of the division and resignation of his successor.

Hayden White argues that the sense of compulsion I felt in the need to frame these descriptions, or stories, or organizational biographies, derives from "the impulse to moralize reality, that is, to identify it [the story, description, etc.] with the social system that is the source of any morality that we can imagine" (White 1981, 14). White continues,

> ... The reality of events does not consist in the fact that they occurred but that, first of all, they were remembered, and, second, that they are capable of finding a place in a chronologically ordered sequence. . . . Narrative appeals to our desire for "formed coherency" that only stories possess. Reality wears the mask of meaning.

White argues that "the demand for closure in the historical story is a demand . . . for moral meaning, a demand that sequences of real events be assessed as to their significance as elements of a *moral drama*." Narrative has become a convention or form, a discourse that "signals at once its objectivity, its seriousness, and its realism," a value that "arises out of a desire to have real events display the coherence, integrity, fullness, and closure of an image of life that is and can only be imaginary" (White 1981, 19–20, 23).

If, for White, narrative is a convention expressing an imaginary image of life, it is an extraordinarily important convention, "a primary and irreducible form of human comprehension, an article in the constitution of common sense" (White 1981, 252). Stories allow us "to accommodate the notion of human intentions, aims, and purposes in our representations of human affairs . . . [and] permit us to judge the moral significance of human projects [and] provide the means by which to judge them, even while we pretend to be merely describing them" (White 1981, 253).

If, in Hayden White's sense of that activity, my function consisted of "narrativizing" the interviews with members of these various organizations, the results sometimes emerged with startling coherency to the subjects of my inquiry. My writing can perhaps best be characterized as description constructed out of listening to and observing lawyers in conversation about their practices. Its cognitive authority was first put to the test when I circulated a full description to the entire firm or organization. I wrote descriptions I felt were favorable to every organization I visited. I found myself attracted to, I liked, the vigorous and effective people doing interesting work in every organization I described. I had convinced people in the organization that I had gone about my work honestly in creating an organizational self-portrait. In one respect, I saw myself writing *their* story, the story they would write if they were being honest about their practice. They could not write the story off as something other than what they had told me: the protocol was too strict to allow them to be angry at me for misusing them or misquoting them, or being unfair to them. And the effect was sometimes extraordinarily powerful.

It was not uncommon for people to be disturbed by what they read. Symptoms included depression over what I wrote, strong efforts to convince me to sanitize the script and eliminate important elements of the story, or the expression of anxiety that I had not captured the special character of the organization—an anxiety corresponding to an inability to respond to my willingness to enrich the story to meet perceptions of its inadequacy. To some extent I take these rather unhappy reactions as a partial testimonial that the stories struck home as being real, or at least vital to the characters portrayed in them, animated by their perception that there was little room for criticism of the unfairness or partiality of my methods. And reactions were mixed: at one organization where several people were most disturbed with the description, another lawyer asked my permission to use it to recruit a new lawyer who would be given the text to learn about the practice in some depth.

At least one organization was largely indifferent about what I wrote. A disadvantage of being a dean was that I had difficulty finding time to write. Some of my subjects therefore did not see a complete description until two, three, or as much as four years after I interviewed at the organization. The passage of time made some critics grow fonder of, or less interested in editing, the portrait I painted of them, a blessing I came to appreciate. Change in the practice had made my description "historical," and therefore less threatening.

If, as White argues, in a way I find convincing, storytelling is of necessity a morality tale, then perhaps the exercise of writing these stories is best seen as a form of descriptive ethics. The style of the telling is crucial to whether these nonfictional tales carry conviction. I have tried to describe lawyers' lives in organizations as honestly as I know how, without denunciation or acclaim. My hope is that these stories will form part of the "constitution of common sense" about

the contemporary profession, a modest contribution to our understanding of people pursuing this special endeavor, and a basis on
which readers can make thoughtful judgments about the lives of
lawyers.

References

Adler, Stephen J., and Donald Baer. 1986. "The Final Shake Out." *American Lawyer,* June, 1, 23-26.

Ainsworth, Bill. 1991. "Tilting at Windmills?" *The Recorder,* 9 December, 1.

American Law Institute–American Bar Association. 1980. *A Model Peer Review System.* Part 1. Philadelphia: American Law Institute.

American Bar Association. 1986. *In the Spirit of Public Service: A Blueprint for the Rekindling of Lawyer Professionalism.* Chicago: American Bar Association.

———. 1991. *At the Breaking Point: The Emerging Crisis in the Quality of Lawyers' Health and Lives—Its Impact on Law Firms and Client Services.* Chicago: American Bar Association.

———. "The AM Law 100." 1985. *American Lawyer,* July–August, Special pull-out section.

———. 1986. *American Lawyer,* June, Special pull-out section.

———. 1990a. *American Lawyer,* July–August, Special pull-out section.

———. 1990b. *American Lawyer,* September, Special pull-out section.

———. 1991. *American Lawyer,* June, Special pull-out section.

———. 1993. *American Lawyer,* July–August, Special pull-out section.

Bellis, Jonathan P., and Rees W. Morrison. 1991. "Inside Looking Out." *National Law Journal,* 2 December, S1-4.

Bellon, Lee Ann. 1991. "Firms Need to Regroup for 1992: Getting Back on Track." *National Law Journal,* 30 December, 38.

Bickel and Brewer. 1991. Firm Brochure. Dallas.

Blumberg, Abraham S. 1967. *Criminal Justice.* Chicago: Quadrangle Books.

Booth, Eva E., and Susan Raridon. 1991. "A Support Staff Can Cast a Lasting Impression." *Massachusetts Lawyers Weekly,* 25 December, S8.

Brill, Steven. 1985. "The AM Law 50: America's Fifty Highest-Grossing Firms." *American Lawyer,* July–August, supplement, 1-15.

———. 1991a. "Inside View." *American Lawyer,* June, supplement, 6-42.

———. 1991b. "Short-Term Pressures, Long-Term Opportunities: Balancing Business and Intangibles; Ways to Preserve Culture When Money's Tight." *American Lawyer,* September, supplement, 6-50.

Calhoun, Daniel H. 1965. *Professional Lives in America: Structure and Aspiration 1750-1850.* Cambridge, Mass.: Harvard University Press.

Chayes, Abram, and Antonia Chayes. 1985. "Corporate Counsel and the Elite Firm." *Stanford Law Review* 32:277-300.

Clark, Burton R. 1970. *The Distinctive College: Antioch, Reed, and Swarthmore.* Chicago: Aldine Publishing.

————. 1972. "The Organizational Saga in Higher Education." *Administrative Science Quarterly* 17:178–84.

Clarke, Caroline V. 1991. "Keeping Reebok Running." *American Lawyer,* September, 60–64.

Clifford, James. 1988. *The Predicament of Culture: Twentieth-Century Ethnography, Literature, and Art.* Cambridge, Mass.: Harvard University Press.

Covington and Burling. 1991. Firm Brochure. Washington, D.C. March.

Curran, Barbara A., and Clara N. Carson. 1991. *Supplement to the Lawyer Statistical Report: The U.S. Legal Profession in 1988.* Chicago: American Bar Foundation.

Curran, Barbara A., Katherine Rosich, Clara Carson, and Mark Puccetti. 1985. *Lawyer Statistical Report: A Statistical Profile of the U.S. Legal Profession in the 1980s.* Chicago: American Bar Foundation.

Dahl, Dick. 1991. "Leaner, Meaner, Nicer." *Massachusetts Lawyers Weekly,* 7 October, 33.

David, Irwin T. 1991. "Establishing a Foundation for Business Development." *New York Law Journal,* 30 September, 40–41.

Davis, Polk, and Wardwell. 1990. Firm Brochure. New York. June.

Dietel, J. Edwin. 1992. *Leading a Law Practice to Excellence and Sustaining Law Practice Excellence: Bringing Extraordinary Leadership to a Law Practice by Doing the Right Things Right.* Chicago: American Bar Association.

Dorsey and Whitney. 1991. Firm Brochure. Minneapolis.

"Enter Mr. Barr." 1991. *National Law Journal,* 25 November, 12.

Escher, W. Jon. 1991. "Research Is the Key to Courting In-House Counsel." *Massachusetts Lawyers Weekly,* 18 November, S1.

Felstiner, William L. F., and Austin Sarat. 1986. "Law and Strategy in the Divorce Lawyer's Office." *Law and Society Review* 20:90–134.

Freund, James C. 1985. "Comment." *Stanford Law Review* 37:301–04.

Friedman, Lawrence. 1973. *A History of American Law.* New York: Simon and Schuster.

Galanter, Marc. 1989. Review of *Two Jewish Justices,* by Robert Burt. *Law and Social Inquiry* 14:507–26.

Galanter, Marc, and Thomas Palay. 1991. *The Tournament of Lawyers: The Growth and Transformation of the Big Law Firm.* Chicago: University of Chicago Press.

Geary, Paul J. 1991. "Today's Technology Can Increase Law Officer Productivity." *Massachusetts Lawyers Weekly,* 23 December, S1.

Geertz, Clifford. 1988. *Works and Lives: The Anthropologist as Author.* Stanford, Calif.: Stanford University Press.

Gilson, Ronald, and Robert Mnookin. 1985. "Sharing Among the Human Capitalists: An Economic Inquiry into the Corporate Law Firm and How Partners Split Profits." *Stanford Law Review* 37:313–92.

Gordon, Robert W. 1984. "The Ideal and the Actual in the Law: Fantasies and

Practices of New York City Lawyers: 1870–1910." In *The New High Priests: Lawyers in Post-Civil War America*, ed. Gerard W. Gawalt. Westport, Conn.: Greenwood Press.

———. 1988. "The Independence of Lawyers." *Boston University Law Review* 68:1–83.

———. 1990. "Corporate Law Practice as a Public Calling." *Maryland Law Review* 49:255–92.

Gould, Steven J. 1990. "Theory and Empirical Observation." *New York Review of Books*, 18 January, 26.

Greene, Robert Michael. 1990. *Managing Partner 101: A Primer on Firm Leadership*. Chicago: American Bar Association.

Grossbard, Paul D. 1991. "The IRS Doesn't Have to Take Everything." *Texas Lawyer*, 11 November, 24.

Haserot, Phyllis Weiss. 1991. "Promotion and Ethics May Clash; Guidelines Vary." *National Law Journal*, 15 July, 15, 17–18.

Heinz, John P., and Edward O. Laumann. 1982. *Chicago Lawyers: The Social Structure of the Bar*. New York and Chicago: Russell Sage Foundation and American Bar Foundation.

Heller, Jamie. 1991. "Creditor's King Is an Arbiter and a Gentleman." *Connecticut Law Tribune*, 12 August, 1.

Henning, Joel. 1991. "Associates Tell It All." *Illinois Legal Times*, June, 1.

Heymann, Philip B., and Lance Liebman. 1988. *The Social Responsibilities of Lawyers: Case Studies*. Westbury, N.Y.: Foundation Press.

Hildebrandt, Bradford W. 1991a. "In Collections, Take a Tip from Vendors," *Connecticut Law Tribune*, 30 September, 20.

———. 1991b. "Strategic Thinking: A New Direction." *Legal Economics* 17:46.

Jackall, Robert. 1988. *Moral Mazes: The World of Corporate Managers*. New York: Oxford University Press.

Jefferson, Jon. 1991. "But What Role for the Soul?" *American Bar Association Journal* 77:60–64.

Kaitz, Mitzi. 1991. "Don't Underestimate the Power of Vogue." *Massachusetts Lawyers Weekly*, 16 September, 33.

Kaplan, Sheila. 1991. "Foxes in the Henhouse?" *The Recorder*, 5 September, 1.

Kaufman, Jack, and Joel Henning. 1990. "End Runs and Other Pay Scale Strategies." *American Lawyer*, September, 42.

King, A., ed. 1974. *The Papers of Daniel Webster*. Hanover, N.H.: University Press of New England.

Kornstein, Daniel J. 1991. *Guide to New York Law Firms*. New York: St. Martin's Press.

Kronman, Anthony T. 1987. "Living in the Law." *University of Chicago Law Review* 54:835–76.

"Lawyer's Creed of Professionalism." 1988. In *1991 Selected Standards on Professional Responsibility*, 460–62. Westbury, N.Y.: Foundation Press.

LeVan, Gerald. 1991. "Practicing Law Is Not What It Used to Be." *Massachusetts Lawyers Weekly*, 24 June, 52.

Lochna, Philip R., Jr. 1985. "Comment." *Stanford Law Review* 37:305–12.

Luban, David. 1981. "Paternalism and the Legal Profession." *Wisconsin Law Review* 1981:454–93.

———. 1988. *Lawyers and Justice.* Princeton: Princeton University Press.

———. 1989. "Difference Made Legal: The Court and Dr. King." *Michigan Law Review* 87:2152–2224.

MacIntyre, Alasdair C. 1984. *After Virtue.* Notre Dame, Ind.: University of Notre Dame Press.

Maister, David. 1985. "The One-Firm Firm." *Sloan Management Review* 27:3–13.

———. 1991. "How's Your Asset?" *American Lawyer,* 15 December, 30–33.

Mann, Kenneth. 1985. *Defending White Collar Crime: A Portrait of Attorneys at Work.* New Haven, Conn.: Yale University Press.

Mestel, Lynn. 1991. "Recruiters Struggle through the Recession." *New York Law Journal,* 18 November, 46.

Metzger, Walter P. 1975. *What Is a Profession?* Seminar Reports: Columbia University, Program of General Education in the Humanities 3:1–12.

Monk, Ray. 1990. *Ludwig Wittgenstein: The Duty of Genius.* New York: Penguin Books.

Nelson, Robert. 1988. *Partners with Power: The Social Transformation of the Large Law Firm.* Berkeley and Los Angeles: University of California Press.

Novachicik, Deborah. 1991. "No Longer a Back Office Function: Sophisticated Computers Need Sophisticated Management." *Connecticut Law Tribune,* 28 October, 20.

Orenstein, Susan. 1991. "Crosby, Heafey Places Focus Close to Home." *The Recorder,* 12 November, 1.

Orey, Michael. 1991. "Take Me to Your Leader." *American Lawyer,* December, 3.

Oseil, Mark J. 1990. "Lawyers as Monopolists, Aristocrats, and Entrepreneurs." *Harvard Law Review* 103:2009–66.

Parsons, Talcott. 1954. "The Professions and Special Structure." In *Essays in Sociological Theory.* Glencoe, Ill.: Free Press.

Pildes, Richard H. 1992. "Conceptions of Value in Legal Thought." *Michigan Law Review* 90:1520–29.

Rhode, Deborah, and David Luban. 1992. *Legal Ethics.* New York: Foundation Press.

Rose, Joel A. 1991a. "The Well-Planned Merger." *New York Law Journal,* 6 August, 4, 28.

———. 1991b. "The Changing Nature of a Firm's Culture." *New York Law Journal,* 1 October, 4.

Rosen, Robert. 1984. "Lawyers in Corporate Decision Making." Ph.D. diss., University of California, Berkeley.

———. 1989. "The Inside Counsel Movement, Professional Judgement, and Organizational Representation." *Indiana Law Journal* 64:479–90.

Rubenstein, David K. 1991. "Corporate Work Still Moving In-House; It Will Reconfigure the Triangle?" *Illinois Legal Times,* August, 1.

Sander, Richard H., and Douglas Williams. 1989. "Why Are There So Many

Lawyers? Perspectives on a Turbulent Market." *Law and Social Inquiry* 14:431–79.

Saniborn, Randall, and Marianne Lavell. 1991. "Subsidiaries, Dan Quayle Dominate ABA in Atlanta." *National Law Journal*, 26 August, 3, 31.

Schon, Donald. 1987. "The Crisis of Professional Knowledge and the Pursuit of an Epistemology of Practice." In *Teaching by the Case Method*, ed. C. Roland Christenson. Boston: Harvard Business School.

Scott, W. Richard. 1966. "Professionals in Bureaucracies: Areas of Conflict." In *Professionalization*, ed. H. M. Vollmer and D. L. Mills. Englewood Cliffs, N.J.: Prentice-Hall.

Sells, Benjamin. 1991. "How Professional Obligations Undermine Personal Relationships." *Illinois Legal Times*, November, 30.

Selznick, Philip. 1957. *Leadership in Administration*. Evanston, Ill.: Row, Peterson.

Sitzman, G. Neil. 1991. "Legal Assistant Calls For Credit Where Credit Is Due." *The Recorder*, 11 November, 7.

Solomon, Rayman. 1992. "Five Crises or One: The Concept of Legal Professionalism 1925–1960." In *Lawyers' Ideals/Lawyers' Practices: Transformation in American Legal Profession*, ed. Robert L. Nelson, David M. Trubek, and Rayman L. Solomon. Ithaca, N.Y.: Cornell University Press.

Sterett, Susan. 1990. "Comparing Legal Professions." *Law and Social Inquiry* 15:363–84.

Stocker, Michael. 1990. *Plural and Conflicting Values*. New York: Oxford University Press.

Stout, Jeffrey. 1990. *Ethics after Babel*. Boston: Beacon Press.

Studley, Jamienne S. 1991a. "The Art of Networking." *Manhattan Lawyer*, October, 36.

———. 1991b. "Building on the Assets of Midsize Firms." *Manhattan Lawyer*, November, 45.

Swaine, Robert. 1946. *The Cravath Firm and Its Predecessors*. Vol. 2. New York: Baker and Voorhis.

Taylor, Charles. 1989. *Sources of the Self: The Making of Modern Identity*. Cambridge, Mass.: Harvard University Press.

United States Census Bureau. 1992. *Statistical Abstract of the United States*. Washington, D.C.: U.S. Government Printing Office.

Wehmann, Carolyn O. 1991. "Firms Focus on Evaluations; Getting the Most From Associate Performance Reviews." *New York Law Journal*, 30 September, 39, 48.

White, Hayden. 1981. "The Value of Narrativity in the Representation of Reality." In *On Narrative*, ed. W. T. J. Mitchell. Chicago: University of Chicago Press.

Wiggin and Dana. 1991. Firm Brochure. New Haven, Conn. April.

Wilber, James. 1990. "Inside Track to Cost Containment." *American Lawyer*, December, 40.

Wilensky, Harold. 1964. "Professionalization of Everyone." *American Journal of Sociology* 70:137–58.

Winter, Steven. 1990. "Indeterminacy and Incommensurability in Constitutional Law." *California Law Review* 78:1441–1541.

Wolfram, Charles H. 1986. *Modern Legal Ethics.* St. Paul, Minn.: West Publishing.

Wollheim, Richard. 1988. *The Thread of Life.* Cambridge, Mass.: Harvard University Press.

Index